ASSESSMENT FOR READING INSTRUCTION

SOLVING PROBLEMS IN THE TEACHING OF LITERACY
Cathy Collins Block, Series Editor

Recent Volumes

Tools for Matching Readers to Texts: Research-Based Practices
Heidi Anne E. Mesmer

Achieving Excellence in Preschool Literacy Instruction
Edited by Laura M. Justice and Carol Vukelich

Reading Success for Struggling Adolescent Learners
Edited by Susan Lenski and Jill Lewis

Best Practices in Adolescent Literacy Instruction
Edited by Kathleen A. Hinchman and Heather K. Sheridan-Thomas

Comprehension Assessment: A Classroom Guide
JoAnne Schudt Caldwell

Comprehension Instruction, Second Edition: Research-Based Best Practices
Edited by Cathy Collins Block and Sheri R. Parris

The Literacy Coaching Challenge: Models and Methods for Grades K–8
Michael C. McKenna and Sharon Walpole

Creating Robust Vocabulary: Frequently Asked Questions and Extended Examples
Isabel L. Beck, Margaret G. McKeown, and Linda Kucan

Mindful of Words: Spelling and Vocabulary Explorations 4–8
Kathy Ganske

Finding the Right Texts: What Works for Beginning and Struggling Readers
Edited by Elfrieda H. Hiebert and Misty Sailors

Fostering Comprehension in English Classes: Beyond the Basics
Raymond Philippot and Michael F. Graves

Language and Literacy Development: What Educators Need to Know
James P. Byrnes and Barbara A. Wasik

Independent Reading: Practical Strategies for Grades K–3
Denise N. Morgan, Maryann Mraz, Nancy D. Padak, and Timothy Rasinski

Assessment for Reading Instruction, Second Edition
Michael C. McKenna and Katherine A. Dougherty Stahl

ASSESSMENT *for* READING INSTRUCTION

SECOND EDITION

MICHAEL C. McKENNA
KATHERINE A. DOUGHERTY STAHL

THE GUILFORD PRESS
New York   London

Library of Congress Cataloging-in-Publication Data

McKenna, Michael C.
    Assessment for reading instruction / by Michael C. McKenna, Katherine A. Dougherty Stahl.—2nd ed.
        p. cm.—(Solving problems in the teaching of literacy)
    Includes bibliographical references and index.
    ISBN 978-1-60623-035-0 (pbk.)
    1. Reading—Ability testing.   2. Reading.   I. Stahl, Katherine A. Dougherty.   II. Title
LB1056.46.M35 2009
372.48—dc22

                                                              2008027889

In memory of
Steven A. Stahl

About the Authors

Michael C. McKenna, PhD, is Thomas G. Jewell Professor of Reading at the University of Virginia. He has authored, coauthored, or edited 15 books and more than 100 articles, chapters, and technical reports on a range of literacy topics. Dr. McKenna's books include *The Literacy Coach's Handbook*, *Help for Struggling Readers*, *Teaching through Text*, and *Issues and Trends in Literacy Education*, among others. His research has been sponsored by the National Reading Research Center and the Center for the Improvement of Early Reading Achievement. Dr. McKenna is the cowinner of the National Reading Conference's Edward Fry Book Award and the American Library Association's Award for Outstanding Academic Books. His articles have appeared in *Reading Research Quarterly*, the *Journal of Educational Psychology*, *Educational Researcher*, *The Reading Teacher*, and others. Dr. McKenna's research interests include reading assessment, comprehension in content settings, reading attitudes, technology applications, and beginning reading.

Katherine A. Dougherty Stahl, EdD, is Assistant Professor of Reading at New York University, where she serves as Literacy Education Program Director and teaches graduate courses. Her research focuses on reading acquisition, struggling readers, and comprehension. Dr. Dougherty Stahl's articles have appeared in *Reading Research Quarterly*, *The Reading Teacher*, and the *Journal of Literacy Research*. In addition to teaching in public elementary school classrooms for over 25 years, she has extensive experience working with struggling readers in clinical settings. These experiences have led to her research interests and her ongoing collaborations with teachers translating research into practice to improve classroom literacy instruction.

Preface

This second edition has been written after an unusual change of authorship. Because of the death of Steven A. Stahl in 2004, the role of coauthor was taken on by Kay, Steve's widow and longtime writing partner. We have worked hard to preserve the original insights Steve provided and at the same time make this second edition still more useful than the first. To accomplish this goal, we have made a number of changes.

THE COGNITIVE MODEL

We began by updating the cognitive model of reading assessment. Its logic is the same, but the component skill areas are grouped a little differently. We moved print concepts to the upper tier, because we felt this concept relates more directly to word recognition than to strategy use. We combined decoding and sight-word knowledge into a single step. Previously, these were considered in sequence and it was easy to get the impression that if sight-word knowledge were adequate there was no need to inquire about decoding. By combining them in the same step, we hope to make clear that both must be considered. Finally, we added knowledge of sentence structures to that of text structures. Taken together, these modifications are minor. They do not alter the basic idea of the model but make it easier to implement.

CHAPTER ORDER

We changed the order of Chapters 4, 5, and 6. In the first edition, Chapter 4 was devoted to fluency, followed by emergent literacy in Chapter 5 and word recognition and spelling in Chapter 6. The new ordering reflects the developmental order of these skill areas. Emergent literacy is now treated in Chapter 4 because it is the cornerstone of more advanced proficiencies. It is followed by word recognition and spelling in Chapter 5 and fluency in Chapter 6. After using the book in many settings, we became convinced that this order will help convey the idea that oral proficiency is developmental in nature and that it proceeds through predictable stages. Although both editions make this point in the opening chapter, it is now reflected in the sequence of chapters.

REPRODUCIBLE FORMS

We have made a number of changes in the forms available for copying. A few of the forms appearing in the first edition have been removed, some have been modified, and some new ones have been added. Gone are the Developmental Test of Word Recognition, the Spelling Skills Test, the sample Dynamic Indicators of Basic Early Literacy Skills (DIBELS) protocols, and the Stahl–Murray Test of Phonemic Awareness. For each of these, we have substituted a more effective alternative based on feedback from teachers and our own experience.

We have made light edits in a number of the forms appearing in the first edition and have made significant revisions in three of them:

- *Informal Phonics Inventory.* We previously referred to this instrument as a survey, but we have expanded it so that it includes virtually all phonics skills. It is still possible for teachers to use it as a survey, but they may also use it to keep track of specific skill acquisition over time. A chart for this purpose has been added.
- *Elementary Spelling Inventory, Feature Guide,* and *Qualitative Spelling Checklist.* A version of these instruments appeared in the first edition. Since then, however, a new edition of *Words Their Way* has appeared, and we have reprinted the revised versions with permission of Pearson and the authors.
- *Wordless Picture Book.* We have explained this useful tool more fully within the text of Chapter 4. For easy reference we have also added to the form itself user-friendly directions for administration.

Several forms appear for the first time here, and we believe they add considerably to the usefulness of the book. They include:

- *Tests of Phonemic Awareness.* This checklist is more comprehensive than the Stahl–Murray instrument—targeting all levels, not just two. At the same time it is more flexible, allowing teachers to gather and record a variety of evidence.
- *Checklist of Internet Strategies.* This tool recognizes that reading successfully in online settings requires that students apply additional strategies. It organizes these strategies by subcategory and makes it easy to document evidence.
- *Adolescent Reading Attitudes Survey.* This new instrument complements the Elementary Reading Attitude Survey by addressing the attitudes of middle and secondary students. It also distinguishes between attitudes toward reading in print versus digital settings.

NEW FEATURES, NEW FOCUS

In the 6 years since the first edition appeared, the field of reading assessment has evolved in a variety of ways. The changes in reproducibles listed above are a reflection of recent trends, but they have also guided us in revising our discussion of topics. As you read, you will notice these changes:

- The phonemic awareness assessment tasks have been expanded and made more explicit, and are in compliance with the areas and tasks defined in the Report of the National Reading Panel and the National Institute for Literacy's *Put Reading First*.
- We have added a discussion of the use of alphabet books based on recent research.
- In light of the popularity of DIBELS and the increasing use of Maze to document response to intervention, we added sections on these tasks. Information on DIBELS can now be found in Chapter 4, on emergent literacy, and in Chapter 6, on fluency.
- Our discussion of fluency culminates in the Multidimensional Fluency Scale, adapted from Jerry Zutell and Timothy Rasinski. We believe readers will find this an excellent means of pulling together the components.
- We replaced the case study of Mel in the Appendix with a brand-new case study of Lee. This case is consistent with the tests and recommendations in other parts of the second edition.
- We modified our discussion of miscue analysis to bring it into better alignment with research and to explain what it can and cannot tell teachers.
- Finally, we added a table to the last chapter that categorizes the many instruments provided in the book. This retrospective listing serves both as a capstone to the previous chapters and as a quick reference that will help teachers find what they need.

Our goal has been to make this second edition more current, more broadly based, and more useful to teachers and specialists. We hope you agree that we have succeeded.

Contents

Contents

CHAPTER ONE

Introduction to Reading Assessment

THREE STRUGGLING READERS: A PREFACE

Consider these three children:

Josh is a third grader reading approximately at the mid-first-grade level. He struggles to pronounce unfamiliar words, sometimes by making guesses from their first letter and sometimes attempting to sound them out from left to right. He does, however, know a fair number of words by sight, and whenever he encounters one of them, he can pronounce it immediately.

Latrelle, a fourth grader reading at a second-grade level, has acquired a good store of words that she recognizes at sight, and she can successfully pronounce almost any familiar word she encounters while reading. Her pace is slow, however, and her oral reading is expressionless. She does not group words into meaningful phrases as she reads, and she tends to ignore punctuation.

Sean, another fourth grader, is a proficient oral reader who can read aloud just about anything he is given, but he often has problems comprehending new material. This difficulty is especially evident when he is asked to read nonfiction and when he is expected to draw conclusions about what he reads. He is a fair student when new content is explained by his teacher, but he has problems whenever he must learn it on his own from print.

The term *struggling reader* has become popular precisely because it lacks precision. When students leave the primary grades with significant problems, they present grave challenges to their teachers. They struggle, regardless of the cause, until they either

1

catch up or give up. The children cited above are composites of real cases and represent important patterns that teachers must be prepared to identify and address. Much of this book focuses on the assessment of younger children, but we would like to begin by considering where declining trajectories can lead.

MODELS OF READING ASSESSMENT

All reading assessment is based on a model. This model can be explicitly laid out, as we intend to do here, or haphazardly formulated. Without a model, a reading specialist has no way of making sense of the observations derived from the reading assessment battery. The model helps the reading specialist recognize patterns in the data, determine the course of instruction, identify the child's strengths, and identify which aspects of reading knowledge are obstructing the child with reading problems.

A model should provide a roadmap, a set of directions to help the reading specialist navigate the assessment procedure and provide guidelines for interpretation. Not every child needs to receive every assessment. An effective model helps you determine which measures may best inform you about the child's needs.

The Deficit Model

The term *diagnosis*, as you might suspect, has a medical origin. Its use is based on the assumption that reading difficulties are much like physiological disorders. This conventional view, sometimes called the "medical model," assumes that the difficulty, or deficiency, resides within the student, and that the teacher, like a physician, must identify it and respond appropriately with instructional techniques designed to have a medicinal or therapeutic effect. This thinking has led, predictably, to terms such as *remediation* and *remedial reader*.

Very few in the field of reading still explicitly defend this model. There is little evidence that most children's reading problems are due to a single remediable cause. Even though research in the field of neuropsychology continues to identify possible neurological causes for reading problems (Pugh et al., 2001; Riccio & Hynd, 1996; Shaywitz, 1996), this work has not produced definitive results, nor does it show promise of "remediating" children with reading problems in the near future.

The Contextual Model

An alternative view of reading assessment does not deny that reading difficulties often reflect deficits within students, but it broadens the perspective to include two other possibilities. One is the notion that there may be a mismatch between the type of instruction provided and the manner in which a given child learns. The second possibility is that contextual factors beyond the scope of the school (such as a disadvantaged or emotionally troubled home life) may impair reading development. The contextual model suggests that reading difficulties can be traced to an interaction between the student, the methods or materials used with the student, and the broader context in which the student functions.

This model is quite different from a "learning style" model, which suggests that children have individual "learning styles" that can be diagnosed and matched to appropriate instruction (e.g., Carbo, Dunn, & Dunn, 1986). In the learning style model, children are classified as either visual or auditory learners and matched with either more holistic or more phonics-oriented instruction. This model has been tested repeatedly and not found to be valid (Stahl, 1999a). The contextual model, in contrast, views individual students as well as instructional methods as more complex than the learning model concept, with students having individual needs that are, or are not, met by the instruction they receive. Student needs may be attitudinal, motivational, or cognitive, and instruction may or may not meet any of those needs.

Stage Models

Stages of Reading Development

The first of the stage models that may be used in assessing children was formulated by Chall (1996), who characterized reading development as progressing through six stages as the child moves from emergent literacy, or the beginning period of becoming aware of print, to advanced literacy activity, such as that needed to assimilate material in a graduate course. An overview of Chall's model is presented in Table 1.1, in which we have slightly adapted her terminology.

Although Chall's model provides a blueprint for overall reading development, it was not developed specifically for analysis of reading difficulties. For that purpose, we prefer the model of Spear-Swerling and Sternberg (1996), who combined Chall's model of overall reading stages with Ehri's (1998) discussion of the development of word recognition and their own observations of struggling readers to suggest a roadmap of reading achievement that pinpoints areas where children get "off track" from the normal course of development. This model is shown in Figure 1.1.

Growth of Word Recognition

The first four stages of Spear-Swerling and Sternberg's model rely on Ehri's (1998) model of the growth of word recognition. Ehri describes the growth of children's knowledge of words as progressing through four qualitatively different phases. At first, children recognize words through distinctive visual features, such as the "tail" in *monkey* or the two "eyes" in *look*. Ehri has called this stage *visual cue reading*. In one study (Gough, Juel, & Griffith, 1992), a group of prereaders learned words presented on a series of flashcards, one of which had a thumbprint in the corner. When shown the cards again, this time with the thumbprint on a different card, they tended to misread the thumbprinted card as the word in the first set, suggesting that they were attending to the thumbprint rather than to the letters.

TABLE 1.1. Jeanne Chall's (1996) Model of the Stages of Reading Development

Stage	Name	What child is learning	Typical activities	Materials
Stage 0 Birth to grade 1	Emergent literacy	Functions of written language, alphabet, phonemic awareness	Story reading, "pseudoreading," alphabet activities, rhyming, nursery rhymes, invented spelling	Books (including predictable stories), letters, writing materials, *Sesame Street*
Stage 1 Beginning grade 1	Decoding	Letter–sound correspondences	Teacher-directed reading instruction, phonics instruction	Preprimers and primers, phonics materials, writing materials, trade books
Stage 2 End of grade 1 to end of grade 3	Confirmation and fluency	Automatic word recognition, use of context	Reading narratives, generally about known topics	Basal readers, trade books, workbooks
Stage 3 Grades 4 to 8	Learning the new (single viewpoint)	How to learn from text, vocabulary knowledge, strategies	Reading and studying content-area materials, use of encyclopedias, strategy instruction	Basal readers, novels, encyclopedias, textbooks in content areas
Stage 4 High school and early college	Multiple viewpoints	Reconciling different views	Critical reading, discourse synthesis, report writing	Texts containing multiple views, encyclopedias and other reference materials, magazines and journals, nonfiction books, etc.
Stage 5 Late college and graduate school	A worldview	Developing a well-rounded view of the world	Learning what not to read as well as what to read	Professional materials

As children learn more and more words, a purely visual system of identification, such as the one these children were using, becomes unwieldy. As children develop rudimentary phonemic awareness, they begin to use individual letters, usually the first but sometimes the last, to identify words. This stage is called *phonemic cue reading* or *partial alphabetic coding.* To get to this stage, the child needs to have an "alphabetic insight," or the realization that letters correspond to sounds in words. This requires both rudimentary phonological awareness as well as some letter–sound knowledge.

As children's written vocabulary increases, they need to further analyze words, examining more parts of an unfamiliar word to identify it. This leads to *full alphabetic coding,* in which the child examines each letter in the word. This ability may come as the result of receiving instruction in decoding, or children can develop it on their own. This letter-by-letter decoding gives way, with practice, to *consolidated word recognition,* in which a reader uses groups of letters, either as chunks or through analogies, to recognize words automatically, as proficient readers do (Chall, 1996; LaBerge & Samuels, 1974).

This development of word recognition occurs not in a vacuum but in conjunction with growth in phonemic awareness and exposure to different types of text. Phonemic awareness is a part of phonological awareness, which "refers to a broad class of skills that

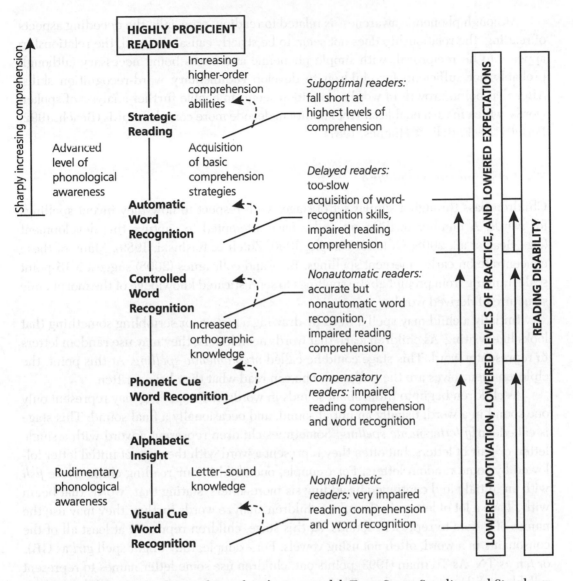

FIGURE 1.1. Spear-Swerling and Sternberg's stage model. From Spear-Swerling and Sternberg (1996). Copyright 1996 by Westview Press, a member of Perseus Books Group. Reprinted by permission.

involve attending to, thinking about, and intentionally manipulating the phonological aspects of spoken language" (Scarborough & Brady, 2001, p. 25). Phonemic awareness is that part of phonological awareness that processes phonemes rather than syllables or onsets and rimes. We (Stahl & McKenna, 2001; Stahl & Murray, 1998) suggest that phonological awareness develops first from an awareness of syllables, onsets, and rimes, to an awareness of initial phonemes, final phonemes, and, lastly, vowels. We also have found a parallel development in spelling (see also Bear, Invernizzi, Templeton, & Johnston, 2008).

Although phonemic awareness is related to reading, especially the decoding aspects of reading, the relationship does not seem to be strictly causal. Instead, the relationship appears to be reciprocal, with simple phonemic awareness being necessary (although probably not sufficient) for children to develop rudimentary word-recognition skills. After that point, growth in word recognition seems to enable further analysis of spoken words, which in turn enables further ability to decode more complex words (Beach, 1992; Perfetti, Beck, Bell, & Hughes, 1987).

The Development of Spelling

Children pass through a similar set of stages with respect to how they invent spellings for words. A number of different scales have attempted to capture this development (e.g., Bear et al., 2008; Gillet & Temple, 1990; Zutell & Rasinski, 1989). Many of these concentrate on early emergent spellings. Bear and colleagues (2008) suggest a 15-point scale, ranging from prealphabetic spellings to sophisticated knowledge of the morphemic structure of derived words.

Initially a child may spell a word by drawing a picture or scribbling something that looks like writing. As children learn that words need letters, they may use random letters to represent a word. This stage could be called *prephonemic spelling*. At this point, the children themselves are the only ones who can read what they have written.

As children begin to think about sounds in words, their spelling may represent only one sound in a word, usually an initial sound, and occasionally a final sound. This stage is called *early letter-name spelling*. Sometimes children represent a word with a single letter, or pair of letters, but often they represent a word with the correct initial letter followed by some random letters. For example, one child in our reading clinic wrote *fish* with an initial *f* and continued by adding six more letters, stating that "words that begin with *f* have a lot of letters in them." As children analyze words further, they may use the names of letters to represent sounds. At this stage, children represent at least all of the consonants in a word, often not using vowels. For example, they might spell *girl* as GRL or *ten* as TN. As Treiman (1993) points out, children use some letter names to represent syllables, while not using others. This stage seems to represent a beginning of the analysis of words into phonemes, usually consonants.

As children learn more about how words are spelled, they use vowels, and the words they write resemble the actual word, like DRAGUN for *dragon*. Children usually master short vowels first, then long vowel patterns. This may reflect instruction, or it may reflect the simplicity of short vowel codings. Bear and colleagues (2008) call the stage in which children are including vowels, although not always correctly, *letter-name spelling*. At this point, children realize that all words need vowels, although they still have not mastered correct spelling of short vowels. When they can spell short vowels consistently, but not yet long vowels, Bear and colleagues term their spelling *within-word pattern spelling*. Their scale continues, but this is the appropriate range to discuss struggling readers, because this is the range of their spelling abilities. Table 1.2 summarizes these first four stages.

TABLE 1.2. Early Stages of Spelling Development

Spelling stage	Characteristics	Example
Prephonemic spelling	Child uses random letters, without regard to the sounds they may represent.	JNVW for *hat*
Early letter-name spelling	Child begins this stage by representing only one sound in a word, usually the first, but eventually represents all consonant sounds.	Early: FDZWD for *fish* Late: GRL for *girl*
Letter-name spelling	Child uses vowels but often does so incorrectly.	DRAGUN for *dragon*
Within-word pattern spelling	Child can consistently spell words with short vowels but not words with long vowels.	HOT for *hot* METE for *meet*

(A caveat before we leave the topic of spelling: It is our experience that children's spelling difficulties linger long after their reading problems have disappeared. We see college students who have a history of reading problems and who have compensated for, or have even overcome, these problems, but are still dreadful spellers.)

Although Spear-Swerling and Sternberg (1996) describe reading development throughout the grades, most of their discussion is focused on word recognition and the early stages of reading. We find that this model serves as a good lens through which to view children with reading problems, but it is limited, and we feel the need to complement the model with a more fine-tuned cognitive view of reading. We use the stage model to roughly identify the stage of the child's reading and to determine where the child went "off track" (and how we can bring him or her back on track), but we use the cognitive model to guide more specific assessments.

Josh, Latrelle, and Sean Revisited

Returning to the three struggling readers described at the beginning of this chapter, the Spear-Swerling and Sternberg model can help us understand some of their needs. We suggest that, before proceeding, you go back to the beginning of the chapter and try to place each of these children at the appropriate stage.

Josh seems to be in the beginning stages of acquiring alphabetic insight, in spite of his 3 years in school. In general, he seems to be a compensatory reader who uses his sight-word knowledge to compensate for his rudimentary decoding ability. We would want to know more about his specific abilities in decoding, and we might want to know more about his ability to comprehend. Latrelle would be classified as a nonautomatic reader because she can read accurately but extremely slowly and without expression. Sean is a word-caller who does not comprehend what he is reading, in spite of quick and accurate word reading.

The stage model is useful for giving us a general idea about these children, but it does not tell us specifically about what we need to teach them. The cognitive model, discussed below, provides a more accurate roadmap.

A Cognitive Model

A fourth model suggests that reading is composed of three separate components. Reading comprehension, the purpose of reading, depends on (1) automatic recognition of the words in the text, (2) comprehension of the language in the text, and (3) the ability to use the strategies needed to achieve one's purpose in reading the text. A child will have difficulties with comprehension if he or she has difficulty with any of these three components. If a child's word recognition is not automatic or sufficiently accurate, then comprehension will suffer. If the child does not understand the vocabulary, lacks appropriate background knowledge, or lacks knowledge of text structure or genre, comprehension will suffer. Children read different texts for different purposes. Sometimes these purposes are general, such as enjoyment or literal comprehension. But sometimes the purposes are specific, such as studying for a test or learning facts to include in a report. If the child can read the text but does not achieve the purpose of reading, then comprehension also will suffer.

This model, shown in Figure 1.2, is discussed in the sections that follow. We use this model to ask ourselves a series of questions, such as, "Does the child have difficulty with automatic word recognition?" or "Is the child's vocabulary knowledge an impediment to comprehension?" The answers to these questions suggest areas of strengths and weaknesses in the child with whom we are working. We call this model "cognitive" simply

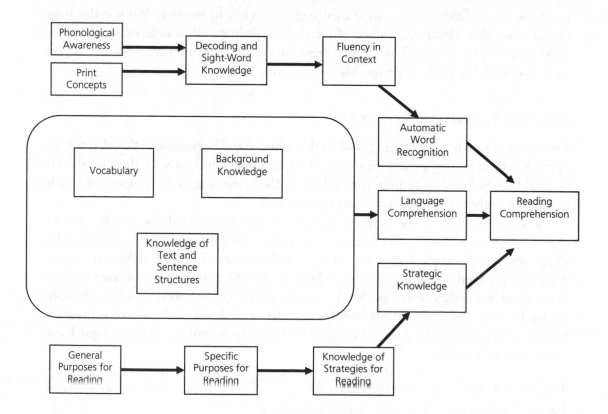

FIGURE 1.2. Cognitive model.

because it requires thinking systematically about these questions and reaching justifiable inferences based on the answers.

The first question to ask is whether the child has a reading problem. Often, teachers or reading specialists are told (by parents or other teachers) that a child has a reading problem when, in fact, the child does not. Sometimes a child does poorly on a standardized test, even when he or she is able to read grade-level material in the classroom without difficulty. Remember that a standardized test is one observation, for 1 or 2 days. Sometimes children simply have a hard time with testing or have difficulties on the day of that test. Children who come to school without breakfast or after witnessing an argument, or with some other problem, may not do as well on a standardized test as they might have. As we note in the next chapter, such tests should not be the only source of information about a child's reading (or math, for that matter). Instead, a compilation of multiple sources of information is needed to understand whether the child's reading performance is part of a consistent pattern. This compilation involves not only standardized test results, but also how the child reads the book used in the classroom, informal reading inventory results, and other information.

To answer this question, one must keep in mind that the purpose of reading is comprehension. If a child can comprehend texts at a level appropriate for his or her grade, then it may not matter whether the child can demonstrate mastery of other reading skills. Often, a child may do relatively poorly on a measure of phonics or decoding but still be able to comprehend acceptably. This discrepancy may reflect a problem with the assessment rather than a deficit in the child's skills. Observe the child closely to see whether he or she can use the skills in connected text, even though he or she may have difficulties applying them in isolation or with stating a rule.

So, Step 1 in the assessment process is to look at the reason a problem is suspected.

- If you have seen the child struggle with books in the classroom, then check the child's standardized test scores.
- If the child scored poorly on standardized tests, then closely observe the child in class.
- If further observation suggests that the child has difficulties both on standardized measures and in reading classroom texts, then give an informal reading inventory.

If a child has a significant problem with comprehension of age-appropriate texts, then the teacher should further examine the child's reading. Following our model, the teacher needs to ask the following questions about the child:

- Is the child able to read texts at his or her grade placement level, using automatic word recognition and adequate expression?
- Is the child able to comprehend the language of the text?
- Does the child have adequate knowledge of the purposes for reading?
- Does the child have strategies available to achieve those purposes?

These questions are explored in the remainder of this chapter.

AUTOMATIC WORD RECOGNITION

If a child struggles with word recognition, comprehension will inevitably suffer (LaBerge & Samuels, 1974). Word recognition needs to be automatic, so that the child does not have to devote conscious attention to the words in the text and can devote all of his or her cognitive effort to understanding what is read. When a child stumbles over words or s-s-s-sounds out many words, the child's understanding typically suffers.

To answer the first question about automatic word recognition—Is the child able to read texts at his or her grade placement level using automatic word recognition and adequate expression?—you must listen to the child read material intended for his or her grade level. This can be done by pulling the child aside and listening to him or her reading from a selected text, or it can be done through an informal reading inventory, as described in Chapter 3. If the child's reading is expressive and he or she can read at an instructional level appropriate to the grade placement, then you can reasonably conclude that the child's problem lies elsewhere. However, our clinical experience suggests that as many as 90% of the children we see have difficulties in this area. Sometimes the problems lie exclusively in this area; at other times the child will have difficulties with language comprehension and strategic knowledge as well. But word recognition difficulties underlie the vast majority of reading problems, so we spend a lot of time assessing them.

If a child is deemed to have difficulties in automatic word recognition, then the question that follows is:

- Is the child fluent in context?

Context

Some educators (e.g., Goodman, 1993) suggest that children use context as a means of predicting words in a passage. According to these theorists, readers use information from context to minimize the use of letter–sound information to recognize words. For example, for the sentence

The boy pulled the red _____.

a reader may predict the word *wagon* before recognizing the word. If the first letter is *w*, then the reader may move on, without sounding out the word or using other word-recognition skills. Other educators (e.g., Clay, 1993a) suggest that children use three types of cues to recognize words—graphophonemic, syntactic (part-of-speech), and semantic (meaning) information—and that effective word recognition involves the use of these three cueing systems. In the above example, a reader would predict the word to be a noun, because nouns always follow *the* and adjectives such as *red*. The reader would predict *wagon*, since wagons are pulled, typically by young children, and they are often red. If, instead of a *w*, the initial letter were a *c*, the reader might mentally search for words that begin with *c* and satisfy those semantic (meaning) constraints and come up with *cart*. A substitution like *wagging* would violate both syntactic and semantic constraints and might indicate that the child was paying more attention to sounding out the word than to the context.

This model is intuitively appealing, but research does not support it as a model of reading behavior. Effective readers would recognize the word *wagon* more quickly and reliably than they would be able to predict the word through the use of syntactic and semantic information (Stanovich, 1991). Research using a number of different approaches has found that good readers do not predict words but, instead, use their automatic word recognition processes to propel reading (Adams, 1990, 1998).

Although we do not feel that research supports this model (see Adams, 1998), we have found that good readers do use context in two principal ways. First, they use context to monitor their reading. A reader who produces *wagging* for *wagon* in the target sentence would realize that the word does not make sense and would go back and self-correct. Thus a good reader's miscues tend to make sense in context because of active monitoring, not predicting.

Good readers also use context to rapidly select the intended meaning of multiple-meaning words. Consider this sentence:

The rancher hired a new hand.

The word *hand* has several meanings, but proficient readers have no trouble discerning the correct one. They do so after the word is located in memory, not before. That is to say, the good reader uses context not to predict the word but to select the appropriate meaning once the word has been located.

Our experience is that all children, even struggling readers, tend to use context quite well. Stanovich (1980) suggests that struggling readers make greater use of context than good readers because they have less word-recognition skill and need to rely more on context. When we evaluate children in our clinic, usually 80% or more of their miscues are syntactically acceptable (the same part of speech as the text word), and 70% or more are semantically acceptable (make sense in the context of the sentence, even if their meaning is not the same as the word in the text). When children do not use context effectively, either the text is extremely difficult for them and they make random guesses, or they are not focused on context.

When children do not view connected text as meaningful, they do not consider context. Sometimes, if children are taught to overrely on words (which especially occurs in radical phonics programs), then they may lose sight of the importance of textual meaning, and reading becomes nothing more than a rote exercise. This extreme position is rare, but occasionally we do see children who have been taught to focus in this manner. These children also tend to be significantly better at calling words than comprehending text. If the text is within the child's instructional level, and the child is not making contextually acceptable miscues, then the child's attention needs to be redirected to the meaning of the text, and he or she needs to be taught that texts are meaningful.

If a child is poor at using context, we would look at the child's interview data to see how he or she perceives reading, and we would evaluate the child's comprehension of texts read orally, to see whether he or she is focusing on comprehension during reading.

Fluency

Many children with reading problems can read accurately but cannot read quickly enough to make sense of what they are reading. If reading is not fluent, then comprehension usually suffers. We learn about the child's degree of fluency through observation of oral reading. Sometimes this observation is done through an informal reading inventory, but it also can be done by observing the child read a tradebook, by using benchmark texts for running records, or by using leveled passages as in the DIBELS battery. In Chapter 3, we include a rubric or scoring guide that might be used to decide whether reading is fluent. Generally, however, the criteria can be stated simply, as whether the child's reading sounds like language:

- Is the child halting or smooth in his or her reading?
- Does the child stop to sound out words excessively?
- Does the child have to repeat phrases excessively or self-correct excessively?

If a child engages in halting reading, with excessive sounding out, repetition, or self-correction, then he or she may need work in fluency.

If the child is not fluent or accurate at reading texts written at the his or her grade placement level, then we need to ask two questions about the child's word recognition:

- Does the child have adequate sight-word knowledge?
- Does the child have adequate knowledge of decoding strategies?

Sight Words

The term *sight words* can be defined in two principal ways. Ehri (1998) uses the phrase *sight words* to refer to all the words that a child recognizes "at sight," or automatically. Under this definition, both common words, such as *the* and *what*, and uncommon words, such as *wolf* and *rescue*, might all be sight words for a given individual. Although we see the utility of an inclusive definition such as Ehri's, in this book we reserve the term *sight words* for the most frequently used words in the English language. Adams (1990) points out that the 105 most common words account for about 50% of running text. This is as true for adult text as it is for children's text. Furthermore, these words are often irregular or use rare sound–symbol correspondences and need to be memorized so that they can be retrieved quickly and automatically.

There are several lists of the most frequently used words in English, notably the lists developed by Dolch (1936) and Fry (cited in Fry, 1980). As one might expect, there is considerable overlap among lists. In addition, the words on any of these lists are worth assessing and teaching. Therefore, we do not recommend any particular list. We do include the Fry Sight-Word Inventory of 300 high-frequency words in Chapter 5.

In assessing children's sight-word knowledge, it is important to note both speed and accuracy. Because so many textual words are sight words, slow recognition entails slow text reading in general. Sounding out a word like *with*, even if the child arrived at the correct pronunciation, would still impair comprehension, as would a halting pronunciation after a long pause. Therefore, one should note both the accuracy and speed of recognition. Each sight word on a list should be recognized in roughly half a second—that is, without hesitation.

In addition, one should observe children's recognition of sight words in context. Since sight words account for such a large percent of words in text, an informal reading inventory also gives ample opportunity to observe children's sight-word recognition skills in context. Again, sight words should be recognized *automatically*, without hesitation or sounding out.

Decoding

We are also interested in whether a child has the ability to decode unknown words. The ability to decode requires both a knowledge of the processes involved in decoding as well as knowledge of specific letter–sound relationships. We need to assess both.

Assessing the Process of Decoding

As suggested by Ehri's model, the process of decoding involves three successive understandings: acquisition of the alphabetic principle, the ability to blend letters into sounds, and the ability to use both phonograms and analogies. Children's acquisition of the alphabetic principle—the principle that letters can be used to represent sounds—is revealed by their use of letters as cues for words in both word recognition and spelling. Spelling may be a better assessment for a child's knowledge of the alphabetic principle, since children may use the first letter as a visual rather than phonemic cue.

Letter-by-letter decoding—the ability to blend letters together to make words—is the hallmark of Ehri's "full alphabetic coding" phase and Spear-Swerling and Sternberg's "controlled word recognition" stage. Although this phase is fairly short-lived, it is critical: Children need to appreciate individual letter–sound correspondences in order to move toward automatic word recognition. This ability can be evaluated by measures that tap children's knowledge of individual letter sounds as well as their decoding of short-vowel words. Because short vowels are usually taught first in most phonics curricula, we use short vowels as the test of children's blending ability.

The last stage involves being able to use both phonograms, or chunks of letters (such as *ick, ill, and*, etc.), and analogies (decoding *strike* by comparing it with *like*). Proficient readers decode words using these strategies. Studies have found that children must be able to understand letter-by-letter decoding before they are able to benefit from analogy or phonogram instruction, but children need to use phonograms in order to read proficiently (e.g., Ehri & Robbins, 1992). Children are first able to use phonograms and analogies to decode monosyllabic words; later, they can use them to decode polysyllabic words.

Assessing the Content of Decoding

Even if a child has knowledge of a process such as letter-by-letter decoding, he or she still needs to learn certain linguistic facts. For letter-by-letter decoding, these facts would be:

- Consonant sounds (<u>s</u>un, <u>f</u>an, <u>t</u>oy, <u>d</u>og)
- Consonant digraphs (<u>th</u>at, <u>th</u>in, <u>sh</u>eep, <u>ch</u>ick, <u>wh</u>o, <u>ph</u>one)
- Consonant blends (<u>bl</u>ue, <u>st</u>ar, <u>sl</u>eep, <u>dr</u>ink, <u>str</u>ipe)
- Short vowels in consonant–vowel–consonant (CVC) words (c<u>a</u>t, p<u>e</u>t, p<u>i</u>n, d<u>u</u>ck, l<u>o</u>g)
- Vowel digraphs (b<u>oa</u>t, gr<u>ee</u>n, w<u>ai</u>t, p<u>ea</u>)
- Rule of silent <u>e</u> (rac<u>e</u>, hos<u>e</u>, bik<u>e</u>)
- Vowel diphthongs (j<u>oi</u>n, c<u>ow</u>, b<u>oy</u>, p<u>aw</u>)
- *R*-controlled vowels (st<u>ar</u>, b<u>ir</u>d, w<u>or</u>ld, h<u>er</u>)
- *L*-controlled *a* (b<u>all</u>, c<u>all</u>)
- Other variant vowels (caught, put)

This list does not mean that children need to learn rules. The "rules" often do not apply to enough words to render them clear cut. For example, the rule "when two vowels go walking, the first one does the talking" works only about 45% of the time (Adams, 1990). It works for *boat* but not for *bread* or *join* or *does*. And the "rule" of silent *e* only applies about 60% of the time. It works in *home* but not in *come*, in *drove* but not in *dove* or *love*, in *save* but not in *have*. Instead, children need to know *patterns* to help them identify individual words. Rather than presenting a rule, present lists of words that adhere to the pattern, so that children can internalize the pattern and do not have to think about the rule. As Cunningham (2001) has observed, the brain is more comfortable recognizing patterns than applying rules.

As for phonograms, or rimes, there are hundreds in the English language. Wylie and Durrell (1970) found 286 phonograms in their examination of primary-grade text, 272 of which are pronounced the same way in every word in which they appear, and they found 37 rimes that account for nearly 500 words. These rimes were used as a basis for the Z-test presented in Chapter 5. Clearly, these phonograms could be the start of a phonogram-based program, but they should be seen as only a start. One cannot teach all 272 phonograms, but one might expand beyond the initial set. If a child has difficulties in decoding, then the next question we ask is:

- Does the child have adequate phonological awareness?

Phonological Awareness

Phonological awareness—or the awareness of sounds in spoken words—is a prerequisite for children to learn to decode. It is not uncommon for young children, kindergarteners, and even some first graders to be unable to think of words as a collection of sounds and, for example, to be unable to provide the first sound of *dog* or *fish*. Stanovich (1986), among many, suggests that early difficulties in phonological awareness underlie later reading problems. Children who do not think of the first sound of *mouse* as /m/ will be unable to use the letter *m* to help recognize the word.

One child in our clinic, Heather, is a wonderful (and cute) example of this problem. Heather was a first grader when we saw her, the daughter of a dentist and a stay-at-home mother, living in a small Midwestern town. Her mother reported that Heather had difficulties in learning phonics, although she had no problems reading easy preprimer text by memorizing the words. From discussions with her mother, we suspected that she had difficulties with phonological awareness. When asked to say *meat* without the /m/, Heather thought for a while, then said, "Chicken." Although nonplussed, we went on, asking her to say *coat* without the /k/. After some thought, she said, "Jacket."

Heather's difficulties came about because she tended to view words as semantic units, as we might, in order to understand them in speech and reading. However, to learn to use an alphabetic language, to reach that vital alphabetic insight, the child needs to recognize that words are both meaningful *and* collections of sounds. Because Heather did not have that alphabetic insight, she could not move forward. She was easy to teach, figured out the relations between letters and sounds, and went on to be a good reader. But she did need initial help to make sense of word recognition.

For beginning readers, it is important to consider one last barrier to automatic word recognition. The following question is critical regardless of the child's level of phonological awareness:

- What concepts of print does the child have?

We want to know about the child's knowledge of basic print concepts, including the left-to-right directionality of English, the fact that spaces are word boundaries, and so forth. These concepts are fundamental to an appreciation of how print works, and they are the foundation on which decoding skills develop. Extremely important is the concept of a printed word: that a word is a collections of letters separated by spaces. For example, Andrew, a second grader who had repeated first grade, was still puzzled by the difference between a word and a letter, despite his experience of 2½ years in primary school. When asked to slide two cards together to show a word, he slid them together to reveal one letter. When asked to show two words, he showed two letters. When asked to show one *letter*, he was puzzled, thinking that he had already done that. This child would have been extremely confused during lessons that talk about the "first letter in the word _____." If his teachers had spotted his confusion and dealt with it early, it is likely that many of Andrew's current problems would not have developed. We have provided several measures that evaluate children's concept of what a word is in this book.

We have placed print concepts and phonological awareness together in our schematic (Figure 1.2) because they are unrelated and one does not depend on the other. It is important to consider both.

We have now traced word recognition back to its roots, from automatic word recognition, to fluency in context, to knowledge of sight words and decoding, to phonological awareness and print concepts. This cognitive view complements the stage view of Spear-Swerling and Sternberg. Put together, one can see how a reader can fall behind, and how a teacher can target instruction to put the reader back on the road to proficiency.

LANGUAGE COMPREHENSION

Even if a reader is a proficient word-caller, the child also must be able to comprehend what is read. We encounter children who are able to read fluently but cannot understand what they read. Often, this is just a matter of not attending to meaning. When children are given intensive phonics instruction without being asked to attend to meaning, they may not focus on the meaning. This situation is rare and easily fixed.

Most other children who have comprehension problems have difficulties understanding the language of the text, even if they can read the words. Although language comprehension involves a great number of elements, we find that the problems we see occur largely in three areas. Put as questions, we ask ourselves:

- Does the child have an adequate *vocabulary* for his or her age and grade?
- Does the child have the *background knowledge* necessary to understand the particular passage that he or she is reading?
- Is the child able to use common *text and sentence structures* to aid in comprehension?

Vocabulary

Children's knowledge of word meanings is the best predictor of their comprehension, both of passages containing those words and of passages in general (Stahl, 1999a). This factor may be predictive because knowledge of words enables children to comprehend passages, or because vocabulary knowledge is a measure of children's general knowledge or their general intelligence. Either way, children with reading problems tend to have problems with word meanings.

These problems also tend to worsen as children progress through school. Stanovich (1986) attributes this decline to what he calls *Matthew effects*, based on the notion from the Bible that the "rich will get richer and the poor will get poorer" (Matthew 25:29). The notion of Matthew effects stems from Stanovich's observation that the gap between proficient and struggling readers widens over time (see Figure 1.3).

Stanovich suggests that many of the problems struggling readers encounter are not due to underlying causes but to these children's increasing lack of reading experience. In the case of vocabulary, children who have reading problems both read less text and read less-challenging texts. Because they read increasingly less-challenging material, they are exposed to fewer words of increasing difficulty. Because most words are learned from exposure in context, children with reading problems learn fewer words. Because they know fewer words, they are less able to read challenging texts and therefore encounter

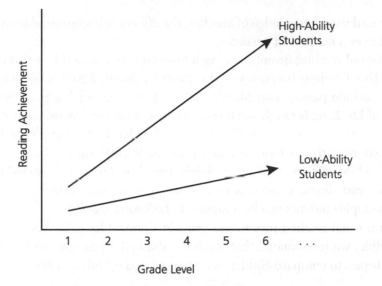

FIGURE 1.3. An example of the Matthew effect.

fewer difficult words—thus engaging a downward cycle that exacerbates the differences between proficient and struggling readers.

Because vocabulary knowledge constitutes an important component of intelligence tests, we find that children with reading problems produce intelligence test scores that decline over time. This finding does not mean that they have less native intelligence, just that they have a relatively smaller vocabulary than their peers. But the decline in intelligence test scores can mean that these children lose a legal categorization, such as "learning disability," that is determined by intelligence test scores.

Over the school years, children learn an impressive number of word meanings. Estimates are that children typically enter first grade knowing between 3,000 and 6,000 words and learn between 1,000 and 3,000 new words per year, knowing as many as 45,000 words by the end of 12th grade (Nagy, 1988). This large number of words cannot be tested directly. Instead, tests are based on samples of words. We suggest a number of standardized tests that assess vocabulary, but we do not provide one in this book because of the difficulties of accurately sampling such a large number of words.

Background Knowledge

Much has been written about the contribution of background knowledge to children's reading comprehension (e.g., Anderson & Pearson, 1984). Because the purpose of this book is to talk about assessment, we limit our discussion of background knowledge to its effects on assessment.

Children obviously differ in terms of background knowledge, and these differences affect their performance on reading tasks. Standardized measures deal with the issue of background knowledge by utilizing many short passages. If a child has strong knowledge of one topic and weak knowledge of another, the effects of background knowledge should average out over a number of passages.

On informal reading inventories, each level can be assessed in a single passage. On the Qualitative Reading Inventory–4 (Leslie & Caldwell, 2005), selections at the fifth-grade level include passages on Martin Luther King, Jr., and Margaret Mead. Because knowledge of Dr. King is taught each year, whereas Margaret Mead is rarely taught prior to high school, the passage on Dr. King is more familiar to most students. Children may answer questions correctly based on their prior knowledge, rather than on what they just read. Often, children's answers seem plainly based on previous knowledge rather than on what was read. Teachers need to be cautious in interpreting the scores from passages about whose topic students can be assumed to be knowledgeable.

Some informal reading inventories provide a pretest for prior knowledge; others do not. If possible, we recommend that teachers administer passages on familiar as well as unfamiliar topics to compare children's responses under both conditions.

Sentence Structures

The texts that children encounter as they move through school contain progressively more complicated sentences. On average, sentences grow longer and are likely to contain multiple clauses and phrases. Because these structures are seldom heard in conversation, children must learn them by reading. Because there is no sequence that we can use to predict which grammatical structures are likely to be encountered at which grades, it is important for teachers to be aware of the occurrence of challenging syntax. This make an excellent target for questioning and for think-alouds.

The length of a sentence and its complexity are highly correlated, so that examining the average sentence length of a text is a shortcut to appraising its grammatical complexity. This is the approach taken by most readability formulas, and we feel that by attempting to create a good match between a student's instructional reading level and the readability level of a text, a teacher can do much to ensure that the grammatical structures the student faces are appropriate.

Text Structures

We also see children in the clinic who differ in terms of their knowledge of text structure. By *text structure*, we mean structural patterns in text that are common to particular genres. For example, one can identify the following elements for narratives:

- Setting and characters including
  - Time
  - Place
  - Major characters
  - Minor characters
- Problem that major character encounters
- Goal that major character is trying to achieve

- Events
  - Event 1
  - Event 2 . . .
- Resolution

Research has found that children tend to include these elements in their recall of narratives (e.g., Yussen & Ozcan, 1996). Narratives also can be thought of as comprising chains of events, with one event causing the next. These causal chains form the plot of the narrative.

Other genres have different elements. Most expository genres are structured around main ideas and supporting information. Sometimes the main idea is a cause-and-effect relationship or the presentation of a problem and solution, whereas other times the main idea is the topic around which the passage provides supporting and descriptive information.

We find that children who have reading problems also have difficulties perceiving text structures. This difficulty could be due to labored decoding that renders them unable to integrate information into a coherent whole, or because they do not understand how to discern the overall structure of a text. Either way, such children can benefit from instruction on text structure.

We assess children's knowledge of text structure through free recall. As discussed in Chapter 7, this recall involves having a child "tell you back" what he or she has read. Ordinarily, we expect the recall to include most of the important information, be it important story elements (narrative text) or main idea information (expository text). We ordinarily expect the recall to roughly mirror the order the information was presented in the text. Any significant divergence from either inclusion of important information or text order is a cause for concern. Some children recall information haphazardly, as if they were picking out random facts, suggesting poor recall and the need for work in this area.

A word of caution is in order. Some children, because of a shy nature or a lack of understanding of the task, simply do not recall text well. In other words, their response may lead a teacher to underestimate how well they have comprehended. Interpretation of poor recall should involve considering whether a limited response may have been the result of reticence or failure to grasp the task.

STRATEGIC KNOWLEDGE

Consider how you, as a proficient reader, are probably reading this text. Chances are, you are in a comfortable, but not too comfortable, place, one you typically reserve for studying. The lighting is good. As to the actual process of studying, there is considerable variation. Some people study with music; others need quiet. Some people use highlighters; others write in the margins, use notecards, or nothing at all. Some people gain an overview by skimming the whole text; others read it carefully from start to finish. Whatever approach you are taking, chances are that it is the same approach you have taken to reading textbooks in the past. You have found a set of strategies that work for you while studying.

Contrast this set of strategies with those used for reading a recreational novel. You probably read the novel in a different place, possibly in bed or in a noisier environment. The contrast between the two activities shows how you, as a proficient reader, have different strategies for reading different types of texts for different purposes. Prior to reading, you decided what your purpose was and chose a set of strategies to help you achieve your purpose. The strategies are both related to environment and learning set (i.e., place to work, quiet or noise) and cognitive strategies for remembering (i.e., highlighter, notecards, reading end-of-chapter summaries first).

We find that children with reading problems often have difficulties assimilating different strategies and knowing which should be used for a given purpose. For example, Cameron is a sixth grader with severe reading difficulties. His primary problems involve his slow reading rate and his ponderous process of word recognition. When given the textbook interview (in Chapter 8) and asked how he would study a chapter for a test, he replied that he would read it straight through. Because of his slow reading rate, we doubted he would be able to finish it in a week or that he would remember much of what he had read because of his labored focus on the individual words. When we asked him, he confirmed that he rarely finished half of his weekly reading assignment. When asked what kind of grades he got, he replied, "D's and F's." Cameron was not successful at studying and did not know how to modify his behaviors so that he could succeed. There are techniques that can be used to help children who have reading problems study more effectively, even material they might have difficulty reading straight through (see Schumaker, Deshler, Alley, Warner, & Denton, 1982), and we did teach him to use these techniques, which improved his grades somewhat.

The first question we ask is:

- Does the child have a set of strategies that he or she can apply to achieve different purposes in reading?

This question is largely answered by interviews and self-assessments. We have provided a textbook interview, but with older children we often spend a great deal of time talking about how the child deals with content-area texts. Older children often have a great deal of insight into their difficulties, and we try to take advantage of that insight.

Not only do children with reading problems often not know specific strategies, but they often do not understand general purposes for reading. In one study, proficient readers were asked, "If I gave you something to read, how would you know you were reading it well?" They responded that they would know they were reading it well if they understood what they read, if they "got the big ideas," and so on. Struggling readers, on the other hand, often responded that they were reading well when "they said the words correctly" or when they were not corrected by the teacher. Worse yet, many struggling readers were unable to identify how they knew they were not reading a passage successfully. If readers do not know that the general purpose for reading is to get meaning from print, but instead view reading as a decoding act, they will experience difficulties.

To ascertain the child's understanding of the general purposes of reading, we need to ask a question such as:

- What does the child view as the goal of reading, in general?

As adults, we recognize that the general goal of reading is to comprehend text. Our specific goals inevitably affect how we comprehend, of course, but we are clear about why we read. Many children, on the other hand, harbor vague ideas about the general goal of reading. Many believe that the goal is to say all of the words correctly or simply to arrive at the last word. They might not deny that understanding what they read is important, but in reality this goal is dwarfed by the lesser goal of word recognition. Rather than viewing word recognition as a means to an end, they view it as an end in itself. Instruction and programs that overemphasize decoding may exacerbate this perception, but it is common among struggling readers everywhere. It is therefore important for teachers to learn about children's views concerning reading and to attempt to broaden their outlook if need be.

PUTTING IT ALL TOGETHER

Listing all the questions that we ask, we arrive at the following:

- Is the child able to read texts at his or her grade placement level with automatic word recognition and adequate expression?
  - Is the child fluent in context?
  - Does the child have adequate sight-word knowledge?
  - Does the child have adequate knowledge of decoding strategies?
  - Does the child have adequate phonological awareness?
  - What concepts of print does the child have?
- Is the child able to comprehend the language of the text?
  - Does the child have an adequate vocabulary for his or her age and grade?
  - Does the child have the background knowledge necessary to understand the particular passage that he or she is reading?
  - Is the child able to use common text and sentence structures to aid in comprehension?
- Does the child have adequate knowledge of the purposes for reading and possess strategies to achieve those purposes?
  - Does the child have a set of strategies that can be used to achieve different purposes in reading?
  - What does the child view as the goal of reading in general?

These questions can be used to guide us through the assessment process. By the time we finish a complete assessment of a child, we should have answered most or all of these questions. (Some of the questions may prove unnecessary once we begin. For example, a child with strong decoding skills can be assumed to have acquired adequate phonological awareness.)

Form 1.1 (p. 23) is a modified version of Figure 1.2, with larger boxes for note taking. Many teachers have found it useful to make notes about a child in each of the boxes. Having to fill out the chart forces one to examine all aspects of the child's reading.

Now let's return to our three cases. For Josh, we are concerned about his decoding ability. The first questions we would ask concern his ability to decode and his phonological awareness, because we suspect that difficulties in this area underlie difficulties in automatic word recognition and reading connected text. We also would want to know about his ability to use context to support fluent reading, his comprehension ability, and his listening comprehension. As for Latrelle, we suspect that her decoding skills are adequate, although we would still want to assess them. We are more concerned about her automaticity and her ability to use context. We also want to know about her comprehension, and since she is required increasingly to read different kinds of text in fourth grade, we would want to know about her knowledge of strategies. For Sean, we are not as concerned with his word recognition as we are with his comprehension and strategic knowledge.

Chapter 2 focuses on general issues in assessment. Chapter 3 introduces the informal reading inventory, the keystone of classroom reading assessment because it is so important in answering many of the questions we have raised here. The remainder of the book deals with more fine-grained assessment in the particular areas we have discussed.

Modified Cognitive Model

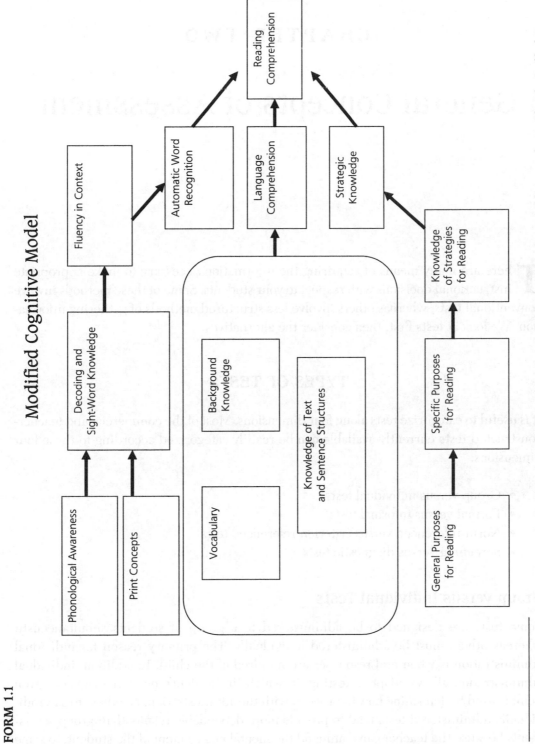

CHAPTER TWO

General Concepts of Assessment

There are many means of acquiring the information necessary to make appropriate instructional decisions with respect to your students. Some of these methods involve conventional tests, whereas others involve less structured methods of gathering information. We look at tests first, then consider the alternatives.

TYPES OF TESTS

It is useful to categorize tests along four dimensions. Most of the commercial and teacher-constructed tests currently available can be readily categorized according to these four dimensions:

- Group versus individual tests
- Formal versus informal tests
- Norm-referenced versus criterion-referenced tests
- Screening versus diagnostic tests

Group versus Individual Tests

Some tests are designed to be administered to a group of students simultaneously, whereas others must be administered individually. The primary reason for individual administration is when oral responses are required of the child. In addition, individual administration allows adaptive testing, in which the student's performance to a given point is used to determine how to proceed with the administration. Needless to say, individually administered tests tend to provide more dependable results than group assessments because the teacher can command the mental engagement of the student, to some extent, during the testing process. On the other hand, of course, group tests are far more efficient, even if their results are less dependable.

Formal versus Informal Tests

Tests differ with respect to how rigidly they are administered and interpreted. A formal test is one in which the directions for administration are clear cut and allow little, if any, discretion on the part of the teacher. Moreover, formal tests are scored in a carefully pre- scribed manner. A group standardized achievement test, such as those often mandated by state or local education agencies, is a good example of a formal test. An informal test, on the other hand, is one in which teacher discretion plays a major part. For example, the teacher may decide to modify how the test is given, based on early responses given by the student. Moreover, the teacher may exercise wide latitude in determining how to interpret the results. An essay test is one example of an informal test, and so is an infor- mal reading inventory, which we discuss in Chapter 3.

Norm-Referenced versus Criterion-Referenced Tests

There are two major ways of bringing meaning to test scores. One way is to compare one child's result with the results of other children. In other words, we can compare one child's performance with what might be normally expected of other children, hence the word *norm*. Norms such as percentile ranks, grade equivalents, stanines, normal curve equivalents, scale scores, and many others are commonplace in educational parlance. (We discuss norms in greater detail later in this chapter.)

A second way to interpret a child's performance is to compare his or her test score against a preestablished criterion or benchmark. A good example is the written portion of the state driver's examination. An examinee is permitted to miss a predetermined number of questions and still pass the exam. This criterion has nothing to do with how others performed on the same test. The comparison is between the individual driver and the criterion established by the Department of Motor Vehicles.

As a general rule, norm-referenced tests are useful in determining the overall devel- opmental level of a child with respect to others. Criterion-referenced tests are useful for mastery-level learning or competency-based assessment. A curriculum that consists of many specific skills to be learned is probably well served by a series of criterion- referenced tests (one per skill).

Screening versus Diagnostic Tests

Another useful way to categorize tests is by the use that is made of them. Two types are particularly important—screening and diagnostic tests. Screening tests attempt to pro- vide a broadly defined estimate of a student's overall achievement level in a given area. Screening tests are generally administered individually and are used to identify areas where more fine-grained assessments should be administered. These tests are brief and fairly general. Above all, the results indicate the next step to be taken in reading assessment: the administration of diagnostic instruments. Group achievement tests, such as the Stanford Achievement Test, the Iowa Tests of Basic Skills, and others can serve as screening tests, although their results are more often used as outcome measures for large groups of children.

Diagnostic tests, on the other hand, provide detailed information useful in planning instruction. These tests may involve multiple dimensions, possibly represented by subtests or by a variety of tasks a student is asked to perform. By the same token, a test designed to tell whether a student has mastered a particular objective is also an example of a diagnostic test. This is because the result documents progress in terms specific enough to help in planning instruction.

INTERPRETING NORM-REFERENCED READING TESTS

Perhaps the most important part of giving a test is making sense of the scores. In the case of a norm-referenced test, interpretation is guided by comparing a student's raw score (the number of items correct) with the scores of other students. In other words, we are interested in what a "normal" score might be and to what extent the score for a particular student differs from it. To make such a comparison, the student's raw score is converted into another score, called a norm. Many types of norms are in common use today; some of the most frequently encountered are presented in Table 2.1.

Figure 2.1 illustrates how some of these norms are related to one another in terms of the normal (what else?) curve. Notice, for example, that the fifth stanine always contains 20% of the group used to norm the test and extends from the 40th through the 59th percentile ranks. Also note that the nine stanines are perfectly symmetrical, so that the first and ninth stanine always contain 4% of the population, the second and eighth always contain 7%, and so on.

TABLE 2.1. Common Norms and What They Mean

Norm	Definition
Percentile rank	Percentage of children the same age whose scores a given child's equals or exceeds. (This is an approximate definition, not the one used in computation.) Percentile ranks cannot be averaged.
Stanine	One of nine statistically comparable divisions of the population tested, with the fifth positioned in the middle of the normal curve and accounting for 20% of those tested. (Short for "standard nine.")
Grade-equivalent score	An estimate of the grade level corresponding to a given student's raw score—a highly dubious norm whose use is officially discouraged by the International Reading Association.
Normal curve equivalent	The score resulting from partitioning the normal distribution into 99 statistically equivalent sections. NCEs can be averaged, unlike percentile ranks.
Scale score	A statistically converted score, usually computed to combine the results of different tests or to weight items differentially.
Quartile	One-quarter of the norming group, permitting a given child's score to be grossly categorized as falling in one of four sections.

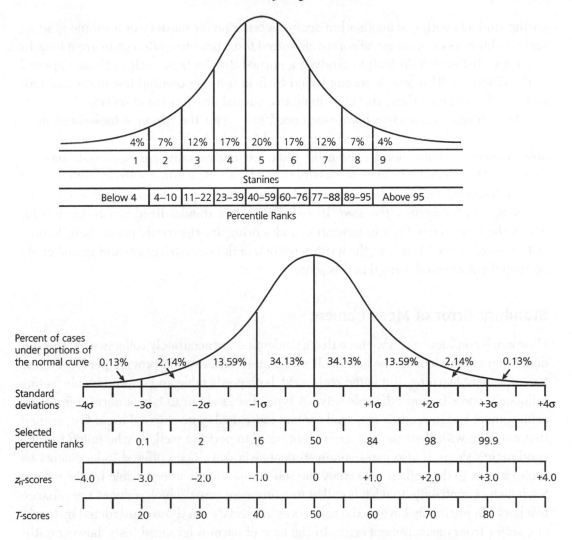

FIGURE 2.1. Common norms in relation to the normal distribution.

The lower graph in Figure 2.1 illustrates how a population of students varies from its own mean (average) score. The Greek letter *sigma* (σ) is used to represent the standard deviation of the group (that is, the extent to which the scores made by group members tend to vary). You will observe that more than 68% of the population (about two-thirds) have scores that fall within one standard deviation of the group mean. The farther we get from this mean, the fewer individuals we find. For example, only 13.59% of those tested typically score more than one standard deviation above the mean and far fewer than 1% score more than three standard deviations above it.

Not all tests produce these symmetrical, bell-shaped curves. Imagine a weekly spelling test of 20 words, on which all of the students in a gifted class score either 19 or 20. Results of such a test would be skewed to the right, which should be of no concern to the teacher. The results of classroom tests of this nature are usually interpreted not by comparing students with one another but against a criterion for mastery or a simple grading scale. Publishers of commercial norm-referenced tests, however, often go to great lengths to ensure that scores do tend to produce a normal distribution, such as those depicted in the diagrams. This goal is accomplished by field testing potential test items and ultimately selecting only those that contribute to a normal distribution of scores.

Most teachers associate norm-referenced tests with the group achievement measures they may be required to administer and for which they are often held accountable. However, many norm-referenced tests are individually administered, such as those used by special educators to classify students. Another minor misconception about norm-referenced tests concerns the word *standardized*. This term is frequently used as a synonym for *norm-referenced*. In fact, however, a standardized test is any test for which the procedures for administration and scoring are rigorously prescribed. Even a criterion-referenced test (e.g., the written portion of the state driver's examination) could be thought of as standardized in this sense.

Standard Error of Measurement

How much confidence can we have that a student's score accurately reflects what the student knows or can do? In the best of all worlds, test scores would provide perfect indicators of student learning. But in the real world, both predictable and unpredictable factors influence scores in unpredictable ways. A typical class about to take a norm-referenced achievement test in reading may well contain individuals who skipped breakfast, argued that morning with their parents, are unmotivated to perform well, or who failed to get a good night's sleep. It also may contain students who have been offered inducements by their parents to do well, or who enjoy the self-competition made possible by the norms. Such factors contribute to what is called measurement error, which reduces the reliance teachers can justifiably have on the test scores. All tests, even those constructed by teachers, suffer from measurement error. In the case of norm-referenced tests, however, it is possible to estimate just how large this error may be.

A simple equation may help us conceptualize the error factor. This equation depicts the relationship between a student's "true score" (that is, the score the student should have received based on the area being assessed) and the student's "actual score" (the score the student actually makes on the test).

$$\text{Actual score} = \text{True score} \pm \text{Error}$$

The true score can never be directly measured, only estimated. We hope the actual score is reasonably close to the true score, but we can never be certain that this is the case. The standard error of measurement provides a way of estimating how far "off" the actual score may be. This we can accomplish by creating a zone, or interval, around the actual score. First we add the standard error of measurement to the actual score to form the high point of the interval. Then we subtract the standard error from the actual score to find the low point. Because of the statistical properties of a test that has a normal distribution, we can conclude that there is roughly a 67% chance that the individual's true score falls somewhere within this interval. We call this region a "confidence interval," because it permits us to make a statement, with reasonable confidence, about the true score. To say that there are roughly two chances in three that an individual's true score lies within one standard error of the actual score sounds appealing, but it also means that there is one chance in three that the true score is either above the interval or below it—with no way to tell which!

If you desire to have more confidence in your conclusion, you simply construct a larger confidence interval by adding and subtracting twice the standard error from the actual score. The result is a 95% interval. In other words, we can be 95% certain that an individual's true score lies within two standard errors of the actual score. This seems very useful, indeed—except that the 95% interval can be so large that the statement is virtually meaningless.

As an example, consider the diagram in Figure 2.2. In this case, a student has earned a raw score of 20 on a test that has a standard error of measurement of 2 raw score points. The 67% confidence interval is constructed by adding and subtracting 2 points from the raw score of 20, so that the interval extends from 18 to 22. The 95% interval is constructed by doubling the standard error before adding and subtracting, so that this interval extends from 16 to 24. When the end points of the interval (that is, 16 and 24) are translated into norms such as percentile ranks, the range is disappointingly large.

One may well wonder, given the difficulties involved in attempting to estimate the true score, just why group achievement tests are given. Surely there is so much error involved that the results cannot be meaningfully interpreted. The response to this objection is that group achievement tests are not designed to assess individual students with a high level of accuracy. Rather, they are designed to assess groups and to answer educational questions concerning the achievement of groups. When large numbers of scores are averaged, the measurement error is diminished. A question such as "How well is the fifth grade doing in our school district?" is far better suited to group achievement testing than a question such as "How well is Johnny doing in reading?" Such tests provide us with only the most tentative measures of an individual student's learning, useful only for screening in the areas assessed.

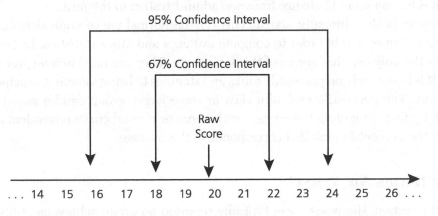

FIGURE 2.2. Examples of confidence intervals (standard error of measurement = 2).

Which Norms Are Best?

For the purpose of interpreting the results of group achievement testing, percentile ranks and stanines are perhaps the most useful norms for teachers. Percentile ranks give an indication of where an individual student's performance falls relative to other students the same age. Stanines do this as well, but because there are only nine possible stanine scores, they are not as precise as percentile ranks. Why, then, report stanines at all? The reason is that stanines are statistically equivalent, allowing certain conclusions to be reached. It takes as much effort to move from the first to the second stanine as it does from the sixth to the seventh, for example. This is not true of percentile ranks, however, rendering stanines preferable for making pretest–posttest comparisons or for comparing the results of two subtests.

The Two-Stanine Rule

If the difference between the scores made by a student on two different subtests (or on the pre- and postadministrations of the same test) is two stanines or greater, the difference is probably real. A difference of two stanines is typically sufficient to overcome measurement error. For example, if a child scores at the fourth stanine on a subtest of reading comprehension, and at the sixth stanine on a subtest of vocabulary, it is reasonable to conclude that achievement in the area of reading comprehension is lower than achievement in vocabulary, compared with the norming group. On the other hand, if the stanine for one of these two areas is 3 and for the other area 4, we are statistically prevented from concluding that there is any real difference whatsoever.

A Limitation of Percentile Ranks

Some educators make the mistake of computing class or school averages using percentile ranks. Doing so is not statistically appropriate, because percentile ranks are not on an equal-interval scale. That is to say, the "distance" between the second and third percentile ranks is not the same as the "distance" between the 32nd and 33rd percentile ranks. The closer a score is to the 50th percentile rank, the more volatile it becomes and the easier it is for the score to change from one administration to the next.

Because of this difficulty, statisticians rely on normal curve equivalents and scale scores (see Figure 2.1) in order to compute averages and other statistics. In fact, this is virtually the only use that norms of this kind serve. They are hard to interpret in themselves. It is best to rely on percentile ranks and stanines to bring meaning to achievement test scores. The percentile rank of a class or some larger group can be ascertained, if desired, by first computing the average scale score or normal curve equivalent and *then* locating the percentile rank that corresponds to this average.

Which Norms Are Worst?

Without question, the worst norm typically reported on group achievement tests is the grade-equivalent score. This norm purports to indicate the grade level at which the student has performed on a particular subtest. A common way of interpreting a grade-equivalent score is by relating it to that of "average children" at a particular level. For example, if a seventh grader produces a grade-equivalent score of 2.6 on a subtest of reading comprehension, it is common for teachers to conclude that this student comprehends as well as the average second grader who is in the sixth month of school. This conclusion is very difficult to defend, however. For one thing, a test that is appropriate for middle schoolers is unlikely to have been given to second graders simply in order to establish norms. Indeed, many grade-equivalent scores are merely statistical projections that permit a student to be compared with students of other ages.

Another difficulty of grade-equivalent scores is that for most tests they have "floors" and "ceilings." A floor is simply the lowest grade-equivalent score it is possible to make, because grade equivalents have not been projected below a certain level. For example, if the floor for a reading comprehension subtest is 2.0, then even a student who is a nonreader may be judged to be reading as well as the average beginning second grader (Silvaroli, 1977). Problems with floors are not as troublesome as they once were, but the potential for difficulties still exists.

A ceiling, on the other hand, is the highest grade-equivalent score a student can earn. It is rare for an achievement test to have a ceiling higher than 12th grade. Although ceilings could lead us to underestimate the achievement of advanced students, this possibility is not as troublesome as that of overestimating the achievement of struggling readers due to the effects of floors.

The International Reading Association, in a 1980 Board of Directors position statement that is still in effect, officially condemned the use of grade-equivalent scores for all of these reasons. You may well ask, if such scores are so bad, why are they computed by test publishers in the first place? The answer publishers often give is that educators demand grade-equivalent scores. The publishers are well aware of their limitations, of course, but contend that eliminating them would put them at a competitive disadvantage. Perhaps the solution to this dilemma lies in fostering better awareness in educators, policymakers, and other stakeholders who use test results. Until awareness is heightened, however, the best advice that can be offered to practitioners in the position of interpreting test results is simply to ignore grade-equivalent scores.

An important exception to the problematic nature of grade equivalents is the case of individually administered tests that have a large sequence of items progressing in difficulty. Such tests are often used by special educators. An example is the Peabody Picture Vocabulary Test–IV, which has items ranging from very simple to very difficult. Because of this range and because easier items have actually been administered to younger students and the harder ones to older students, age and grade equivalents are much more meaningful.

Suggestions for "Reading" a Student Profile

The array of data contained in the score report for an individual student can be perplexing. The following suggestions are offered as a means of navigating through this maze of data.

1. Ignore grade-equivalent scores. For all of the reasons we have discussed, such scores offer no usable information to teachers.
2. Consider the reading comprehension score as the best indicator of overall reading achievement.
3. In the case of low scores, note whether the number of items attempted is the same as the number possible, especially for subtests that are out of line with the general profile.
4. Be skeptical of specific skill results based on very few items. It is common for skill breakdowns to include results based on only a handful of items corresponding to a particular skill. The reliability of these embedded subtests is extremely low, and daily classwork constitutes a far better indicator of skill deficits. (See the sample contained in Figure 2.3.)
5. Use the national stanine to interpret achievement for each subtest. The percentile rank is more precise in some ways, but stanines can be more easily interpreted, as follows:

   Stanines 7–9 = Above average
   Stanine 6 = Borderline
   Stanine 5 = Average
   Stanine 4 = Borderline
   Stanine 1–3 = Below average

6. Use the two-stanine rule to compare subtest scores. Remember that if the difference is at least two stanines, there is a statistically good chance that a real difference exists. You cannot know precisely how large the difference is, however.

Student: Joe Kelly
School: Kashinkerry Elementary
Grade: 03
Test Date: March

	Reading Subtests		
	Total Reading	Reading Vocabulary	Reading Comprehension
Number Possible	84	30	54
Raw Score	45	17	28
Scaled Score	590	582	595
National Percentile Rank	23–4	23–4	26–4
National Stanine	4	4	4
National NCE	34.4	34.4	34.4
Grade Equivalent	2.7	2.7	2.7

FIGURE 2.3. Sample reading profile from a fictitious nationally norm-referenced group achievement test.

7. Use group achievement scores for broad-based screening purposes only. Be prepared to reinterpret results based on other evidence that may be more dependable. Such evidence might include classroom performance, results of individual assessments, and teacher observations.

8. Be on the lookout for students who do not take the testing seriously. It is unfortunately commonplace for some students to expend only minimal effort on taking achievement tests. The scores they produce are virtually worthless, and it is important to know who these students are. Otherwise, mistakes can be made when evaluating their achievement. Make a point of giving their names to next year's teachers if the results of the testing arrive too late in the year for you to make any use of them yourself.

The National Assessment of Educational Progress

The National Assessment of Educational Progress (NAEP) in reading is "our nation's report card," an assessment periodically given to students across the country to assess growth in reading achievement over time. It has been administered since 1969, allowing policymakers to examine trends in achievement. The scores on the NAEP are reported on a scale from 0 to 500. These scores are developed separately for each subject area.

The NAEP does not report individual student scores, and it does not report school-wide scores for participating schools. Since 1990, scores have been reported for individual states, so that states who participate (all states now do, but this has not always been the case) can compare their achievement to that of other states and to the national averages.

If the test cannot be used for individual assessment, because the results are never reported that way, why discuss it here? We do so for two reasons. First, these results are widely reported in newspapers and other media, and it is important to understand what they are, and are not, so that teachers can respond intelligently. Second, the NAEP provides some benchmarks for judging children's performance, rather than only discussing how children scored in relation to a norming sample.

The NAEP reports scores in two ways. The first is the average scale score for the nation and for the states. A state's average can be compared with the nation's or with that of other states. For example, Table 2.2 indicates that Georgia's statewide average for grade 4 was below the national average in 1992 and 2007, whereas Connecticut was above average both years. Delaware was below the national average in 1992 but above it in 2007. The reverse was true for Rhode Island, which was above the national average in 1992 but below it in 2007.

The second way results are reported are by benchmarks. The NAEP governing board has divided performance into three levels: basic, proficient, and advanced. These performance levels are translated into specific benchmarks for each grade.

Although these are listed as "benchmarks," they were designed as high standards for children to reach. The point of setting standards so high was that teachers would push their students toward these standards, rather than toward a more modest level of attainment. But children can fail to reach the "basic" level for fourth grade, for example, and

TABLE 2.2. Fifteen-Year NAEP Comparison by State for Grade 4 Reading (Public Schools Only)

	Average scale score	
	1992	2007
The nation	215	220
Alabama	207	216
Arizona	209	210
Arkansas	211	217
California	202	209
Colorado	217	224
Connecticut	222	227
Delaware	213	225
Florida	208	224
Georgia	212	219
Hawaii	203	213
Iowa	225	225
Kansas	—	225
Kentucky	213	222
Louisiana	204	207
Maine	227	226
Maryland	211	225
Massachusetts	226	236
Michigan	216	220
Minnesota	221	225
Mississippi	199	208
Missouri	220	221
Montana	—	227
Nevada	—	211
New Hampshire	228	229
New Mexico	211	212
New York	215	224
North Carolina	212	218
Oklahoma	220	217
Oregon	—	215
Pennsylvania	221	226
Rhode Island	217	219
South Carolina	210	214
South Dakota	—	223
Tennessee	212	216
Texas	213	220
Utah	220	221
Virginia	221	227
Washington	—	224
West Virginia	216	215
Wisconsin	224	223
Wyoming	223	225
District of Columbia	188	197

still demonstrate a literal understanding of what they read, understand a main idea from expository text, or follow a simple plot (Donahue, Voelkl, Campbell, & Mazzeo, 1999). These are all listed as "below basic" skills at the fourth-grade level. At the eighth- and 12th-grade levels, "below basic" implies an even higher level of skill. We need high standards to propel our students (and us) to higher achievement, but we are concerned that statements such as "40% of our fourth graders are reading below the basic level" can be misinterpreted. (See Table 2.3 for definitions of levels at each grade.)

Finally, the NAEP is a measure that is both standardized and formal, with aspects of a criterion-referenced measure. Item difficulties are calculated by comparing the numbers of children who got each item correct, creating a scale score. The test is formally administered by a set of administration rules, but there also are criteria that were used to develop the test (the achievement level definitions). Many state tests have been based on this model, being both formal and criterion-referenced.

RELIABILITY AND VALIDITY

Perhaps the most important statistical evaluators associated with tests are reliability and validity. These two related criteria are frequently confused. *Reliability* refers to the consistency of results, that is, the general dependability of a test: A test that produces similar results under similar conditions is said to be reliable. *Validity* refers to the degree to which a test measures what it purports to measure and what the examiner wishes to measure. Reliability is a prerequisite of validity, but validity is not needed for reliability. To put it another way, a valid test is always reliable, but a reliable test is not necessarily valid.

Consider an everyday analogy: McDonald's hamburgers. McDonald's hamburgers, we suggest, are reliable but not valid. If you walk into a McDonald's anywhere in the world, from Savannah to Hong Kong, you receive precisely the same product. Now that's reliability! But are these sandwiches what you really want when you think of a good hamburger? In our view, they are not. In other words, they are not valid examples of "true" hamburgers. To put it in testing terms, there is high reliability and low validity. The same can be true of a test. To use an extreme example, a math test may be highly reliable, but if used to assess reading ability, it would produce results that are clearly invalid.

Reliability is computed in various ways and is usually expressed as a decimal. The closer the reliability coefficient is to 1.0, the more reliable the test. Reliability coefficients of .90 or higher are considered extremely high and are hallmarks of reliable testing. Reliability is influenced by such factors as (1) the length of the test (the longer the test, the more reliable it is), (2) the clarity of directions, and (3) the objectivity of scoring.

Validity is a murkier concept and usually has no numerical translation. Rather, the producers of a commercial test simply make a case for its validity by presenting the evidence they have accumulated. It is up to consumers (i.e., teachers and administrators) to decide whether the test is truly valid for their purposes. Several types of validity are important; a quick overview may help clarify the general concept of validity.

TABLE 2.3. NAEP Performance Level Definitions and Descriptions

Achievement-level policy definitions

Basic   Partial mastery of prerequisite knowledge and skills that are fundamental for proficient work at each grade.

Proficient   Solid academic performance for each grade assessed. Students reaching this level have demonstrated competency over challenging subject matter, including subject-matter knowledge, application of such knowledge to real-world situations, and analytical skills appropriate to the subject matter.

Advanced   Superior performance.

Fourth grade

Basic   Fourth-grade students performing at the Basic level should demonstrate an understanding of the overall meaning of what they read. When reading text appropriate for fourth-graders, they should be able to make relatively obvious connections between the text and their own experiences and extend the ideas in the text by making simple inferences.

Proficient   Fourth-grade students performing at the Proficient level should be able to demonstrate an overall understanding of the text, providing inferential as well as literal information. When reading text appropriate to fourth grade, they should be able to extend the ideas in the text by making inferences, drawing conclusions, and making connections to their own experiences. The connection between the text and what the student infers should be clear.

Advanced   Fourth-grade students performing at the Advanced level should be able to generalize about topics in the reading selection and demonstrate an awareness of how authors compose and use literary devices. When reading text appropriate to fourth grade, they should be able to judge text critically and, in general, to give thorough answers that indicate careful thought.

Eighth grade

Basic   Eighth-grade students performing at the Basic level should demonstrate a literal understanding of what they read and be able to make some interpretations. When reading text appropriate to eighth grade, they should be able to identify specific aspects of the text that reflect overall meaning, extend the ideas in the text by making simple inferences, recognize and relate interpretations and connections among ideas in the text to personal experience, and draw conclusions based on the text.

Proficient   Eighth-grade students performing at the Proficient level should be able to show an overall understanding of the text, including inferential as well as literal information. When reading text appropriate to eighth grade, they should be able to extend the ideas in the text by making clear inferences from it, by drawing conclusions, and by making connections to their own experiences—including other reading experiences. Proficient eighth graders should be able to identify some of the devices authors use in composing text.

Advanced   Eighth-grade students performing at the Advanced level should be able to describe the more abstract themes and ideas of the overall text. When reading text appropriate to eighth grade, they should be able to analyze both meaning and form and support their analyses explicitly with examples from the text; they should be able to extend text information by relating it to their experiences and to world events. At this level, student responses should be thorough, thoughtful, and extensive.

12th grade

Basic   Twelfth-grade students performing at the Basic level should be able to demonstrate an overall understanding and make some interpretations of the text. When reading text appropriate to 12th grade, they should be able to identify and relate aspects of the text to its overall meaning, extend the ideas in the text by making simple inferences, recognize interpretations, make connections among and relate ideas in the text to their personal experiences, and draw conclusions. They should be able to identify elements of an author's style.

Proficient   Twelfth-grade students performing at the Proficient level should be able to show an overall understanding of the text, which includes inferential as well as literal information. When reading text appropriate to 12th grade, they should be able to extend the ideas of the text by making inferences, drawing conclusions, and making connections to their own personal experiences and other readings. Connections between inferences and the text should be clear, even when implicit. These students should be able to analyze the author's use of literary devices.

Advanced   Twelfth-grade students performing at the Advanced level should be able to describe more abstract themes and ideas in the overall text. When reading text appropriate to 12th grade, they should be able to analyze both the meaning and the form of the text and implicitly support their analyses with specific examples from the text. They should be able to extend the information from the text by relating it to their experiences and to the world. Their responses should be thorough, thoughtful, and extensive.

Content Validity

A test that reflects the curriculum that is taught is said to possess *content validity*. The process of curriculum alignment, advocated by Fenwick English and others (English & Frase, 1999), is designed to ensure a good match between what is taught and what is tested, and is a popular means of improving content validity. Imagine a teacher who invests many hours trying to foster critical reading comprehension ability merely to find that students will be given only low-level questions on an achievement test. Such a test would have limited content validity for that teacher.

Construct Validity

When a test produces results that conform well to real-world applications, it is said to possess *construct validity*. For example, assume that the results of a reading achievement test show that students who did well had already been placed in advanced reading groups by their teachers, that students who performed poorly had been placed in below-average groups, and so forth. This would be evidence of construct validity.

Predictive Validity

Some tests are expressly designed to predict future performance or success. Results of the SAT and ACT, for instance, correlate well with the later college GPAs of the students who take them. College admissions officers use the results in the confidence that they do a good job of predicting success. That is to say, the tests possess good predictive validity.

In considering predictive validity, Paris (2005) theorizes that it may be important to distinguish among constrained and unconstrained skills. According to Paris, *constrained skills* are those skills that "develop from nonexistent to high or ceiling levels in childhood" (p. 187). Concepts about print, alphabetic knowledge, and phonics are highly constrained. Phonemic awareness and oral reading fluency are less constrained. However, comprehension and vocabulary are unconstrained due to their scope, importance, and range of influence in domain and time span. They tend to develop over a lifetime. Simply put, some skills are mastered while others continue to develop. This distinction can cause problems when the two types are both treated in the same way. As a result, we advise caution in using data analysis related to constrained skills to form developmental trajectories for more general reading proficiency (Paris, 2005; Riedel, 2007).

Concurrent Validity

If a new measure and an established measure are administered at about the same time to the same students, and if the two scores turn out to be highly correlated, this result could be regarded as evidence of validity for the new test. Because the two measures are administered at almost the same time, we call a strong relationship evidence of *concurrent validity*. When, for example, a convenient, easy-to-give measure, such as the San Diego Quick Assessment, is shown to provide reading-level estimates that are the same or similar to those provided by more complex tests, evidence of concurrent validity is established.

Consequential Validity

Consequential validity addresses the consequences of test administration and score interpretation. Messick (1993) states that "the appraisal of the functional worth of the testing in pursuit of the intended ends should take into account all of the ends, both intended and unintended, that are advanced by the testing application, including not only individual and institutional effects but societal and systemic effects as well" (p. 85). Considering the consequences of the administration of a test and interpreting test results as a validation of educational tests is a new and somewhat controversial idea in psychometrics. What are the intended and unintended consequences of a particular assessment? Does the administration of a particular high-stakes test minimize the reading curriculum to skill-based instruction? Does the administration of a particular test yield instruction that supports a standards-based curriculum? Does the utilization of the assessment result in differentiated instruction that is targeted to each student's needs? These are a few questions that might be asked when considering the consequential validity of an assessment.

WHEN IS A TEST NOT A TEST?

Information useful in planning reading instruction does not always come in the form of test results. In fact, many teachers would argue that the most important information about students does not come from tests at all, but from other sources. These sources include written work, classroom observations, parent input, and portfolios.

Written Work

The products of written class assignments can provide important clues to a student's literacy development. Such products include compositions, journal entries, worksheets, e-mails, class notes, and many others. For younger children, written work samples may include scribbling and early writing, potentially rich in data about spelling development and phonological awareness.

Classroom Observations

As students engage in reading and writing activities during the school day, observant teachers often discern patterns useful in monitoring growth and identifying needs. Yetta Goodman has called this process *kidwatching* (e.g., Owocki & Goodman, 2002). In some cases, structured observations can be helpful, such as checklists of key behaviors. Unstructured observations are useful as well, especially for experienced teachers who know what they are looking for in terms of behavioral cues. In this case, the teacher notices a revealing pattern and either makes a mental note of it or (better yet) makes a brief anecdotal record for later reference.

Parent Input

Calls to parents and remarks they make during face-to-face conferences can provide insights into a child's behaviors. Documenting such input by making quick, dated notes for later use can be useful. Occasionally, parent input also comes in written form, as notes or letters sent to the teacher or other educators.

Portfolios

A literacy portfolio is a collection of evidence that enables a teacher to document progress over time. The evidence might include:

- Samples of daily work
- Coded passages read orally by the student
- A chart of reading rate over time
- A record of reading interests and books read
- Journal entries by the teacher (or anecdotal notes)
- Journal entries by the student
- Test results

This list is far from exhaustive. Creative teachers can make portfolios a telling glimpse into the literacy growth and development of individual students. Following are guidelines and suggestions for getting started with portfolio projects.

1. All of the evidence should be dated so that progress over time can be interpreted. Leafing through a portfolio from start to finish can provide an occasional long-term perspective that would otherwise be hard to gain.

2. Unless a teacher is fairly selective about what is included in the portfolio, it can rapidly become cumbersome, difficult to store, and hard to use.

3. Roger Farr (1992) recommends keeping two portfolios for each student. One he terms the *working* portfolio, as described above. This is the portfolio used to monitor progress and guide instructional decision making. The other is the *show* portfolio, a dated collection of the student's best work. It is far smaller than the working portfolio and is used to signal progress during student conferences and to discuss a student's strengths and needs during parent conferences. If you think keeping two portfolios might be unmanageable, a compromise might consist of keeping only the working type and using sticky notes to identify specific entries prior to a conference so that they can be quickly located.

4. Consider passing portfolios along to next year's teachers. Logistics can be troublesome, but putting a well-maintained portfolio into the right hands can provide a wealth

of information at the start of a new school year. Think how you might feel if you were on the receiving end of such a policy!

5. Use portfolios during postobservation conferences with an administrator or literacy coach. Their contents can enrich the discussion considerably and also document why you might have used certain instructional techniques with particular students. The observing administrator will not fail to be impressed, for portfolios are clearly one mark of a reflective teacher intent on using evidence of student performance to guide instructional planning.

SUMMARY

There is a wide variety of options available for assessment and a wide variety of users of educational assessment. From the highest levels, policymakers in the state and federal government might use information from the NAEP to judge the effectiveness of reading instruction in an entire state or the nation. These results can provide a rough estimate of whether policies are improving achievement. Standardized norm- or criterion-referenced tests can provide a school superintendent the same type of data on a smaller scale. These tests can tell the superintendent or the school board about the overall effectiveness of a curriculum in a district, or how well individual schools are performing. Used correctly, standardized tests can provide important information about reading programs used in a district.

For an individual teacher, however, such measures usually do not provide much information above and beyond that available through informal measures and observations. Because of the standard error of measurement, scores on norm-referenced tests are rarely sufficiently accurate, by themselves, for individual interpretation. At best, they may be used to screen children. If a child does particularly poorly or particularly well, the teacher might want to retest, using an informal reading inventory (IRI) to confirm the score of the norm-referenced test. If the IRI produces divergent results, the teacher should at least question the results of the norm-referenced test. IRIs, running records, and other measures are closer to the child's curriculum and may be more relevant for individual diagnosis.

CHAPTER THREE

Informal Reading Inventories
and Other Measures
of Oral Reading

I n reading assessment, we are always asking questions and using the results of our assessments to answer these questions. At the end of Chapter 1, we asked a series of questions about children's reading skills. From our model, we are concerned globally about the child's abilities in the areas of automatic word recognition, language comprehension, and strategic knowledge. An expanded list of questions follows.

WHAT DO WE WANT TO LEARN
FROM A READING ASSESSMENT?

Questions	Sources of information
Automatic word recognition	
Does the child read fluently and naturally?	Oral reading sample, observations
What level material should the child use for instruction?	Oral reading sample, level
Does the child use context to complement inadequate decoding skills?	Miscue analysis of oral reading
Does the child self-correct?	Oral reading sample, observations
Does the child read words better in context or in isolation?	Oral reading sample, observations
With which spelling patterns is the child familiar?	Criterion-referenced decoding test, invented spellings, spelling inventory
Can the child decode words in isolation that he or she cannot decode in context? Or vice versa?	Comparison of decoding test with oral reading sample

41

Does the child have an adequate level of phonemic awareness?	Phonological awareness inventory
What is the child's knowledge of basic print concepts?	Word lists, oral reading sample

Language comprehension

What level material can the child comprehend when reading silently?	Silent reading sample, informal reading inventory (IRI)
What level material can the child comprehend when reading orally?	Oral reading sample, IRI
Does the child comprehend better when reading orally than silently?	Comparison of oral and silent reading
Does the child comprehend what he or she can accurately read?	Oral reading sample, IRI
What types of questions give the child trouble?	Examination of literal, inferential, etc., questions on IRI
Does the child understand material at his or her grade level when it is read aloud by the teacher?	Listening comprehension passage
Does the child have an adequate vocabulary for understanding?	Informal observations during discussions
Does the child use story structure to aid in comprehension?	Retellings
Does the child have adequate background knowledge?	Background knowledge measures (varies with each story read)
What does the child do when he or she lacks background knowledge?	Analysis of IRI responses

Strategic control

Does the child use varied strategies flexibly during reading?	See Chapter 8
Does the child understand the purposes of reading?	See Chapters 8 and 9
How positive is the child's attitude toward reading?	See Chapter 9

A quick review of this table suggests that a great many of the questions we raise about children's reading can be answered through the sensitive use of an oral reading sample. Such a sample can come from an informal reading inventory or running records. Many of the other questions can be answered through the use of other parts of the informal reading inventory—the silent reading and listening comprehension sections and the word list. For that reason, we consider the IRI to be the cornerstone of the reading assessment process. However, Walpole and McKenna (2006) have pointed out that IRIs must be complemented by more targeted measures. Consequently, many of the other assessments in this book are used to confirm, elaborate, or explain the results garnered

from an IRI. Relatively easy to administer (once you have learned some simple notations), an IRI in the hands of a well-trained practitioner provides a great deal of information about a child's reading strengths and weaknesses. In addition, the same processes
involved in interpreting an IRI can be used by teachers in their everyday observations of
children's reading.

What Is an IRI?

An IRI consists mainly of a sequence of graded passages, typically beginning at the
preprimer level. Each passage is followed by comprehension questions and, occasionally,
a retelling scoring guide. Most IRIs are also equipped with graded word lists for estimating where to begin in the passages and for assessing a child's ability to recognize words
in isolation.

For each passage the child reads, the teacher judges whether the passage is on the
child's independent, instructional, or frustration level. (We will define these levels more
precisely in a moment.) This judgment is based on both accuracy of word recognition
and success in answering the comprehension questions posed orally by the teacher. The
teacher shows the child a copy of the passage and makes notations on a separate copy
that includes the questions and scoring guides. Once the child completes a passage, the
teacher must decide which, if any, of the remaining passages in a sequence should be
given next. Following the IRI administration, the teacher must consider the child's performance on all of the passages read and then make an overall judgment as to the child's
instructional reading level.

Form 3.1 presents the teacher's version of a passage that we have developed as an
illustration. Of course, the student version of this passage (Form 3.2) contains no questions and is printed in larger type. The summary form (Form 3.3) is a generic table used
to record in an organized manner some of the most important data produced by an IRI
administration. The tables found in commercial IRIs will vary, of course.

Reading Levels

Traditionally, children were assigned a reading level by means of an informal reading
inventory. These levels were based on those determined by Emmett Betts in the 1930s
(Betts, 1946). A passage of a particular readability level was judged to represent a child's
independent, instructional, or frustration level, as defined below:

- *Independent level* is the highest level at which a child can read the material without assistance.
- *Instructional level* is the highest level at which a child could benefit from instructional support.
- *Frustration level* is the lowest level at which a child is likely to be frustrated, even
  with instructional support.

How are these levels estimated using an IRI? When the results of an IRI are quantified into percentages of questions answered correctly and percentages of words read accurately aloud, these two percentages can be used to estimate a child's reading levels. Conventionally, the independent level has been defined as the highest level at which a child can read with 99% accuracy and with at least 90% comprehension. The instructional level has been defined as the highest passage a child can read with 95–98% oral accuracy and with at least 75% comprehension. The frustration level has been defined as the lowest level at which the child can read with 90% or lower oral accuracy and with 50% comprehension or below. These criteria are presented in Table 3.1.

This classification has been used to the present day in many commercial informal reading inventories (e.g., Johns, 2005). There are problems with a strict application of such criteria, however. To begin with, comprehension assessment depends on the questions used. Some questions are more difficult; some are easier. A child's performance depends on the difficulty of the questions, and asking a different set of questions can lead to a different conclusion about whether a particular passage is on a child's independent, instructional, or frustration level (Peterson, Greenlaw, & Tierney, 1978).

Others have questioned the oral accuracy levels. Clay (1993a) uses a 90% accuracy level for the early reading books in Reading Recovery. This level makes sense for the predictable picture books used in early first grade. It also makes sense, given the level of support provided to children in Reading Recovery.

It is also not clear whether the 95% cutoff for the instructional level should include self-corrections or how semantically acceptable miscues should be handled (e.g., substituting *crimson* for *scarlet*). Some informal reading inventories recommend that semantically acceptable miscues be considered acceptable deviations from the text and not counted as errors. Others instruct users to count all miscues as errors. Some commercial IRIs, such as the Qualitative Reading Inventory–4 (Leslie & Caldwell, 2005), provide two ways of determining the instructional level: (1) counting all miscues, and (2) counting only those that significantly change the meaning of the text.

It may strike you that Betts set a very high standard for oral accuracy, including high percentages and verbatim-only acceptability. Keep in mind that Betts based his notion of instructional levels on the instruction typical of the time. During that era, the directed reading activity (also developed by Betts) was the most commonly used instructional model. In this model, prior to reading, the teacher provides background information; preteaches key vocabulary; and provides a purpose, or focus, for reading. Children read

TABLE 3.1. The Betts Criteria for Interpreting the Level of an IRI Passage

Level	Word recognition		Comprehension
Independent	99–100%	*and*	90–100%
Instructional	95–98%	*and*	75–89%
Frustration	90% or lower	*or*	50% or lower

segments of the text silently, stopping to discuss teacher-posed questions. Children reread the text that addresses the answer of the question orally. Following the reading of the whole selection, children answer a series of postreading questions. The directed reading activity provides relatively minimal instruction compared to more recent models. In fluency-oriented reading instruction (Stahl & Heubach, 2005), the entire text is first read and discussed, followed by a number of repeated readings of the text. In this approach, children receive considerably more support in reading the text and thus should be able to benefit from reading more difficult text. Stahl and his colleagues found that children could benefit from reading text with only 85% accuracy—texts that would conventionally be considered to be at the frustration level—at the beginning of instruction.

This finding does not imply that all children can read all texts. Consider Vygotsky's (1978) notion of the zone of proximal development. Vygotsky suggested that children can do their most productive work within a zone. The bottom end of the zone (the easiest material) is the level at which children can work independently. The top end of the zone (the most difficult material) is the most difficult level, at which children can work with teacher support. Above that level, children cannot work productively with material even with teacher support. Our experience is that children can be supported in working with material that is relatively difficult, but still within the zone, if the teacher plans to provide extra support. Sometimes this support is provided through repeated readings or assisted reading of various kinds; at other times it can be provided through direct comprehension support, such as through reciprocal teaching.

We do not have precise guidelines for determining a zone of proximal development for each child. Our rough-and-ready guess is that, if you are using intensive teaching techniques like those described above, you might try starting one year above the child's instructional level, as measured by a conventional informal reading inventory. This is a guess, but it has worked well in our clinic. If you are using classroom techniques like directed reading activities, which do not provide as much support, then you might stay at the instructional level. Either way, you need to monitor what the child is doing and make sure that the child is successful with, but somewhat challenged by, the level of material you are using.

Miscue Analysis

Prior to the 1970s, IRIs were used almost exclusively to estimate a child's instructional level and to place him or her in materials of appropriate difficulty. More recently, educators have attempted to extract more information from an IRI by analyzing the oral errors a child makes and drawing conclusions about the use of context to decode words. This focus was the result of Kenneth Goodman's notion that word identification relies on three types of "cues": those located within the word itself (graphophonic cues), those associated with sentence structure (syntactic cues), and those emanating from the meaning of the surrounding text (semantic cues). His model suggested that all three types of cues are used in concert and that readers resort to graphophonic cues as a last resort, when the predictions they make about the identity of word are not supported by context. Goodman viewed readers as merely sampling the letters of a word in order to confirm a prediction about its identity. This reasoning led him to suggest that when a reader substitutes one word for another, it should not be regarded as a problem as long as the substitution is similar in meaning. For example, when the reader says *pony* for *horse*, the teacher knows that syntactic and semantic cues are being used, something Goodman saw as the hallmark of proficient reading. This is why Goodman preferred the term *miscue* to *error*. It is also why some IRIs have criteria based on "semantically acceptable" errors—or miscues, if you like.

Later research, however, revealed beyond question that Goodman's model was wrong (e.g., see Adams, 1990; Rayner & Pollatsek, 1989). Proficient readers process nearly every letter of every word, but for the most part they do so automatically, at an unconscious level. In contrast, miscues based on context are made by beginning readers who are not yet rapid decoders or by older students with decoding difficulties. This finding raises practical issues for a teacher listening to a student read aloud. When the child hesitates at an unfamiliar word, a teacher following the Goodman model might ask the child what word makes sense or encourage the child to read to the end of the sentence to obtain more clues. On the other hand, a teacher familiar with current research would call the child's attention to the structure of the word, to letter–sound relationships, rimes, affixes, and so forth.

This development creates a dilemma for those wishing to administer an IRI. If a teacher makes a simple tally of actual errors, scoring criteria can be quickly applied. But doing so ignores the *kinds* of errors the child makes. Is there not important information residing in the patterns of miscues? We contend that there is, but our approach differs considerably from the one popularized by Goodman (McKenna & Picard, 2006/2007). Consequently, we do recommend that miscues be recorded by type, but we outline a new approach to interpretation later in this chapter.

GUIDELINES FOR ADMINISTERING AN IRI

There is no single best way to give an IRI. Much depends on what you want to know. The IRI is like a toolkit that can be used for a variety of purposes—not all of it may be appropriate on a given occasion, and the way you use it will vary.

This does not mean that there is no consensus about useful approaches to giving IRIs, however. If your goal is to estimate a child's instructional reading level and, in the process, gather data about how the child decodes words, then the following general steps may be helpful. But remember, as a teacher you are empowered to "veto" any of these steps if the specific circumstances appear to warrant it.

Overall Strategy for Giving the IRI

1. *Estimate the child's independent reading level.* One way of doing this is by examining any available evidence you may have, such as classroom performance, results of a previous IRI, and so on. Another way is to give the graded word lists

of the IRI and to consider the highest word list on which no words are missed to be a tentative estimate of the independent reading level.

2. *Administer the passage corresponding to your estimate of the independent level.* Have the child read this passage orally while you code miscues. Then ask the comprehension questions. At this point you must judge whether the passage is at the independent reading level by considering both the word-recognition accuracy (number of oral reading errors) and the child's comprehension performance (number of questions missed).

3. *Decide which passage to administer next.* If the initial passage is above the child's independent reading level, you must proceed to simpler passages until the independent level is reached. If the initial passage is judged to be at the student's independent reading level, you should proceed to more difficult passages until frustration is reached or appears to be imminent. In any case, each time you complete a passage, you must decide which passage to give next or whether to discontinue the IRI.

Strategy for Giving Each Passage

1. Briefly prepare the student by asking a question that taps prior knowledge or by identifying the topic.
2. Ask the student to read the passage silently.
3. Ask the student to read the passage aloud.
4. If you are interested in reading rate, note the exact beginning time.
5. Code oral miscues as the child reads.
6. If the child hesitates too long, supply the word.
7. Discontinue the passage and do not ask the questions if
   a. the passage is so difficult that you are reasonably sure it would be judged at the frustration level, or
   b. you have had to supply, in your judgment, too many words.
8. If you are interested in reading rate, note the exact ending time.
9. Ask the comprehension questions, giving partial credit where you feel it is warranted and rewording questions if you think it will help communicate what a given question asks.
10. Use the scoring guidelines to determine the level of the passage in terms of (a) oral accuracy and (b) comprehension.
11. Come to an overall judgment as to whether the passage is at the child's independent, instructional, or frustration level. Sometimes this judgment may not be clear-cut.

Coding Oral Reading

As the child reads a passage, the teacher marks departures from the printed text. The goal is to create a record that can be "played back" later. As we have noted, these departures are often called *miscues*, rather than errors, because the reader may be using certain "cues" about a word (graphophonic, syntactic, or semantic). Major types of miscues include the following:

1. *Omission.* A word is skipped during oral reading.
2. *Insertion.* A word or phrase not in the text is spoken by the reader.
3. *Substitution.* The printed word is replaced with another.
4. *Reversal.* The order of the printed words is changed by the reader. (Changing the order of letters within a single word, such as saying *was* for *saw*, is a type of substitution.)
5. *Teacher-supplied word.* The reader hesitates long enough that the teacher steps in and pronounces the word in order to keep the process moving.
6. *Repetition.* A word or phrase is repeated, sometimes for better enunciation, sometimes to monitor comprehension.
7. *Ignoring punctuation.* The reader ignores commas, periods, question marks, and so forth, so that the oral reading is not meaningful and fluent, even though word accuracy may be quite high.
8. *Hesitation.* The reader hesitates but not long enough that the teacher pronounces the word.
9. *Self-correction.* The child rereads one or more words in order to correct an error.

Not everyone agrees on how these miscues should be coded by the teacher. The following examples represent conventional practice. In the end, it matters very little as long as (1) the teacher is consistent, and (2) teachers with whom coded passages may be shared are familiar with the system being used.

1. Text: Jim called me yesterday.
   Child: Jim called me.
   Coding: Jim called me yesterday.

2. Text: Jim called me yesterday.
   Child: Jim called me up yesterday.
                          up
   Coding: Jim called me yesterday.
                          ^

3. Text: Jim called me yesterday.
   Child: Jim called me today.
                            today
   Coding: Jim called me yesterday.

4. Text: Jim called me yesterday.
   Child: Jim called me me yesterday.
   Coding: Jim called <u>me</u> yesterday.

5. Text: Jim called me yesterday.
   Child: Jim called me (*brief pause*) yesterday.
   Coding: Jim called me | yesterday.

6. Text: Jim called me yesterday.
   Child: Jim called me (*pause, word pronounced by teacher*) yesterday.
                                           P
   Coding: Jim called me yesterday.

7. Text: Jim called me yesterday.
   Child: Yesterday Jim called me.
   Coding: Yesterday Jim called me.

8. Text: Jim called me yesterday.
   Child: Jime called me yesterday.
               Jime
   Coding: Jim called me yesterday.
            (Or you could simply write a macron over the *i*.)

9. Text: Jim called me yesterday.
   Child: John phoned me sometime yesterday.
            John phoned sometime
   Coding: Jim called me yesterday.

10. Text: Jim called me yesterday.
   Child: John Jim called me yesterday.
            John ✓
   Coding: Jim called me yesterday.

11. Text: Jim called me yesterday. We talked for an hour.
   Child: Jim called me yesterday we talked for an hour.
   Coding: Jim called me yesterday. We talked for an hour.

Counting Miscues

Which miscues are tallied to determine the oral accuracy percentage? The answer to this question may alter the results and lead to different conclusions about whether the passage is on the child's independent, instructional, or frustration level. The question is really twofold. First, can certain types of miscues be disregarded in counting the total? Conventional wisdom suggests that hesitations and ignoring punctuation should not be counted. This policy leaves the following:

1. Omissions
2. Insertions
3. Substitutions
4. Reversals
5. Teacher-supplied words
6. Repetitions

Authorities (including the authors of commercial IRIs) agree on the first five but remain split on the issue of repetitions. Some studies indicate that counting them lends validity to the scoring criteria developed by Emmett Betts, who created the first IRIs (McKenna, 1983). Others argue that repetitions are healthy signs of comprehension monitoring and, in any case, involve no departure from the printed text. Perhaps the best advice is to adopt the policy recommended by the instrument a teacher is actually using, since it has probably been field tested using that guideline.

The second question is whether to consider the semantic acceptability of a miscue in deciding whether to count it. When a child says *crimson* for *scarlet*, for example, it seems unjust to count it as an error. Unless the passage is from *Gone with the Wind*, the original meaning seems to have been preserved. Some authorities therefore recommend that the acceptability of any departure from the printed text be considered when arriving at an error tally. Our view is that the nature of miscues should be considered subjectively, as a source of potentially useful qualitative evidence, but that semantic acceptability should not be considered in arriving at an error count. There are several reasons for this policy. First, considering semantic acceptability is subjective; different examiners are likely to arrive at different tallies. Second, such a policy is time consuming; IRIs already require a fair amount of time to administer and interpret, without compounding matters unnecessarily. Third, counting semantically acceptable miscues as correct would invalidate the Betts scoring criteria, and although alternate criteria are offered by IRI authors, these certainly do not enjoy the research validation of those recommended by Betts.

Applying Scoring Criteria

At the end of the examiner's copy of each passage are criteria for judging the child's performance. Separate criteria pertain to comprehension and oral accuracy. Simple charts make it possible to arrive at rapid judgments, so that a teacher can decide which passage to administer next. These charts represent the error tallies and are tied to percentage criteria. Although authors differ about which criteria lead to the best estimates of reading levels, the most enduring are those suggested by Emmett Betts (see Table 3.1).

The Betts criteria are somewhat strict. Keep in mind that if more lenient criteria were used, the resulting estimate of a child's instructional level might be higher. Note also that the conjunction (*and* versus *or*) is critically important in Table 3.1. For example, for a passage to be judged on a child's independent reading level, the criteria for both comprehension *and* word recognition would need to be met. On the other hand, if either criterion for the frustration level is met, the passage is assumed to be at the frustration level. Later in this chapter we reexamine how these criteria are applied.

GUIDELINES FOR INTERPRETING THE RESULTS OF AN IRI

The following guidelines may be useful for estimating a child's independent, instructional, and frustration level after the IRI has been given.

1. Classify the student's performance on each passage given as independent, instructional, or frustration level. You might find it convenient to use the abbreviations *IND*, *INST*, and *FRUS* for this purpose. Use the lower level of word-recognition accuracy and comprehension, unless you are convinced to the contrary for reasons that are apparent during the testing. Borderline results may cloud the picture, but that is a natural consequence of IRI assessment.

   Examples:

Word recognition	Comprehension	Overall
IND	IND	IND
INST	INST	INST
FRUS	FRUS	FRUS
IND	INST	INST
INST	IND	INST
FRUS	IND	FRUS
INST	FRUS	FRUS

2. Estimate the independent level to be the highest level at which the overall judgment is IND.
3. Estimate the instructional level to be the highest level at which the overall judgment is INST.
4. Estimate the frustration level to be the lowest level at which the overall judgment is FRUS.

   Example 1

Passage	Word recognition	Comprehension	Overall
PP	IND	IND	IND
P	INST	INST	INST
1	FRUS	FRUS	FRUS

   Independent level: PP
   Instructional level: P
   Frustration level: 1

   Example 2

Passage	Word recognition	Comprehension	Overall
PP	IND	IND	IND
P	IND	INST	INST
1	INST	INST	INST
2	INST	FRUS	FRUS

   Independent level: PP
   Instructional level: 1
   Frustration level: 2

Example 3

Passage	Word recognition	Comprehension	Overall
2	IND	INST	INST
3	IND	IND	IND
4	IND	INST	INST
5	INST	FRUS	FRUS

Independent level: 3
Instructional level: 4
Frustration level: 5

Example 4

Passage	Word recognition	Comprehension	Overall
PP	INST	IND	INST
P	INST	INST	INST
1	FRUS	FRUS	FRUS

Independent level: Not Determined
Instructional level: P
Frustration level: 1

A NEW APPROACH
TO MISCUE ANALYSIS

Considering the nature of miscues can sometimes lead to (1) insights about how reading is developing and (2) indications of the kind of instruction a child needs. Looking for trends within and across passages is a subjective process, one that is informed by experience. Research can also help, and becoming knowledgeable about some of the major findings from studies of miscue analysis is useful. Here are just a few:

1. About half of first graders' miscues are omissions.
2. As children mature, substitutions become more common.
3. Initially, substitutions may amount to mere guesses, often with a word beginning with the same letter.
4. Substitutions gradually become more sophisticated, bearing greater phonic resemblance to the actual word.
5. Substitutions begin as real words (for beginning readers) but often become nonwords (i.e., phonic approximations).
6. Insertions are always rare (10% or fewer of all miscues).
7. Letter reversals (such as *was* for *saw*) are common in first grade but typically disappear during second grade.
8. Reliance on context is heaviest for beginning readers and older poor readers.
9. Repetitions can be a mark of comprehension monitoring—that is, of a reader's attempt to make print make sense.
10. Word-perfect reading does not always mean good comprehension.

Form 3.4 (p. 74) is a worksheet that can be used to examine children's miscues. Basically we take each substitution and ask ourselves questions about it. First, we ask whether the miscue was graphically similar to the text word at the beginning (B), middle (M), or end (E) of the word. Next, we ask whether the word is syntactically similar to the text word, or whether it was the same part of speech as the text word. Then we ask whether the word has a similar meaning to the text word. For this, we use a fairly liberal criterion: whether the substitution would force the child to go back and correct the meaning. Thus a word can make sense, even if it is not a synonym for the text word. (For example, in the sentence "She wore a blue dress," substituting *beautiful* for *blue* would be semantically consistent with context.) Finally, we ask whether the word was self-corrected. We expect children to monitor their reading, and if a miscue does not make sense, we expect a child to notice and at least attempt to correct it. If a miscue does not make sense and the child does not attempt to correct it, it is likely that the child is not monitoring the reading for sense.

In the example given in Figure 3.1, taken from a first grader reading a preprimer passage at his frustration level, six of the eight miscues were graphically similar in the first position, four were syntactically similar, and three were semantically similar to the text word. This pattern suggests (1) that the child is relying on the first letter to identify words (because of the predominance of correct first letters) and (2) that the child is not using context to support or monitor word identification (since few of the words are syntactically or semantically acceptable). This pattern is especially troublesome, since the passage had a clear predictable pattern.

RUNNING RECORDS

Running records are coded notations of text reading, used as a vehicle for error analysis. After coding the student's reading, the errors are evaluated to determine their type or reason. Although used widely in classrooms today, running records were originally used

Text says	Child says	Graphically similar?			Syntactically similar?	Semantically similar?	Self-corrected?
		B	M	E			
lost	like	✓			✓		
inside	in	✓			✓	✓	
looked	lood	✓		✓			
was	w-	✓					
he	him	✓			✓	✓	
under	your			✓			
same	school	✓					
pony	horse				✓	✓	

FIGURE 3.1. Sample miscue analysis.

as a daily assessment procedure in Reading Recovery lessons (Clay, 1993b). Running records share several similarities with informal reading inventories. However, running records can be generated from any text, not only prepared text.

Functions of Running Records

Teachers and researchers can use both types of assessments as authentic process measures of children's reading. In this case, *authentic* means that the measure duplicates reading that the child is likely to be doing in a classroom or independently. The one-on-one setting required for these measures may contribute to increased focus by some readers or performance anxiety for others. The student is asked to read aloud, and the examiner records the student's reading of the text using a coding system. This procedure enables the researcher or teacher to get a "snapshot" of the reader engaged in the reading process, rather than the product evaluation obtained with commercially produced theme tests or standardized reading tests.

Errors are analyzed in relation to the reader's use of the semantic, syntactic, and graphic cues, called "meaning, syntactic, and visual (graphophonic) cueing systems" by Clay (1993a). Although the examiner may ask a few comprehension questions after the reading, the error analysis constitutes the primary evaluation of meaningful reading. This information may be used to make immediate teaching decisions or at a later time to develop a plan of instruction.

Teachers who use leveled texts in reading instruction can use running records to track progress over time. By *leveled* texts we mean any texts that increase in difficulty along a gradient that is sensitive to characteristics that reflect reading challenges. Teachers can use running records over time to demonstrate children's increasing competencies with increasingly difficult texts. Running records provide evidence of children's developing knowledge of the reading process (see examples in Figures 3.2, 3.3, and 3.4).

Taking a Running Record

Texts

Two advantages of running records are the ease and flexibility of administration. The coding format of running records enables teachers to use them without a typescript. However, because a typescript is not used, the coding of a running record is slightly more complex than the coding system employed for informal reading inventories.

Text length is not dictated, but generally a sample should have between 100 and 200 words. This length enables teachers to conduct running records with a wide variety of texts. Running records can be taken more frequently than a miscue analysis or an informal reading inventory because of the ease and adaptability of the measure to an authentic setting where a variety of materials are used. Clay (1993a, 1993b) recommends that running records be administered using any texts that children can read with 90–95% accuracy. Typically, authentic texts are used. "Little books" that contain complete, cohe-

John Smith
9/6

Come On
Level B / 22 wds.

Page	Accuracy = 91 % Error Rate = 1/11 SC Rate = 1/3	E	SC	Information Used	
				E MSV	SC MSV
2	✔ ✔ Get / wake ✔	1		ⓜⓈ v	
3	✔ ✔ eat |sc / to ✔	+	1	ⓜ s v	m Ⓢ v
4	✔ ✔ ✔ R				
5	✔ ✔ ✔				
6	✔ ✔ ✔				
7	✔ ✔ supper / dinner	1		ⓜⓈ v	
8	✔ ✔ ✔				

FIGURE 3.2. Running record taken at the beginning of the year.

John Smith   Hairy Bear
     1/18   Level G / 109 wds.

Page	Accuracy = 93% Error Rate = 1/13 SC Rate = 1/5	E	SC	Information Used	
				E MSV	SC MSV
2	✓✓ ✓✓ ✓✓✓✓				
3	✓✓✓ ✓✓✓ ✓✓✓ ✓✓				
4	✓✓ ✓✓ ✓✓ silly/still ✓ the/– ✓	2		m s (v) m (s) v	
5	✓✓✓ ✓–✓ ✓✓✓ ✓✓				
6	✓✓ ✓ fighting/frightened –/of	2		m (s)(v) m (s) v	
7	✓–✓ ✓–✓ ✓ cim/crim cam/cram cash/crash ✓	3		m (s) v m (s) ✓ m (s) v	
8	✓ ✓				
9	✓ mit/might |SC .	+	1	m s (v)	(m)(s)✓
10	✓✓ ✓✓ ✓✓✓✓				
11	✓←✓✓✓⌐ ✓✓ money/morning |SC R	+	1	m s (v)	(m)(s)✓
12	✓✓ ✓✓				
13	✓✓✓ scare/scaredy ✓	1		m s (v)	
	pp. 14–16	0 8	0 2		

FIGURE 3.3. Running record taken near midyear.

John Smith   Frog & Toad Together — The Garden
5/12   Level K / 210 wds.

Page	Accuracy = 94% Error Rate = 1/16 SC Rate = 1/53	E	SC	Information Used	
				E MSV	SC MSV
18	✓✓✓✓✓ ✓✓✓✓ ✓✓✓✓ ✓✓✓ had / sc ⌐ hand ⌐ R	+	1	m s (v)	(m) (s) v
	✓✓✓✓✓✓ ✓✓✓✓ ✓✓✓ garden ✓✓ ground		1	(m) (s) v	
	✓✓✓✓ ✓✓				
19	✓ son / sc ✓✓ soon	+	1	m s (v)	(m) (s) v
	Quit ✓✓✓ Quite		1	m s (v)	
20	✓✓✓ ✓✓✓✓ ✓✓✓✓				
	stut / strat ✓ start		1	m s (v)	
	✓✓✓✓✓				
	— — — a few times		3		
	✓✓✓✓ stat / A start / T ✓✓		1	m s (v)	
21	✓✓✓ hand head		1	(m) (s) v	
	✓✓✓ garden ground		1	(m) (s) v	
	✓✓✓✓				
	New ✓✓✓ Now		1	m s (v)	
	✓✓✓✓✓✓ ✓✓✓✓✓✓✓				
	pp. 22–23	3	1		
		13	3		

FIGURE 3.4. Running record at the end of the year.

sive stories or informational text that has been leveled using qualitative criteria (Peterson, 1991; Rhodes, 1981) are often selected as benchmark texts for systematic assessment.

Recording the Reading

Competence in recording running records requires time and practice. Clay (2000) advises beginners to practice tracking running records with average readers first. The fluency of good readers and the complex error patterns of struggling readers may be difficult for a novice to record. It is a good idea for teachers to practice making running records with texts that are overly familiar to them. Although the examiner sits next to the child and looks at the text with him or her, it is less of a juggling act if the examiner has prior experience with the text and its challenges. Clay advises teachers to practice making running records until they feel comfortable and can get a "true account" of student reading with "any text, any time" (p. 6).

A teacher sets the stage for making a running record by asking a child to read to him or her and informing the child that he or she will be writing down some notes. For assessment purposes, the text should be completely unfamiliar to the child; the examiner gives a brief introduction to the story and then asks the child to read. In an instructional setting, the selected book would more likely be one previously introduced by the teacher and perhaps read once or twice the preceding day. For instructional decision making, children should be able to read a text at between 90 and 95% accuracy. This level enables the child to maintain fluent reading, but also allows the teacher to see what material challenges the child and how the child solves any difficulties with text.

Coding the Reading

Coding becomes easier with time and practice. The ability to code becomes refined with each running record made on a child. It is OK to ask a child to hesitate before starting a new page if the examiner needs to catch up. While learning how to make running records, focus on recording the child's reading; you can go back later and record the text that was omitted or substituted. Among the variety of codes used to record errors, we use Clay's (1993a, 2000). Standard coding procedures are important so that teachers can share information about a child. Coding can be done on a blank piece of paper, index card, or running record sheet. The book *Rosie's Walk* by Pat Hutchins (1968) is used to demonstrate the coding system.

1. Mark every word read correctly with a check. Make lines of checks correspond to lines of text. Clay uses a solid line to indicate page breaks.

Rosie the hen went for a walk	✓✓✓✓✓✓
Across the yard	✓✓✓
Around the pond	✓✓✓
Over the haystack	✓✓✓

2. Record an incorrect response with the text under it. Each substitution is scored as an error.

Rosie the hen went for a walk	✓✓ <u>chicken</u> ✓✓✓✓ hen
Across the yard	<u>Around</u>✓✓ Across
Around the pond	✓✓✓
Over the haystack	✓✓ <u>hay</u> haystack

3. Record an omission with a dash over the omitted word. Each omission is scored as an error.

Rosie the hen went for a walk	✓ — — ✓✓✓✓ the hen
Across the yard	✓✓✓
Around the pond	✓✓✓
Over the haystack	✓✓✓

4. Record insertions by writing the word on top and putting a dash beneath. Each insertion is scored as an error.

Rosie the hen went for a walk	✓✓✓✓✓ <u>long</u> ✓ —
Across the yard	✓✓✓
Around the pond	✓✓ <u>fish</u> ✓ —
Over the haystack	✓✓✓

5. A self-correction occurs when a child has made an error and then corrects it. This self-correction is usually evidence that a child is cross-checking one set of cues against another (Johnston, 2000). A self-correction is recorded by using the letters *SC* and is *not* considered an error.

Rosie the hen went for a walk	✓✓ <u>chicken/SC</u> ✓✓✓✓ hen
Across the yard	<u>Around/SC</u> ✓✓✓ Across

| Around the pond | ✓✓✓ |
| Over the haystack | ✓✓✓ |

6. A repetition is recorded with a line above the repeated segment of text but is *not* scored as an error. Repetitions may be demonstrations that a child is sorting out a point of some confusion, either because something did not make sense or was a difficult word or to gain fluency and meaning (Clay, 2000; Johnston, 2000). A numerical superscript may be used to show multiple repetitions.

Rosie the hen went for a walk	✓✓✓✓✓✓
Across the yard	$\overline{✓\ R^2\ ✓✓}$
Around the pond	Across/SC ✓✓ R
Over the haystack	✓✓✓

7. If a child hesitates for longer than 5 seconds because he or she has made an error and does not know how to correct it, or if the child stops and makes no attempts, he or she is told the word. This pause is coded with a *T* (for *told*) on the bottom and scored as an error.

Rosie the hen went for a walk	✓✓✓✓✓✓
Across the yard	$\dfrac{\text{In}}{\text{Across/T}}$ ✓✓
Around the pond	$\dfrac{—}{\text{Around/T}}$ ✓✓
Over the haystack	✓✓✓

8. If a child asks (A) for help, the teacher responds, "Try something" and waits 3–5 seconds for an attempt before telling the child the correct word. This strategy enables the teacher to observe what problem-solving strategies the child is likely to use when facing challenges in text.

Rosie the hen went for a walk	✓✓✓✓✓✓
Across the yard	$\dfrac{—\ /A/\ —}{\text{Across/ /T}}$ ✓✓
Around the pond	$\dfrac{—\ /A/\text{Across}}{\text{Around/ /T}}$ ✓✓
Over the haystack	✓✓✓

9. Sometimes a child loses his or her place or goes off on a tangent that is far removed from the text. In such a case, the teacher should say "Try that again" (TTA), and indicate the line, paragraph, or page where the child should restart. Record by putting brackets around the faulty section of reading and code *TTA*. The entire section is only coded as one error.

Rosie the hen went for a walk	[✓✓✓ <u>wanted to get away</u>]
	went for a walk TTA
	✓✓✓✓✓
Across the yard	✓✓✓
Around the pond	✓✓✓
Over the haystack	✓✓✓

10. Other behaviors may be noted but not scored. Pausing, sounding out parts of the word, finger pointing, unusually fast or slow reading rates, and word-by-word reading should be noted on the running record and considered in the analysis but not included in quantitative scoring. If there are alternative ways of scoring responses, one would usually choose the method that gives the fewest possible errors. According to Clay's (1993a) system, with the exception of proper names, repeated errors are scored as errors each time. For example, if a child substitutes *will* for *would* multiple times, each counts as a separate error. However, it only counts once if a child substitutes *Joey* for *Jerry* throughout a story.

Table 3.2 provides a review of the scoring of errors in a running record.

Analysis and Interpretation of the Running Record

Quantifying the Running Record

The accuracy rate, error rate, and self-correction rate are calculated. First, the number of running words (RW) in the text (excluding the title), the number of errors (E), and the number of self-corrections (SC) are counted. The accuracy rate is the percentage of words read correctly, or $100 - (E/RW \times 100)$. We prefer the use of an accuracy rate rather than an error rate. An accuracy rate allows one to see the positive skills that readers

TABLE 3.2. Scoring of Errors in a Running Record

Scored errors	Non-error behaviors
Substitutions	Self-corrections
Omissions	Repetitions
Insertions	Hesitations
Told the word or told to "try that again"	Ignored punctuation
Repeated errors	

have instead of focusing on the errors they make. This rate relates to the independent, instructional, and frustration levels described earlier. The error ratio is the ratio of errors to running words (E/RW). According to Clay (2000), error rates lower than 1:10 provide the best opportunities for observing children interacting with text. Students who have error rates higher than 1:9 with the text selection may be too frustrated to demonstrate their typical reading processes.

The self-correction ratio is the ratio of self-corrections to the total of errors and self-corrections (SC/E + SC). Self-corrections may indicate the degree to which a reader is monitoring his or her reading or using multiple cueing systems to process text. Self-corrections can provide an important window into the reader's thinking. Which errors does the reader think need fixing? Some readers fix errors that interrupt meaningful reading. Other readers are more in tune to the visual system and only correct errors that don't look right. Typically, if readers have a low error ratio, they are able to use multiple sources of information to self-monitor. However, as error rates become higher, they may neglect information that they would normally be able to use to monitor and adjust their reading.

Miscue Analysis

Typically the miscue analysis of an IRI or the Reading Miscue Inventory (Goodman, Watson, & Burke, 1987) are done on a separate worksheet. However, a running record worksheet usually includes columns for the miscue analysis. When an error is made, write the letters *MSV* (i.e., meaning, structure, visual) in the error column and circle the letters that indicate the source of information most likely used by the child up to the point of error. Miscues are analyzed by asking a series of questions about the miscues and any self-corrections. The questions may be asked about acceptability at the passage level, sentence level, partial sentence level, and the word level. The question areas include:

- *Meaning (M).* Did the reader choose a substitution or phrasing that makes sense in the passage or sentence or part of the sentence?
- *Structure cues (S).* Did the reading sound like language that follows a grammatical form? (The grammatical form may be a dialect form used by the reader.) Did the reader follow the structure of the text? (Sometimes the reader continues with the earlier pattern in a predictable text, even when the structure of the text has changed.)
- *Visual (V).* Did the child read a word that has graphic similarity or sound similarity to the word in the text? Was the graphophonic system being used?
- *Self-correction column (write the letters MSV).* What cueing systems did the reader use to fix the error?

Interpretation of Errors and Self-Corrections

The pattern of errors and self-corrections provides important insights into a child's developing awareness of the reading process. Do the child's errors reflect that he or she is reading for meaning or simply sounding out the words? Does the child's awareness of the graphophonic system extend to scanning the entire word and chunking, or is he or she limited to saying the first sound and making a wild guess? A brief summary of observations and interpretations can be included on the running record sheet. The teacher who can observe these patterns in a written format possesses a powerful guide to instruction. Lesson plans for a child or small group of children should be based on behaviors represented in the running records.

Memories of even the most experienced, capable reading teachers are not always accurate. Observing by listening without recording may make it difficult to detect patterns of errors. Furthermore, undocumented observations cannot be shared or used to trace changes over time. In an era when teacher accountability is becoming increasingly important in the lowest grade levels, running records can be an effective tool for documenting student progress.

One measure that has adapted the procedures for making running records but given them the structure of an informal reading inventory is the Developmental Reading Assessment (DRA—Beaver, 2001; for a similar test, see Rigby Education, 2001). This measure uses a set of leveled texts, similar to those used in running records, but provides a single text for each level. It also provides a printed version of the text, similar to an IRI, so that a teacher not trained in giving running records can administer the test. It does contain guidelines and a rubric for judging recall. Comprehension questions are used only to prompt recall, not as the primary means of judging comprehension. Functionally, the DRA works like an informal reading inventory but uses leveled texts. The leveled texts may resemble more closely the little books that children use in their classrooms.

ESTIMATING A CHILD'S LISTENING LEVEL

The listening level is conventionally defined as the highest passage at which comprehension of the passage read aloud to the child is at least 75%. Generally, the teacher first estimates the frustration level from the passages administered and then selects the next-higher passage to administer on a listening basis. Both the passage and the questions are read aloud to the child. As with the reading passages, the teacher may need to administer more than one listening passage, either above or below the starting point, in order to determine the listening level.

Knowing a child's listening level can be useful in discerning whether comprehension difficulties are the result of decoding problems. In the following example, the listening level of this fourth grader is fourth grade, whereas the instructional level is only second grade. The teacher might justifiably conclude that this child's low reading level is primarily the result of inadequate word-recognition skills.

Example 1

Passage	Word recognition	Comprehension	Overall	Listening
1	IND	IND	IND	
2	INST	IND	INST	
3	FRUS	INST	FRUS	
4				80%

Independent level: 1
Instructional level: 2
Frustration level: 3
Listening level: 4

On the other hand, consider a hypothetical second grader whose listening level is no higher than the instructional level. In this case, the teacher has first administered the second-grade passage on a listening basis. This task was clearly too difficult, however, so the teacher readministered the first-grade passage and then the primer passage, this time reading them to the child. (An alternate form at these levels might have been used.)

Example 2

Passage	Word recognition	Comprehension	Overall	Listening
PP	IND	IND	IND	
P	INST	INST	INST	80%
1	FRUS	INST	FRUS	60%
2				50%

Independent level: PP
Instructional level: P
Frustration level: 1
Listening level: P

For this student, it would be incorrect to conclude that merely improving decoding ability would lead to a substantial gain in reading level. More must be done. This student will require work in comprehension strategies and perhaps oral language development in order to make good progress.

ISSUES CONCERNING IRIs

IRIs are among the best tools available for estimating reading levels. However, a number of issues surround their structure and use. The questions that follow continue to provoke debate, and authorities undoubtedly will continue to differ.

1. *Which question types should be included?* Studies have shown that different question sets covering the same passage can lead to very different interpretations of a

child's comprehension. Field testing of the actual questions used can help, but there are no commonly accepted guidelines for question selection.

2. *How high should the word lists extend?* As a general rule, the higher the grade level, the less sure we can be that the words on a particular list are representative of that grade level. This uncertainty arises from the fact that the number of words used by older children multiplies dramatically and is difficult to sample. Word lists past the primary grades become increasingly suspect.

3. *Are the questions dependent on having read the passage?* Sometimes children can answer questions on the basis of prior knowledge rather than having understood the content of a passage. Ideally, each question should only be answerable after having read the passage, but it is difficult for test developers to predict what a child might or might not know. We explore this issue further in Chapter 7.

4. *Which scoring criteria should be used?* Through the years, debate has centered on the best criteria to use in interpreting IRI results. Johns (2005) argues that alternatives to the Betts criteria have proved unsatisfactory, and indeed they have. As long as we view the criteria as guidelines that can be overruled by teacher judgment, this issue will remain in perspective.

5. *Which readability levels should be represented?* As with word lists, the higher the passage, the more difficult it is to assert that a given passage represents a particular grade level. The difference, for example, between a sixth- and a seventh-grade passage is less than the difference between a second- and a third-grade passage. Again, we rely on field testing to assure an ordered sequence of passage difficulty, but the higher the passage, the greater the likelihood that anomalous results might occur. For example, if a child has more prior knowledge of the topic discussed in the sixth-grade passage than the topic in the fifth-grade passage, it might appear from the IRI that the child comprehends better at the sixth-grade level than at the fifth-grade level. Teachers must not be discouraged by anomalies of this kind, but they do need to interpret such results subjectively. Of course, anomalies are less likely to occur in the lower grades, where differences in difficulty level are clearer.

6. *How long should the passages be?* The passages on some IRIs gradually increase in length as grade level increases, on the rationale that fluency and attention span enable the student to handle longer samples of text. Authors of other instruments have elected to maintain the same length, except perhaps for the simplest passage, so that it is easier to apply scoring criteria and to compare a child's performance across passages of different difficulty levels.

7. *Are IRIs sufficiently situated?* Because the experience of an IRI is so different from classroom activities, some have argued that IRI results may not adequately predict what a child is likely to do in the classroom. According to this argument, it would be preferable to observe and interpret reading performance during day-to-day classroom activities. We contend, however, that the IRI reveals the child's proficiency under more favorable circumstances (e.g., one-on-one engagement with the teacher, few distractions) and is therefore more likely to display what the child is truly capable of than classroom activities would.

8. *Should IRIs include pictures?* Including pictures might provide the child with clues that lessen the need to read carefully and comprehend. That is, pictures may inflate scores and lead us to overestimate a child's reading levels. On the other hand, pictures are very much a part of the reading children do, especially younger children. Is it reasonable to ask them to read passages without illustrations? Is a pictureless environment likely to be too unnatural? Authors of commercial IRIs have come down on both sides of this issue.

9. *Should a number of teacher prompts lead to discontinuing a passage?* When a child pauses at a difficult word, the teacher steps in to keep the process moving. The more times a teacher supplies unfamiliar words, however, the less representative the results will be of the child's ability. In extreme cases, the passage is more akin to a listening than a reading experience. The teacher must judge when this line is crossed and either halt the administration or discount the results afterward.

10. *Should semantically acceptable miscues not be counted in word-recognition accuracy?* As we have noted, many commercial IRIs provide dual systems of scoring, affording a choice to the teacher about whether to count all miscues or only those that depart from meaning. As we noted earlier in this chapter, considering the semantic acceptability of miscues has a number of drawbacks: (a) increased administration time, (b) unreliable scoring criteria, and (c) overly subjective standards for judging. Looking to semantic acceptability also hearkens back to a model of reading that has been repudiated by research. For all of these reasons, we discourage it.

11. *Should IRI passages be narrative or expository?* Research tells us that, other factors being equal, expository prose is more difficult to process and comprehend than narrative prose. Some IRI developers approach this problem by intermingling narrative and expository passages, so that both types are represented in the inventory. (As we noted in Chapter 2, this approach is also the one taken by developers of group achievement tests.) IRI authors who intersperse the two types rely on field testing to ensure a clear sequence of passage difficulty. An alternative approach is to separate expository and narrative passages into distinct strands. In the Qualitative Reading Inventory–4 (Leslie & Caldwell, 2005), for example, the teacher can choose in advance which passage type to present.

12. *Are questions of reliability and validity adequately addressed by IRI developers?* It is a concern that IRIs do not generally report reliability and validity evidence. Often their reliability is contingent on trust in the author rather than standardization. One study (Paris et al., 2004) found different forms of one popular IRI to be so different that the authors needed to create their own scaling of the results. Teacher consumers of IRIs should examine, in advance, the evidence the authors provide of the psychometric properties of their instruments.

STEPS TO A SHORTENED IRI

An IRI can be given on an abbreviated basis by limiting the assessment to a single passage. For example, a second-grade teacher might wish to know which students are reading at or near grade level by the end of the year. By administering only the second-grade passage to each child, the teacher can tell whether it falls at a given child's instructional or independent level. Of course, administering an IRI on this basis will not lead to estimates of the independent, instructional, and frustration levels. More than a single passage would be needed for that purpose.

In order to quickly categorize your students by administering an IRI on a shortened basis, we recommend the following steps:

1. Select the passage corresponding to your grade level. If you teach first grade and will be testing during the spring, use the grade 1 or First Reader passage.
2. Duplicate one copy of the examinee's version per child. (You'll need these for marking the coding and notes.)
3. Assess each child individually.
4. Begin by reading the "prior knowledge" questions, if any. Make a judgment call as to whether limited knowledge of the passage topic may prevent adequate comprehension. Usually, the topics are relatively commonplace, and background knowledge is not an issue. If prior knowledge is, in your judgment, too limited, make a note of this absence.
5. Explain that you want the child to read a story aloud and give him or her the examinee's copy (the one containing only the passage and not the questions).
6. Code the miscues the child makes on the examiner's copy.
7. Use the scoring guide at the bottom of the examiner's copy to determine whether oral reading accuracy is at the independent, instructional, or frustration level.
8. If oral reading accuracy is at the frustration level, stop. Do not ask the questions; the passage is assumed to be at the frustration level.
9. If oral reading accuracy is above the frustration level, ask the comprehension questions.
10. Give full credit, partial credit, or no credit, at your discretion. Reword questions to make them clearer, if you wish, but stop short of prompting.
11. Use the scoring guide at the bottom of the examiner's copy to determine whether comprehension is at the independent, instructional, or frustration level.
12. Compare the results of oral accuracy and comprehension. The passage is judged to be at the lower of these two results. For example, if oral accuracy is independent and comprehension is instructional, the entire passage is judged to be instructional.
13. On your class roster, note each child's performance level on the passage. That is, was it at the child's independent, instructional, or frustration level?

USING IRIs IN PROJECT AND SCHOOL EVALUATION

IRIs tend to provide more reliable information about reading growth than group standardized measures. The fact that they are individually administered, and in a manner that is responsive to student performance, tends to produce valid results. Moreover, they can be administered much more flexibly than achievement tests can, so that pre–post comparisons can be made with reasonable confidence.

Several options are available for project evaluation, depending on the questions project personnel are interested in answering. The two options presented here offer a wide variety of evaluation opportunities.

Option 1: Full Pre–Post Administration

In this option, IRI testing is done at the beginning and end of the project implementation. Our example is from Kashinkerry Elementary, a pre-K–5 school. We will assume that grades 1–5 have been involved in reading-related activities throughout the year. For grades 2–5, this reading activity includes one assessment in early fall and another in late spring. For first graders, however, the preassessment should be delayed until midyear so that more children will be capable of reading at least a preprimer passage.

Two methods can be used to interpret the data. The first is to convert IRI instructional reading levels into continuous grade-level terms by using the following standard equivalencies, used in studies conducted at the National Reading Research Center:

Below preprimer	=	1.0
Preprimer	=	1.3
Primer	=	1.6
1st reader	=	1.8
2nd grade	=	2.5
3rd grade	=	3.5
4th grade	=	4.5
5th grade	=	5.5
6th grade	=	6.5
7th grade	=	7.5
8th grade	=	8.5

The advantage of this method is that parametric statistics, both descriptive and inferential, can be computed, and so growth can be plainly charted in terms of years gained. This indicator is far superior to the grade-equivalent scores produced through standardized achievement testing, because of the individual administration of the IRI and the fact that the data for children of differing chronological ages are not pooled as they are in achievement testing.

The results for Kashinkerry are summarized in Table 3.3. (These results are for a real school, located in an inner-city area and serving predominantly high-risk children.) In grades 2–5, the average gain is in the vicinity of 1 year. Growth at grade 1 reflects only the half year since the January pretesting. Inferential statistics can be computed, if desired. In the case of Kashinkerry, growth at each grade was statistically significant ($p < .001$), and effect sizes (delta) ranged from 0.43 to 0.72. Such effects are considered moderately large and attest to the educational significance of reading growth at Kash-

TABLE 3.3. IRI Instructional Level Results for Kashinkerry Elementary

		Instructional reading level				
		Fall		Spring		
Grade	N	M	SD	M	SD	Mean gain in years
1	123	1.4	0.7	1.9	0.9	0.5
2	106	2.0	1.1	3.3	1.8	1.3
3	79	2.9	1.8	4.3	2.2	1.4
4	97	4.7	1.9	5.7	2.3	1.0
5	92	5.0	1.9	6.1	2.0	1.1

inkerry. (Similar statistics might have been used to compare Kashinkerry with a contrast school in which project activities did not occur.)

A second method of data analysis is to represent the distribution of instructional reading levels at each grade and then, from these distributions, compute the proportion of children at each grade level who finished the school year reading at or above grade level. These results for Kashinkerry are presented in Table 3.4.

Option 2: Single-Passage Administration

In this approach each child is given only one passage, the one at grade level. Only about 5 minutes per child are needed, compared with up to 20 minutes for a full IRI. (See the previous section for suggestions about how to administer an IRI in this way.) Although this approach does not reveal each child's instructional reading level, it can still be used to estimate the percentage of children who are reading at or above grade level versus the percentage who are reading below grade level.

Let's assume that Ms. Johnson, a third-grade teacher, administers the third-grade passage of an IRI to each child in the spring of the year. A child whose performance is judged to be instructional or independent on that passage is counted among those reading at or above grade level. A child whose performance falls below the criteria for the instructional level is counted among those children reading below grade level.

Let's further assume that Ms. Johnson's students have been involved in a reading-related project, whereas Mr. Williams's students, who are demographically similar, have not participated. Mr. Williams's class can be used as a control group by means of the IRI assessment. Table 3.5 presents a hypothetical comparison.

TABLE 3.4. End-of-Year IRI Instructional Levels for Kashinkerry

	Percentage of children at each level							
Grade	None[a]	Preprimer	Primer	1st reader	2	3	4	5+
1	16	15	18	20	19	8	2	1
2	2	7	10	11	23	21	7	18
3	0	5	6	4	19	19	11	35
4	1	0	3	4	8	11	9	63
5	0	1	1	1	8	8	9	73

[a]No level could be determined.

TABLE 3.5. IRI Results for Project and Nonproject Students

	Percentage of students reading below grade level	
Class	Fall	Spring
Project	72.3	30.3
Control	75.6	52.1

These results favor the class that took part in project activities, since fewer students were reading below grade level at year's end. These proportions can be compared statistically, if desired.

It should be noted that the teacher factor in this design has not been controlled. There is a possibility that Ms. Johnson's students might have produced similar results without benefit of the project. This possibility might have been countered by including more than one teacher in each group or by comparing two of Ms. Johnson's classes in successive years (such as the year before the project with the implementation year).

LIST OF COMMON INFORMAL READING INVENTORIES

Bader, L. A. (2004). *Bader reading and language inventory* (5th ed.). Englewood Cliffs, NJ: Prentice Hall.

Colvin, R. J., & Root, J. H. (1999). *Read: Reading evaluation—adult diagnosis: An informal inventory for assessing adult student reading needs and progress* (5th ed.). Syracuse, NY: Literacy Volunteers of America.

Cooter, R., Flynt, E. S., & Cooter, K. S. (2006). *Comprehensive reading inventory.* Englewood Cliffs, NJ: Prentice Hall.

Flynt, E. S., & Cooter, R. B. (1999). *English–Español reading inventory for the classroom.* Englewood Cliffs, NJ: Prentice Hall.

Johns, J. (2005). *Basic reading inventory* (9th ed.). Dubuque, IA: Kendall-Hunt.

Leslie, L., & Caldwell, J. (2005). *Qualitative reading inventory–4.* Boston: Allyn & Bacon.

Roe, B., & Burns, P. C. (2006). *Informal reading inventory* (7th ed.). Boston: Houghton Mifflin.

Shanker, J. L., & Ekwall, E. E. (2008). *Reading inventory* (5th ed.). Boston: Allyn & Bacon.

Stieglitz, E. L. (2001). *Stieglitz informal reading inventory* (3rd ed.). Boston: Allyn & Bacon.

Wheelock, W., Campbell, C., & Silvaroli, N. J. (2008). *Classroom reading inventory* (11th ed.). New York: McGraw-Hill.

Woods, M. L., & Moe, A. J. (2006). *Analytical reading inventory* (8th ed.). Englewood Cliffs, NJ: Prentice Hall.

Sample IRI Passage, Teacher Version

Togo

Togo is a small country in Africa, just north of the Equator. In area, it is about the same size as West Virginia. The people who live there produce coffee, cocoa, cotton, and other crops. The capital of Togo is called Lomé, a city of about a half million.

Togo has three neighbors. To the east is the country of Benin, to the west is Ghana, and to the north is Burkina Faso. Togo's fourth border is the Atlantic Ocean.

The main language of Togo is French, but four African languages are also spoken. Most of the people in Togo belong to one of 37 tribes. Togo is an interesting place, filled with variety and life.

Comprehension Check

_____ 1. Where is Togo? (Africa)

_____ 2. Name a crop grown in Togo. (Accept coffee, cocoa, or cotton.)

_____ 3. What country is west of Togo? (Ghana)

_____ 4. How many tribes live in Togo? (37)

_____ 5. What is the main language of Togo? (French)

_____ 6. If you were in Togo, you'd have to travel in what direction to reach the Atlantic Ocean? (south)

_____ 7. Is Togo as big as the United States? Why? (No. Togo is only as big as one of the states in the United States.)

_____ 8. Do more people live in Togo or Lomé? Why? (Togo, since Lomé is entirely within Togo.)

_____ 9. Do more people live in Togo or West Virginia? (Impossible to say. If the student ventures a guess, ask why. Give credit only for a logical idea.)

_____ 10. Name a crop you think might be grown in Ghana or Benin.

(Accept coffee, cocoa, or cotton, since these two countries are probably similar to Togo. If the student suggests another crop, ask why. Give credit for a reasonable response, such as equatorial crops.)

Scoring Guide

INDEPENDENT LEVEL	**0–2**	Comprehension Errors	AND	**0–2**	Oral Errors
INSTRUCTIONAL LEVEL	**2.5–3**	Comprehension Errors	AND	**3–7**	Oral Errors
FRUSTRATION LEVEL	**5+**	Comprehension Errors	OR	**12+**	Oral Errors

Sample IRI Passage, Student Version

Togo

Togo is a small country in Africa, just north of the Equator. In area, it is about the same size as West Virginia. The people who live there produce coffee, cocoa, cotton, and other crops. The capital of Togo is called Lomé, a city of about a half million.

Togo has three neighbors. To the east is the country of Benin. To the west is Ghana, and to the north is Burkina Faso. Togo's fourth border is the Atlantic Ocean.

The main language of Togo is French, but four African languages are also spoken. Most of the people in Togo belong to one of 37 tribes. Togo is an interesting place, filled with variety and life.

FORM 3.3

IRI Summary Form

Student _____   Date _____

Examiner _____   Grade _____

Level	Word Lists	Word Recognition	Comprehension	Overall Judgment	Listening
PP					
P					
1					
2					
3					
4					
5					

Estimated Levels

Independent Level	
Instructional Level	
Frustration Level	
Listening Level	

Miscue Analysis Chart

Text says	Child says	Graphically similar?			Syntactically similar?	Semantically similar?	Self-corrected?
		B	M	E			

CHAPTER FOUR

Emergent Literacy

During the years prior to school, and into the primary grades as well, we expect to see young children develop behaviors that signal an adequate foundation for formal reading instruction. In order to monitor the development of these emerging literacy behaviors, teachers can apply simple, informal assessment techniques.

What do we expect children to be able to master prior to formal reading instruction? At one time, children were expected to have mastered certain prerequisite perceptual skills before they began a formal reading program. These discretely conceptualized skills—such as auditory discrimination, visual discrimination, visual figure–ground—are now seen as relics of the past. Instead, we view the child as learning continuously about reading from the first exposure to print as an infant. This increasing knowledge of both print and oral language provides the foundation upon which successful reading is built.

Specifically, we examine some ways of assessing three of the major components of emergent literacy: concepts of print, alphabetic recognition, and phonemic awareness.

CONCEPTS OF PRINT

It is easy to take for granted some of the conventions that surround how books are printed and how we read them. These conventions, or common understandings, have little or nothing to do with the processes of word recognition and comprehension. Instead, they are more basic than that, and we hope to see them developed long before formal reading instruction begins. Without them, children will be at a serious disadvantage and are sure to suffer frustration and confusion.

What are these concepts about print? As fluent readers, it has become second nature to us that when we hold a book the spine is on our left. But this is not an inevitable, "natural" state of affairs. For example, books in Arabic or Hebrew are read with the spine to the right. Moreover, when we read a line of print, we start from the left and progress toward the right. Again, however, this is an arbitrary convention, and readers of Arabic and Hebrew, among other languages, begin at the right of each line. Furthermore, when we encounter a page of print, we know from long experience that we must begin reading the uppermost line and proceed downward. Also we must understand that it is the letters and words that convey the message, not the illustrations. A young child's first inclination is to focus on the pictures, which are the only components of a page that seem to have any meaning. Finally, in order to read a line of print, we must know that the white spaces between letter clusters mark the boundaries between *words*. This particular convention is extremely useful in the process of word recognition.

Concept of "Word"

An aspect of print concepts is the child's concept that a word is represented by the marks within the spaces. This is a crucial concept, because it enables children to learn about letters and words through exposure to print. Several studies have found that acquiring the word concept, as measured by accurate finger pointing, is an important marker on the child's road to reading proficiency. Ehri and Sweet (1991), Morris (1993), and Uhry (1999) suggest that children need to have some word knowledge and/or some phonological awareness before they are able to accurately finger point. Other studies have found that finger pointing seems to be a prerequisite for learning about words from text (Clay, 1993b).

The acquisition of the word concept in text, as indicated by finger pointing, is generally measured by having a child memorize a simple rhyme, such as nursery rhyme (e.g., "Baa, Baa, Black Sheep") or a simple song (e.g., "I'm a Little Teapot"). After the rhyme is memorized, the child is asked to read it in a book, pointing to each word as it is spoken.

Assessing Concepts of Print

None of these understandings comes automatically. Children must learn them either through direct instruction or extensive teacher modeling. It is important to assess children's knowledge of these concepts. The following procedure quickly provides a great deal of information through a single, nonthreatening, informal encounter. As the child is seated at a table, place a picture book in front of him or her. Make sure that the book is not positioned in the traditional way. That is, don't place the book with the spine at the left and the front of the book uppermost. Ask the child to show you the front of the book. Then open the book to any page having both a picture and at least two lines of print. Ask the child where you would begin reading. Ideally, the child will point to the leftmost word of the top line. (Do not be surprised, however, if the child points to the illustration or to some vague area within the text.)

Next, open the book to any page containing only a single line of print and place two blank index cards at either end of the line. Using both hands, slide the cards toward each other and say to the child, "I want you to push those cards together until only one word shows. Show me one word." Repeat the process, asking the child to show you one letter. This entire procedure might last only a minute but can give you a great deal of useful data. Simply record the child's responses in a convenient checklist form, making sure to date your entries. Such a checklist might look like the one on Form 4.1 (p. 90). Rather than using a single checkmark, however, it is a good idea to write the date that a child has successfully demonstrated knowledge of a given concept and to write nothing if the child fails to demonstrate it.

A more comprehensive approach involves the book-handling guidelines presented in Form 4.2 (pp. 91–93).

Concept of Story

Another approach to examining children's concept of print is through the use of a word-less picture book, which enables the teacher to examine the child's knowledge of how stories work. Paris and Paris (2001) constructed a narrative comprehension assessment out of wordless picture books that consists of three parts: a "picture walk," story retelling, and prompted comprehension. To do this assessment, first choose a book that has a clear narrative that can be followed just by looking through the pictures. Paris and Paris used *Robot-bot-bot* by Fernando Krahn (1979), but any number of similar books could be used. The picture walk evaluates how the child approaches the text and handles the book, the language he or she uses, and his or her general familiarity with literate, "book-like" language and story structure. A convenient form for evaluating the picture walk appears in Form 4.3 (p. 94).

The picture walk is an effective, informal way of observing the child's familiarity with books, literate language, and story construction. Paris and Paris (2001) use the picture walk to evaluate five behaviors:

- *Book-handling skills*—whether the child has a sense of the appropriate speed and order of reading, and whether pages are skipped or skimmed.
- *Engagement*—whether the child appeared engaged in the story, as indicated by appropriate affect, attention, interest, and effort.
- *Picture comments*—whether the child makes comments about the pictures, including descriptions of objects, characters, emotions, actions, and so on (refers to looking at pictures individually).
- *Storytelling comments*—whether the child makes comments that integrate information across pictures, indicating that he or she is using the pictures to create a coherent story. Comments might include narration, dialogue, or the use of storytelling language.
- *Comprehension strategies*—whether the child uses strategies that indicate monitoring of comprehension. These strategies can include looking back or looking ahead in order to make sense of something, self-correction of story elements or narrative, asking questions for understanding, or making predictions about the story.

Although scores are given for each skill, this procedure is better used as an informal means of assessing children's familiarity with storybooks. Used with an individual child, it can give insights into the child's knowledge of the function of books, experience of being read to, and knowledge of book conventions. These are the five categories provided by Paris and Paris; however, we suggest that one also look at the use of literary language. For example, does the child begin with "Once upon a time . . ." and conclude with "The End"? Does the child use language that sounds like story language, or does the child tell the story in vernacular terms? These observations also can be useful.

The retelling is given immediately after the picture walk. It is a free retelling, in which the child is asked to retell as much of the story as possible without looking back at the pictures. When the child has finished, the teacher can give a neutral prompt, asking the child whether he or she remembers anything else about the story. The teacher should not point to specific pictures or ask specific questions about the story. During the retelling, the teacher should note what is said, possibly tape recording it later for transcription. The retelling is evaluated by the number of story grammar elements included: settings, characters, goal/initiating events, problem/episodes, solution, and resolution/ending. We have provided an evaluation chart in Form 4.4 (p. 95).

Again, this retelling can provide some information about the child's experience with narratives. Children who have a strong story sense, as evidenced by their use of story grammar elements in their retelling, are likely to do better in reading stories than children who lack such a sense. Furthermore, the retelling should be evaluated for overall coherence. Is the child clearly telling a story, or merely recalling bits and pieces of unrelated information? Children without a clear story sense will need additional practice in listening and responding to stories.

Paris and Paris (2001) provide a set of comprehension prompts as the third part of the assessment. Although these prompts are specific to the story that Paris and Paris used, they might be useful in guiding recall for most stories. They are listed below, with directions.

Explicit Questions

1. [Book closed, characters] Who are the characters in this story? (replacement words: *people, animals*)
2. [Book closed, setting] Where does this story happen? (replacement words: *setting, take place*)
3. [Open book to initiating event, usually the first page] What happens at this point in the story? Why is this an important part of the story?
4. [Open book to problem] If you were telling someone this story, what would you say is going on now? Why did this happen?
5. [Go to ending] What happened here? Why did this happen?

Implicit Questions

1. [Feelings] Tell me what the people are feeling in this picture. Why do you think so?

2. [Causal inference] Why do you think this happened?
3. [Go to page with people speaking] What do you think the people would be saying here? Why would they be saying that?
4. [Go to last page of the book] This is the last picture in the story. What do you think happens next? Why do you think so?
5. [Close the book, theme] In thinking about everything that happened in this book, what have you learned from this story?

Overall, this evaluation will give you a sense of the skills that precede being able to read with comprehension. The information from this set of assessments complements the word-level and print-concept measures discussed elsewhere in the chapter. Paris and Paris found that children's scores on the various measures improved through the grades. On the picture walk, the average kindergartner scored a little less than 7, the average first grader about 7, and the average second grader about 8. In the retelling, average scores improved from about 2 in kindergarten, to about 3 in first grade, to about 4–4.5 in second grade. These are guidelines, not absolute norms, since they were based on a small sample.

Emergent Storybook Reading

Another approach to evaluating children's knowledge of storybooks is Sulzby's (1985) Emergent Storybook Reading scale. By observing emergent readers, she noted clear developmental trends in how children approach storybooks, moving from picture-governed attempts at reading to print-governed attempts, with the child finally moving toward near-accurate rendering of the text. Observing a child's attempt to read a storybook can provide valuable insights into the child's knowledge about how books work and can provide direction when considering how to help the child develop the knowledge needed to handle print.

The Emergent Storybook Reading scale can be used in a formal or informal setting. In a formal setting, the teacher might take the child aside, tell the child to pick a favorite book, and then ask the child to "read" the book. It is important that the child be familiar with the book, so that more mature behaviors can be seen. If the child protests that he or she cannot read, then tell him or her to "read as best you can" or "to pretend to read the book." You can encourage the child by making neutral comments, such as "What can I do to help? What do you want me to do? How will that help?" The scale also can be used informally while the teacher observes a child pretend-reading in a natural setting. Either way, understanding the stages that children go through as they learn to handle books will inform the teacher's instruction, by indicating the "next step" in the emergent reading process.

Sulzby (1985) found that children appear to go through nine stages in their approach to storybook reading, as they move from emergent to formal reading levels. This nine-stage scale has been validated repeatedly in her work. For ease of administration, we have compressed the scale to the format shown in Form 4.5 (p. 96).

Picture-Governed Attempts

1. *Labeling and commenting.* In this stage, the child looks at each picture and provides a name or descriptor, such as "doggie," "horse," or "bed," or makes a comment, such as "Go to bed," "That's ugly," or "He's a monster." Sometimes these comments are accompanied by a gesture or by slapping the page. Typically, the speech is less mature than the speech used in other contexts and may represent a storybook reading routine used by parents. In this and the following stage, each page is treated individually, and there are no attempts to link pictures to make a story.

2. *Following the action.* In this stage, children remark on the action in each picture as if it were occurring in the present moment. Comments might be similar to "There he goes. He's gonna get that monkey." The verbs used are typically present tense, present-progressive tense, or "gonna." Again, there is no attempt to link pictures to make a story.

3. *Dialogue storytelling.* This stage is a transition between the "labeling and commenting" and "following the action" stages and the more mature storytelling seen later. It may contain elements of the earlier stages but also includes an attempt to bridge the pages, using dialogue between the adult and child. The "story" may seem disjointed, but a listener can perceive that the child is trying to make a story. Here is an actual example:

CHILD: The children are looking for—for the other children (*turns page*) for one more children. And (*pause*) they looked all over the place (*pause*) for that little children (*turns page*). He went off to the _____. (*Turns page.*) He writed a note to—to the king—and they, uh (*pause*).

ADULT: They wrote a note to the king and then—

CHILD: Then they would. Then the boy bring the note to the king, and then he said to bring it back to here. (*Turns page.*) And then the little girl got peanuts and threw them at everybody.

ADULT: —Oh—

CHILD: And they're making stuff. And that, and that.

ADULT: —Oh—

CHILD: Pushed her into the peanuts.

4. *Monologue storytelling.* At this point, the child is clearly telling a story and uses a storytelling intonation that takes the form of an extended monologue stretching across the pages. The child makes reference to the picture content, but the major emphasis is on a continuous story. Sulzby (1985, p. 468) provides an example of this type of storybook reading:

"This is his house and he is going to sleep. He was reading a book and then after he was reading the book he saw pictures of the mountains up here. Here (*pause*) there's some pictures, here, and then he thought he was going exploring the mountains, he's going to, yeah, about the mountains and he thought I'm going to explore the mountains tomorrow. And then he asked his daddy . . . then he got out of the gate and he saw the mailman coming on the street. And then he went (*pause*) and then he went (*pause*) and then he said to him (*pointing to dog in picture*), Angus. Angus, 'cause that's his name, I know. After this we're gonna come to the mountains (*pause*) and then he got one of his, and then he stuck one flag in there and then this is gonna be his tree."

The story here is primitive, but there is a clear attempt to connect an ongoing plot across the different pages.

Print-Governed Attempts

5. *Print awareness*. This stage is a transition between the purely oral story, governed by picture interpretation, and reading. In this type of reenactment, the child inserts parts that sound like written language, either in intonation or in wording or in both, into parts that sound like oral language. The story may depart from the actual story, but the pretend reading shows a clear sense of audience and a concern with coherence that is missing in the above excerpt. This type of reading also contains parts that are decontextualized or are specified well enough that they could be understood without the pictures. At this stage, the child may refuse to read a section because he or she does not know the words. This stage is similar to Biemiller's (1970) conceptualization of the refusal stage, in which the child knows that print carries the information in the text and knows that she or he cannot read the print. In earlier stages, children may refuse to read, but in this stage the refusal is clearly based on the belief that they need to know more about the print in order to read.

6. *Aspectual reading*. In this stage, the child often uses the patterns of the original story or those in similar books. The child may focus on particular words that he or she knows or may overrely on a particular pattern. One child in Sulzby's study went through the book and read, pointing, "a" "the" "Grandpa" "and," page after page. Other children focus their attention on sounding out individual words. Compared to the earlier stages, this may seem like a regression, but it is an important one. In this stage, the child is trying out new repertoires that will be integrated later on with story knowledge.

7. *Text-governed reading*. In this reading, the child is clearly trying to create a verbatim rendering of the text. Sulzby divides this stage into two parts—reading with strategies unbalanced and reading independently—but we have merged these because both informal reading inventories and running records made of children reading text are better ways to assess children's use of strategies during text-governed reading. What is significant here is that the child is clearly reading the text, not the pictures, often using finger pointing. The child may skip unfamiliar words or insert nonsense words, but most of the words are text words, and the child is using a reading intonation.

This emergent reading scale can provide a great deal of information about a child's knowledge of how books work. If the child's "reading" does not fit clearly into one category or another, assume that the reading is in the lower of the two categories and instruct the child in the next-higher category. Thus if the child's reading is between dialogue and monologue forms of storytelling, assume that the child is in the dialogue stage and prompt him or her to tell extended stories by asking for elaborations and clear transitions between pages.

ALPHABETIC RECOGNITION

It is vital for young children to learn letter names if they are to become proficient readers. Why is this true? It is certainly possible to learn to recognize words by memorizing them as whole units. For example, children with no alphabet knowledge at all could learn to say *cat* whenever they encounter the word in print. But learning words in this way would exert crippling demands on memory, and it would ignore the alphabetic nature of our language. Specifically, there are two important reasons for teaching children letter names at an early age. First, fluent readers do not recognize words as whole units. Rather, they do so by identifying the component letters. This process occurs at an unconscious level, but research leaves no room for doubt. The second reason is that teachers must have some means of referring to the letters during instruction. Although it may be theoretically possible to learn the letters and not their names, this approach would hardly be practical.

Assessing alphabetic knowledge is best accomplished by presenting a child with letters, one at a time, and asking the child to say the name of each. Several questions arise about how best to implement this procedure.

1. *In what order should the letters be presented?* The best way to answer this question may be in the negative. That is, it is important only to avoid presenting the letters in alphabetical order. Doing so would provide the child with a built-in prompt that could lead to inaccurate results. Randomly ordering the letters is preferable.

2. *How should the letters be presented to the child?* We have found that the best way is to present all of the letters on a single sheet of paper in a grid format. Using a blank sheet as a placeholder for each row of letters, the teacher is able to observe the student's awareness of left-to-right directionality. If necessary, the teacher can simply point to each letter with one hand and record the child's response on a separate copy of the grid, using the other hand.

3. *Should capital letters or lowercase letters be assessed?* Because both forms of letters will be encountered continually in printed materials, both forms must be assessed. The random arrangement of letters on the grid should also randomize the appearance of each form. In other words, it would be a poor idea to put the capital and lowercase form of the same letter next to each other.

4. *What font should be used?* There is probably no answer to this question on which everyone would agree. However, common sense suggests that a font that is plain and free of serifs (those extra, decorative marks, such as the short horizontal lines at the top and bottom of a capital *I*) would be less likely to mislead the child. A related issue concerns the letters *a* and *g*. The lowercase forms of these letters often occur in two very different formats, so that children need to be assessed on their knowledge of both. They may encounter *a* or ɑ, *g* or ɡ.

Addressing all of the issues that we have just discussed results in a one-page grid displaying all of the letters, most of them in both their upper- and lowercase forms, plus an extra lowercase form for the letters *a* and *g*. This means that alphabet assessment should tap children's knowledge of 54 symbols. Using such a grid as a method of recording a child's responses is a convenient means of record keeping. By using different markings for repeated assessments, a teacher can document growth in alphabetic recognition on a single sheet of paper over the course of many months. Form 4.6 (p. 97) presents such a grid.

PHONEMIC AWARENESS

It is vital that prereaders become aware of the sounds that comprise spoken words. *Phonemes*, the smallest sounds we hear in words, are the building blocks of our spoken language, and becoming aware of their presence is vital to later successful phonics instruction. It is important to understand, however, that phonemic awareness is not directly linked to phonics. In fact, it is not connected with written language in any direct way. A child may be phonemically aware and yet have no knowledge of the alphabet. Phonemic awareness is entirely an auditory matter.

The research into phonemic awareness instruction is compelling. Findings clearly show that (1) children can be taught to become phonemically aware, and (2) there is a strong causal link between phonemic awareness and later abilities in phonics and spelling. This second finding makes perfect sense. After all, it is difficult to learn letter–sound correspondences if you are unable to hear the component sounds of a spoken word. A certain level of phonemic awareness is a prerequisite to successful phonics and spelling instruction.

Finally, let's examine a minor issue of terminology. Some experts prefer the term *phonological* awareness to *phonemic* awareness. The former term is broader and includes not just speech phonemes but larger units of sound, such as rhymes, syllables, and word duration. For example, a teacher might ask a child to blend the following two sounds: /k/ and /at/. The child would then say the word *cat*. Technically, such an assessment activity is not purely a matter of phonemic awareness. This is because the rime *at* is larger than a single phoneme. It is a chunk of sound comprising two phonemes. Working with rimes and other chunks of sound that are larger than a single phoneme has led some to use the broader phrase, *phonological awareness*. You are likely to encounter either phrase in the literature. It is a small but interesting distinction.

The word *cat* contains three phonemes, each represented by a letter. Learning about how these letters represent phonemes is a matter of phonics. Becoming sensitive to their presence in spoken words is something far more basic. Phonemic awareness should develop prior to school entry or in kindergarten.

How can we tell whether a child is aware of the component sounds of spoken words? How can we assess a child's phonemic awareness? Form 4.7 (p. 98) can be used over time to document the emergent reader's increasing awareness of sounds in words. Mastery might be demonstrated by the child's ability to perform the task with five items fitting the performance description on the form.

Each task is entirely an oral activity, which is why such assessments can be done so readily with 4- and 5-year-olds. Phonemic awareness activities often have game-like formats, and a child's responses can provide a teacher with useful information about the extent of that child's phonemic awareness, even though the child is scarcely aware of being assessed. It is not recommended that all tasks be administered in one sitting unless the child is in first or second grade and experiencing difficulty hearing sounds in words. At that point, the novice reader might be asked to perform several tasks to determine what behaviors are under control and which awarenesses require additional instruction. Dictation for Phonological Awareness (Form 4.8, p. 99) is an adaptation of Hearing Sounds in Words, from the Observation Survey (Clay, 1993a). We include this instrument because invented spelling can be a useful way to evaluate phonological awareness. Although this dictation task provides a lens for viewing phonological awareness, alphabetic knowledge, and some print concepts, it can be a useful supplement to a "pure" test of phonological awareness. Furthermore, it can be given to small groups, as well as individually, thus making it an efficient screening tool.

The Dynamic Indicators of Basic Early Literacy Skills (DIBELS) battery includes two widely used and easily accessible tests for assessing phonological awareness (*dibels. uoregon.edu*). The subtests are Initial Sound Fluency (ISF) and Phoneme Segmentation Fluency (PSF). These are timed, individual measures for determining a child's ability to identify and produce an initial sound of an orally produced word (ISF) and the ability to segment three- and four-phoneme words into their individual sounds. The DIBELS website provides benchmark assessments, alternate forms for progress monitoring, and predictive data for evaluating students' scores. All DIBELS instruments may be downloaded at no cost.

Recent research has indicated that segmentation tasks *reflect* rather than *predict* a child's spelling knowledge. If you need spelling knowledge to complete a task, then, not surprisingly, the task is highly correlated with other measures of word recognition, but it is not a pure task of phonological awareness. This is also true for phoneme deletion. Nevertheless, these tasks are included in many measures of phonological awareness, such as the C-TOPP (Comprehensive Test of Phonological Processing; Torgesen & Wagner, 1999). We feel that such measures should be interpreted carefully.

The increased emphasis on phonemic awareness has led to the development of commercial assessment instruments. The Test of Phonological Awareness (TOPA-2+; Torgesen & Bryant, 2004) is one such instrument. It is a norm-referenced measure that may be administered in individual or group settings. While meeting high standards of reliability and validity, classroom teachers also need to consider factors of cost and time effectiveness. In addition, the C-TOPP (Torgesen & Wagner, 1999) taps several phonological processing abilities across a wide age range.

WHAT TO DO WITH ASSESSMENT RESULTS?

Teaching children in the emergent literacy stage involves providing experience with books and book handling as well as direct instruction in the skills needed for the next stage.

It is important that children develop a foundation in print concept and book handling, because that foundation is the basis for learning how to read connected text. Although we believe very strongly in decoding instruction, placing too much emphasis on decoding early on will lead to confusion later. Instead, we believe that a program for early readers should involve a balance between word work, text experience, and oral language development. A typical program for children reading at the emergent level would involve experience with predictable books, general book handling, phonological awareness instruction, word-recognition work, and responding to a wide variety of teacher read-alouds. It's important to keep in mind that the National Reading Panel determined that over a school year instruction in phonemic awareness should take no more than 20 hours (that's about 6 minutes per day). In addition, they recommended using assessment to determine whether instruction should engage students in the easier tasks like rhyming and initial sound identification or the more difficult manipulation and segmentation tasks. We offer suggestions in the following material.

Predictable Books

Predictable books are books that have a repetitive pattern, which supports the child in learning print conventions (concept of word in text, finger pointing, left-to-right progression, etc.) and to provide what we call "book success." Experiencing book success is essential for children who have initially failed to learn to read, because it convinces them that they *can* learn to read.

Consider a book like *Brown Bear, Brown Bear, What Do You See?* (Martin, 1983). It is a simple pattern, with the pictures supporting the text. On one page is the pattern "[color animal], [color animal], what do you see?" (the animals include a brown bear, a goldfish, a red bird, etc.). These animals are pictured. On the following page is "I see a [color animal] looking at me." Thus reading is propelled by the pattern, which provides an excellent opportunity to teach both directionality and finger pointing during the joint reading. It is easy to memorize the book, so that children can bring it home and demonstrate their "reading" skills to their parents as they develop facility with the alphabetic system.

Following the reading of a predictable book, the teacher can put some of the words on word cards and use these as the basis of word-reading or word-sorting lessons (see Chapter 5). Over the course of the child's program, the teacher works with progressively less predictable books. One metric for predictability is the Reading Recovery levels, now widely used to gauge book levels.

In addition to predictable books, we recommend that each session include some exposure to a nonpredictable storybook, used for comprehension. It is important for all children to develop the vocabulary and comprehension skills needed for success in the later grades. Facilitating the acquisition of these skills might involve an interactive reading session, wherein the teacher reads the book and asks questions or elicits a discussion about the story. Here one should be aware of the child's emergent reading level, as measured by the Sulzby scale. The teacher should try to nudge the child along the scale, so that the child is encouraged to work at the next-higher level, if possible.

Developing Phonological Awareness

Phonological awareness stems from the insight that words can be thought of as an ordered set of sounds. In normal development, this is learned through play or experimentation. For the child with reading problems, however, this experimentation should be directed through activities that encourage the child to think actively about sounds in words. Some of these activities are described in the following material.

Nursery Rhymes

Teaching common nursery rhymes should be part of every kindergarten class. We recommend that nursery rhymes be presented on charts, so that the child can learn basic print concepts as well as the rhyme. Rhymes can be chanted chorally by groups or memorized individually. Children should be encouraged to predict rhymes, write (or orally compose) another line in the rhyme, and so on.

Picture Sorting

Sorting pictures is an effective phonological awareness task. Teachers can gather pictures of objects that begin with the same sound, or, after children are proficient in beginning sounds, end with the same sound. For example, children can sort pictures that begin with the same beginning as *bear* or *mom*. Begin with sorting two sounds, then move to three sounds. This exercise can be integrated with letter work, so that after a letter has been taught, the child can sort pictures that begin with the new sound from pictures that begin with previously taught sounds.

Oddity Tasks

Tasks that require students to identify the "odd man out" from a set of words can also improve phonemic awareness. One might begin with rhyming words but progress to words that differ in beginning consonants, then final consonants. Words that differ in medial consonants can be used but may be too difficult at this level.

Stretch Sounding

Teach children to stretch a word out so that phoneme changes can clearly be heard. For example, *dog* might be stretched to *d-d-d-o-g-g-g*. This can be done by first modeling it, then having the students repeat what you have vocalized. Once students are proficient at stretching out words, try having them clap or place a token in a box as they hear new sounds. For example, if the word is *sad*, you would draw a row of three boxes. Students put a token into a box (moving from left to right, of course!) when they hear the phonemes change. This effective technique was introduced by the Russian psychologist Elkonin (1973).

Caution: We are using the term *phoneme* for clarity. Please do not teach it, or any other technical term, to students. Use *sound* instead, but be clear in your own mind what you mean.

Invented Spelling

Stretch sounding should serve as a natural bridge to invented spelling, since one must stretch a word out in order to spell it. Invented spelling appears to improve phonemic awareness, among other skills. This point is discussed more thoroughly in Chapter 5.

Tongue Twisters

Have students repeat a tongue twister (from Wallach & Wallach, 1979), first in a regular fashion, then separating onset and rime. For example, for the /h/ sound, the tongue twister *Harry had a horrible headache and hated to hear Henry howl* might be separated out as *H-arry h-ad a h-orrible h-eadache and h-ated to h-ear H-arry h-owl.*

Adding Sounds

Take a common rime (-*ear*, -*ake*, -*all*, etc.) and have students add and subtract sounds. For example, one might start by saying, "If I have *ear* and I add /h/, what do I have now? Then, if I take away the /h/ and add /w/, what do I have?" And so forth. This can be done later, using words on the blackboard.

Deletion Tasks

Similar to those described in class, you might have students say *burn* without the *b, pink* without the *p,* and so forth. Rosner (1975), who invented this task, chooses words so that the result is a real word, but we do not employ this limitation—especially after the children get the hang of it.

The Troll

One might use a troll puppet (or any other type of puppet) and say that "the troll will only allow people whose name begins with [ends with, or has in it] the sound of _____ to cross the bridge." Then give names (from the class or outside) and have students determine whether the troll will let this person cross the bridge. If this task proves too difficult, begin with syllables, using the same type of activities. Begin with continuant consonants (*m, s, n, f, z, v*) and vowels, because these can be sounded by themselves. Save stop consonants (such as *t, d, b, c*) until later.

Alphabet Books

Today there are alphabet books based on myriad themes and topics. Using these books as shared reading or interactive teacher read-alouds is an excellent way to extend phonemic awareness and provide reinforcement for letter instruction. Children should be encouraged to repeat some of the words representing letter sounds and to generate their own words for selected pages. Alliterative word play is suggested. Books that draw attention to a clear letter–sound correspondence or letter–picture correspondence are likely to be more effective in teaching about letters and sounds than books that present letters as story characters or within the context of a story (Bradley & Jones, 2007). Alphabet books can provide opportunities for cross-curricular connections and vocabulary development. Children might be encouraged to create pages for a class alphabet book for science and social studies themes.

Alphabetic Work

Although research is not clear as to whether a child needs to know the alphabet prior to learning to read, we recommend that children learn the names and sounds of letters. There is a clear progression in how children normally acquire alphabetic knowledge, at least in the United States. First, they learn the alphabet song. Then they learn to pick out letters from an array of letters in order. Then they learn individual letters. This process can be translated into an instructional sequence:

1. If a child does not know the alphabet song, teach it.
2. If a child knows the alphabet song, ask the child to pick out letters from a letter strip, using the song as a guide.
3. Teach the letters individually. Avoid introducing letters together that have configural similarities and might be easily confused.

There are literally hundreds of approaches to teaching letters individually. We do not know how to distinguish among them. Many teachers use a "letter of the week" approach. Systematically teaching one letter a week seems fine, although we would start with common consonants rather than *a*. We would also continually review all the letters taught, rather than allocating them to the back burner, in essence, at the end of each week. While teaching the letter of the week, we would emphasize the sound of the letter as well as the name. We would have the child cut out pictures of items that contain the letter from old magazines, do picture sorts (see above), do the troll activity using letters rather than sounds, and so on. We also would integrate writing into these lessons, because learning to form the letters provides writing practice as well as important reinforcement for the letter name.

Word Work

Finally, at this emergent stage, we feel that some word learning is useful. This activity might involve asking the children to pick out words that they want to learn or words from their storybooks, either predictable or not. These words can be printed on index cards to be practiced at home and in school. For older children, we have found that the "Three Strikes and You're Out" procedure, described in Chapter 5, works well. If a word is read correctly in three separate sessions, the word is "retired" or placed in some form of word bank. Word cards also can be used for word sorting (see Chapter 5). In using these sorts, we want the child to notice the features of words, not necessarily be able to spell those words.

We also want children to write using invented spelling. This "writing" might be a sentence or a story. In the typical classroom setting, the teacher might encourage the children to attempt to write daily about a topic of their choice. When time permits, a more structured approach might be used. In Reading Recovery (Clay, 1993a), for example, the teacher and student agree on a sentence, and they work on writing the sentence together. On a practice page, the child writes what she or he can. If the child cannot write a word, the teacher may ask the child to write what is known on the practice page, with the teacher filling in what the child does not know, or use Elkonin boxes (see page 86) to break the word into sounds and add letters for the sounds that fit in the boxes. Again, the child can be encouraged to do this by him- or herself or with teacher assistance. Making and breaking words that the teacher has modeled using magnetic letters is also a good way for emergent readers to learn words.

It is important to remember that we want to provide a foundation for the child so that later reading will be successful and at the same time prepare the child quickly for formal reading instruction. For children at the emergent stage in first grade and beyond, we want to be efficient, so that we can get the children at this stage ready to work with their peers; often the children need to make more than a year's progress in a year's time. Indeed, they need to make "accelerated progress," in Clay's (1993a) words, learning more material than they ordinarily might in the same amount of time. Programs such as Reading Recovery are designed to help children make such progress and should be considered as potential learning resources for the child with reading problems at this level.

FORM 4.1

Checklist for Concepts of Print

Concept	Date / /	Date / /	Date / /	Date / /	Date / /
Book orientation					
Left–right directionality					
Top-to-bottom progression					
Word boundaries					
Concept of letter					

Book-Handling Knowledge Guidelines

NAME: AGE: GRADE: DATE:

Before you begin, make sure that you are familiar with the test and the book you will be using. Make sure you select a book that has both pictures and a written story that includes the required punctuation marks. When you begin, be sure to make the child feel comfortable. If you quickly establish rapport, the results will be more valid. If a child shows mastery of a concept, check the provided space. If a child does not show mastery of a concept, leave the space blank or write what the child did.

Say: **I'm going to read you this story, but I want you to help me.**

1. Test: For orientation of book.
    Pass the book to the child. Hold the book vertically by its outside edge,
    spine toward the child. Say:
    Show me the front of the book   Orientation of book

    Concept _____

2. Test: For the concept that print, not pictures, carries the message.
    Turn to the first page of the story. Say:
    I'll read this story. You help me. Show me where to start reading.
    Where do I begin?   Print carries message

    Concept _____

    Read the page. Turn to the next page.

3. Test: For directional understanding (left to right, return sweep). Say:
    Show me where to start.
    (If child goes back to the beginning of the book, turn back to the page under
    discussion and provide the next prompt.)
    Show me where to start on this page.
    Which way do I go? (Child should indicate left-to-right motion.)
    Where do I go after that? (Child should go to beginning of next line.)

                                                        Directional understanding

    Concept _____

    Read the page.

(continued)

---

4. Test: For speech-to-print match/word-by-word pointing. Say:
   Point to it while I read it.

   Read the page slowly but fluently.

   Speech-to-print match

   Concept _____

5. Test: For concept of first and last.

   Read the page. Say:
   Show me the first part of the story.
   Show me the last part of the story.

   First and last (must have both)

   Concept _____

6. Test: A left page is read before a right page.
   Read text until you come to a page that has print on both left and right sides
   of the page. Then ask:
   Where do I start reading?

   Left page read before right

   Concept _____

7. Test: Punctuation.
   Read text, then point to period and ask:
   What is this for?   .

   Period recognition

   Concept _____

   Read text, then point to question mark and ask:
   What is this for?   ?

   Question mark recognition

   Concept _____

   Read text, then point to exclamation point and ask:
   What is this for?   !

   Exclamation point recognition

   Concept _____

   Point to comma and ask:
   What is this for?   ,

   Comma recognition

   Concept _____

   Point to quotation marks and ask:
   What is this for?   " "

   Quotation mark recognition

   Concept _____

(continued)

8. Test: Lowercase letters.
   Point to a capital letter. Say:
   Find a little letter, or a lowercase letter, like this.
   Demonstrate correct match if child does not succeed.
   Point to a different capital letter. Say:
   Find a little letter, or a lowercase letter, like this.   Lowercase letter

   Concept _____

9. Concept of letter, word, first and last letter, capital letter.
   Use two index cards or small pieces of paper that a child can slide easily.
   To start, lay the cards on the page, but leave all the print exposed. Open the
   cards between questions.

   Read the last page of the book, then say:

   I want you to push the cards across the story like this. Demonstrate how
   you can move the cards across the page, coming from opposite directions.
   **Now I want you to push the cards across the page so all you can see is
   just one letter.**

   Now show me two letters.

                                               Letter concept _____

   Now show me just one word.
   Now show me two words.

                                               Word Concept _____

   Take the cards again and show me the first letter of a word.

   Now show me the last letter of a word.   First and last _____

   Show me a capital or uppercase letter.   Capital letter _____

Picture Walk Scoring Guidelines

This book is called _____. In this book the pictures tell the story. There aren't any words written. I'd like you to look at the pictures in the book and use your own words to tell me the story.

Picture walk element	Score description	Score
1. Book-handling skills: Orients book correctly, has sense of appropriate viewing speed and order; viewing errors include skipping pages, speeding through pages, etc.	Incorrectly handles book and makes more than two viewing errors.	0
	Makes one to two viewing errors.	1
	Handles book appropriately, making no viewing errors.	2
2. Engagement: Displays behavioral and emotional involvement during the picture walk, as indicated by attention, interest in book, affect, and effort.	Displays off-task behavior or negative comments.	0
	Displays quiet, sustained behavior.	1
	Shows several examples of attention, affect, interest, or effort (i.e., spontaneous comments).	2
3. Picture comments: Makes discrete comments about a picture, including descriptions of objects, characters, emotions, actions, and options, as well as character vocalizations.	Makes no picture comments.	0
	Makes one picture comment or verbalization.	1
	Makes two or more comments or verbalizations about specific pictures.	2
4. Storytelling comments: Makes comments that encompass several pictures, demonstrating an understanding that the pictures tell a coherent story—can include narration, dialogue, using book language, and storytelling voice.	Makes no storytelling comments.	0
	Provides storytelling elements, but not consistently.	1
	Through narration or dialogue, connects story events and presents a coherent storyline.	2
5. Comprehension strategies: Displays vocalizations or behaviors that show attempts at comprehension, such as self-correcting, looking back/ahead in book, asking questions for understanding, making predictions about story.	Demonstrates no comprehension strategies.	0
	Exhibits one instance of comprehension strategies.	1
	Demonstrates comprehension strategies at least two or more times.	2

FORM 4.4

Retelling Evaluation Guidelines

Did the child include . . .	Yes/No
Setting	
Characters	
A goal or initiating event	
A problem faced by a character, or episodes involving that character	
A solution to the problem	
A clear ending	

Emergent Storybook Reading Scale (After Sulzby, 1985)

	Stage	Characteristics?	Notes
Picture governed	Labeling and commenting	1. Each page is treated as a separate unit. 2. Child either names or describes person/animal on each page or comments on it.	
	Following the action	1. Each page is treated as a separate unit. 2. Child describes the action on each page.	
	Storytelling in dialogue format	1. Child begins to make links between pages. 2. Overall, the listener can perceive a story, although it is disjointed. 3. Storytelling is in dialogue form, propelled by prompts from adult.	
	Storytelling in monologue format	1. Child bridges plot between pages. 2. Tends to take the form of a monologue.	
Print governed	Print awareness	1. Child may refuse to read based on lack of print knowledge. 2. Child points with finger.	
	Aspect-governed reading	1. Child inserts parts that sound like written language. 2. Child may overrely on sounding words out or only read words that are known.	
	Text-governed reading	1. Child attempts to render a verbatim reading of the print.	

Alphabet Recognition Chart

A S D F C B E

R G T Y U H J

M Z P K V Q W

N O I X L

a s d f c b e

r g t y u h j

m z p k v q w

n o i x l a g

Tests of Phonemic Awareness

Administration

For each subtest, provide one or two examples with feedback to be certain that the task is clear to the child. Then assess the student using five items without feedback. Mastery is indicated if the student is able to correctly complete four of the five items. All tasks are performed orally without the use of printed letters or words.

	Task description	Mastery
Rhymes	a. Identifies teacher-generated words that rhyme or don't rhyme. b. Generates words that rhyme with a teacher prompt.	a. b.
Phoneme isolation	Isolates particular sounds from the remainder of the word. The child can identify /k/ as the first sound in the word *cake*.	
Phoneme identity	Given three words, the child can identify a common sound in all three words.	
Phoneme categorization	Say three words to the child, two of which have a common phoneme, such as an initial sound (e.g., *dog, horse, duck*). Ask the child to tell which of the three words does not belong with the other two.	
Blending	Tell the child that you are going to say a word in your own "secret code." Then pronounce the word by saying each phoneme in succession. For example, say "/k/ /a/ /t/." The child must blend these sounds to form the word *cat*.	
Phoneme addition	Provide the child with a common rime. Ask the child to make a word by adding a sound (e.g., add /sh/ to the beginning of *ake*).	
Phoneme deletion	Say a common one-syllable word, such as *cake*. Ask the child to remove the beginning sound, so that the child says *ake*.	
Phoneme substitution	Ask the child to substitute one phoneme for another to make a new word. The word is *shake*. Change /k/ to /d/ to make a new word.	
Phoneme segmentation	a. Segments a word beginning and ending with single consonant into its individual sounds. b. Segments a word beginning with a consonant cluster into its individual sounds. c. Segments a word ending with a consonant cluster into its individual sounds.	a. b. c.

An Adaptation of Hearing Sounds in Words
(After Clay, 1993a)

Dictation for Phonological Awareness

After children are ready with their pencils and paper, say, "I'm going to read this story to you, and you are going to try to write it as best as you can." First read the story in a normal intonation, then read it word by word, so that the children are able to attempt to record each word.

1.   The dog saw Sam. He crossed the road and ran into his arms. (39 phonemes)
2.   I ate a big slice of cake with some ice cream at the party. (37 phonemes)
3.   Dad went to his job at the mill. He is working late today. (39 phonemes)

1. Th e d o g s aw S a m. H e c r o ss ed th e r o a d a n d r a n
    1 2 3 4 5 6 7 8 9 10 11 12 13 14 15 16 17 18 19 20 21 22 23 24 25 26 27 28

    i n t o h i s a r m s
    29 30 31 32 33 34 35 36 37 38 39
                                                    Mastery = 31

2. I a te a b i g s l i ce o f c a ke w i th s o m e i ce c r ea m a t
    1 2 3 4 5 6 7 8 9 10 11 12 13 14 15 16 17 18 19 20 21 22 23 24 25 26 27 28 29 30

    th e p a r t y. (37)
    31 32 33 34 35 36 37
                                                    Mastery = 30

3. D a d w e n t t o h i s j o b a t th e m i ll. H e i s w o r k i ng
    1 2 3 4 5 6 7 8 9 10 11 12 13 14 15 16 17 18 19 20 21 22 23 24 25 26 27 28 29 39 31 32

    l a te t o d ay. (39)
    33 34 35 36 37 38 39
                                                    Mastery = 31

To score the dictation test, count as correct each phoneme (/th/, /s/, /aw/) appropriately represented. It is not necessary that the phoneme be spelled correctly, only that it is represented. Remember that our goal for this measure is phonological awareness. The scoring should be based on an 80% mastery criterion, so for sentence 1, 31 of the 39 phonemes should be correctly represented, even if they are misspelled.

CHAPTER FIVE

Word Recognition and Spelling

Monitoring the development of word-recognition ability is one of the most important tasks of teachers in the primary grades and teachers of struggling readers in the upper grades. The broad area of word recognition is complex, however. There are many contributing skills to track, so it is important that teachers have a solid understanding of the skill areas underlying a student's ability to recognize words.

A useful way of organizing both assessment and instruction in this complex area is to divide it into three components: sight words, structural analysis, and phonics. Let's look at each one of these areas in turn.

SIGHT-WORD KNOWLEDGE

A sight word is any word that can be pronounced automatically, without conscious analysis. There is a tendency to confuse the notion of sight words with that of high-frequency words (such as *of*, *but*, *can*, etc.). It is true that all high-frequency words must eventually become sight words if a reader is to be fluent. However, a reader's sight vocabulary may well include many low-frequency words, such as his or her last name. Sight vocabularies, therefore, differ considerably from one student to the next, although every teacher hopes that they have many words in common.

In order to assess sight words, the teacher must begin with a target list. Primary teachers typically use the Dolch (1936) or Fry (1980) lists or some other compilation of high-frequency words. Next, the teacher must decide on an assessment format in order to gain knowledge about how many of these words each child can pronounce at sight.

One way—a very efficient one—is to assess children as a group. The format presented below is designed for such a group assessment. The children are presented with row after row of words, each row containing four words. In the first example, the teacher leads the children from one row to the next, instructing them to circle one of the words.

Example 1
Teacher says, "Circle *book*." Child sees row of four words.

　　　pear　　book　　bolt　　　napkin

The time saved through group assessment is considerable, of course. However, the accuracy of the results may be compromised, as it often is in group assessments. For example, a child who is familiar with the sound made by the letter *b* will be able to eliminate the first and fourth words of the sample item, even though the word *book* may not yet be a sight word for that child.

In contrast, consider the format presented in Example 2, designed for individual administration. In this case, the teacher shows the child a word and asks for a pronunciation. The words may be presented on flash cards, in list form, or even by means of computer.

Example 2
Teacher says, "Say this word." Child sees flash card.

　　　book

It is important that the teacher remember that the sight word is one that can be pronounced immediately, without analysis. If a student takes more than a second to produce the pronunciation or perceptibly "sounds it out," then that word cannot reasonably be judged a sight word.

It is easy to construct a sight-word inventory once you have decided on which target words to include. Many lists are available. Some include shorter, high-frequency word lists (e.g., the Dolch 220 or Fry lists of 300 and 600 "instant" words). Some are longer lists that include words of lower frequency. Form 5.1 (pp. 116–122) presents Fry's list of 300 instant words in the form of a sight-word inventory. Form 5.2 (pp. 123–124) displays Dolch's list of 220 words categorized by approximate level. You may prefer to construct a simple sight-word inventory on the basis of Dolch's words.

For older students, it is a good idea to use a normed list to compare their results with the results of other students their age. They know many sight words, so it can be difficult to determine whether their sight-word knowledge is hindering their reading fluency and comprehension. The Test of Word Reading Efficiency (TOWRE) is a measure of word-reading accuracy and efficiency (Torgesen, Wagner, & Rashotte, 1999). The TOWRE Sight Word Efficiency task is a list of words that students read individually in 45 seconds. Raw scores can be converted to percentiles, scale scores, and age and grade equivalents.

Regardless of the list you use, it is important to keep in mind that sight-word knowledge consists of individual words. That is to say, each word is a separate skill! Were you to administer a sight-word inventory, it would therefore make little sense to tally the number of words a child can pronounce at sight. Rather, each of the words represents a distinct skill, a word worth knowing in its own right.

Essential Words

For older children, it is useful to know what they know about survival words. These are words that children (and adults) need to know to survive in the real world. For a young person, perhaps the most important words to know, to avoid embarrassment in public restrooms, are *Men* and *Women* (or *Gentlemen* and *Ladies*). We present a list of "essential words," but it is only a beginning and by no means comprehensive. The first part of this list (Table 5.1) contains an older set of words; the next part (Table 5.2) is an updated ver-

TABLE 5.1. The Original Essential Vocabulary

adults only	flammable	noxious
antidote	found	nurse
beware	fragile	office
beware of the dog	gasoline	open
bus station	gate	out
bus stop	gentlemen	out of order
caution	handle with care	pedestrians prohibited
closed	hands off	poison
combustible	help	poisonous
condemned	high voltage	police (station)
contaminated	inflammable	post no bills
deep water	information	post office
dentist	instructions	posted
do not cross, use tunnel	keep away	private
do not crowd	keep closed at all times	private property
do not enter	keep off (the grass)	pull
do not inhale fumes	keep out	push
do not push	ladies	safety first
do not refreeze	live wires	shallow water
do not shove	lost	shelter
do not stand up	men	smoking prohibited
do not use near heat	next (window) (gate)	step down (up)
do not use near open flame	no admittance	taxi stand
doctor (Dr.)	no checks cashed	terms cash
don't walk	no credit	thin ice
down	no diving	this end up
dynamite	no dogs allowed	this side up
elevator	no dumping	up
emergency exit	no fires	use before [date]
employees only	no fishing	use in open air
entrance	no hunting	use other door
exit	no loitering	violators will be prosecuted
exit only	no minors	walk
explosives	no smoking	wanted
external use only	no spitting	warning
fallout shelter	no swimming	watch your step
fire escape	no touching	wet paint
fire extinguisher	no trespassing	women
first aid	not for internal use	

TABLE 5.2. Updated List of Essential Words

10 items or less	falling rock	pay cashier before pumping
30 days same as cash	fasten seat belt	pay here
911	fax machine	pedestrian crossing
airbags	fire alarm	polluted area
alternate route	fire exit	prepare to stop
aluminum cans only	flagger ahead	quiet please
ambulance	flush	radiation hazard
asbestos hazard	for help dial	radioactive materials
automatic	form line here	radioactive waste
biohazard	handicapped parking	railroad crossing
biohazardous waste	hard hat area	read directions before using
blasting zone	harmful	recyclable
bomb threat	hazard	recycle
breakable	hazardous	refrigerate
bridge ices before road	hazardous area	restricted area
buckle up	hazardous chemicals	restrooms
bump	hazardous waste	resume safe speed
business route	help wanted	right of way
by-pass	hospital	right turn only
caffeine	ID required	road closed
cancerous	if swallowed, induce vomiting	school crossing
cash only	in case of fire	school zone
cellular phones prohibited	incinerate	service engine
chemicals	incinerator	self-service
children at play	infectious area	shake well
clearance	insert card (ATM)	shirt and shoes required
construction ahead	irritant	signature
consult physician before use	keep away from water	slippery when wet
danger	keep frozen	slow down
dangerous	keep out of reach of children	soft shoulders
deer crossing	keep refrigerated	speed limit
delay	kerosene	stairs (stairway)
deliveries	lifeguard on duty	stop ahead
detour	loading zone	subway
diesel fuel	makes wide turns	Surgeon General warning
directions	manager	take with food
dispose	may cause birth defects	teller machine
do not bend	may cause dizziness	through traffic
do not block intersection	may cause drowsiness	timecard
do not enter	microwave in use	time clock
do not get in eyes	microwave safe	tornado warning
do not ingest	minimum speed	tornado watch
do not mix	must be 21 years of age	tow away zone
do not take if allergic to . . .	no jet skis allowed	tow zone
do not take with milk	no left turn	toxic
do not use near water, fire, etc.	no littering	toxic waste
dosage	no outlet	turn off cellular phones
drive in	no pagers	turn signal
drive through	no parking	uneven shoulder
drive-up window	no pets	use only as directed
electrical hazard	no photographs permitted	ventilation required
Emergency Medical Services	no refunds	video camera in use
enter only	no returns	video monitor in use
escalator	no through traffic	watch for falling rocks
exact change (needed)	no turn on red	watch for trucks
exit only	no video cameras allowed	wear protective eye gear
expect delays	nonalcoholic	wear safety glasses
expiration	nontoxic	weight limit
expires (EXP)	nuclear waste	wide load
explosives	one way	wrong way
express line	order here	X-ray
evacuate	oxygen in use	yield

sion by Davis and McDaniel (1998). There may be others that are important in your town or for particular children. Use our list as a starting point.

STRUCTURAL ANALYSIS

Structural analysis, also known as *morphemic analysis*, refers to the act of breaking down words into units of meaning (e.g., prefixes, suffixes, root words). Children are required to use structural analysis from an early age, as when they differentiate singular from plural forms or past and present tenses of verbs. As the material they read becomes more complex, a greater array of affixes confronts them. The ability to take apart an unfamiliar word in order to determine its meaning is of increasing importance. Even familiar words containing prefixes and/or suffixes are usually recognized by noting the affixes. This means that structural analysis is useful with both familiar and unfamiliar words.

Assessing Affix Knowledge

Assessing a child's proficiency in this area can be problematic. A simplistic approach would be to assess prefixes and suffixes as we assess vocabulary words. That is, if the child understands that the prefix *un-* means *not*, then that knowledge can be tested the way we might test other vocabulary knowledge. For example, a teacher could simply inventory a child's ability to supply the meanings of familiar affixes. The problem with this approach, however, is that it in no way guarantees that the child could apply this knowledge of affixes to the words encountered in real reading.

Real Words

Another way might be to show the child a sentence containing a word that is subject to structural analysis (i.e., a word that can be structurally analyzed). For example, let's say the child is shown this sentence:

The hot sun made the man uncomfortable.

The teacher asks the child what the word *uncomfortable* means, or perhaps how the man felt. If the child responds by saying that the man felt bad, or words to that effect, would the teacher be justified in assuming that the child used structural analysis? Perhaps, but the word *uncomfortable* is so common that it might well have already been a sight word for that particular child.

Coined Words

An alternative method of assessment would be to coin a few words and present them to children in sentence form. Consider the following sentences, for example:

The mailman likes our street because it is dogless.
The woman wore the dress because of its blueness.

The teacher then asks a child why the mailman likes this street and hopes to hear a response such as, "Because there are no dogs on it." When asked why the woman wore that particular dress, a child who has used structural analysis may well respond, "Because it was blue." These words cannot be sight words, because the teacher has coined them. (As English users, we are permitted to coin words so long as we follow a few simple rules.) By the same token, context is of little use because of the nature of the sentences. It is only by using structural analysis that a child can respond appropriately.

Composing a few age-appropriate sentences containing coined words is easy to do, and it can provide a rapid method of monitoring the development of structural analysis ability.

Common Prefixes and Their Meanings

un-	not	ir-	not	ex-	out
in-	not	il-	not	ante-	before
im-	not	a-	not	anti-	against
sub-	below	kilo-	1000	de-	away
super-	above	mega-	large	dis-	apart from
mono-	one	micro-	small	dis-	opposite
uni-	one	multi-	many	extra-	beyond
bi-	two	over-	above	fore-	in front of
di-	two	poly-	many	mal-	bad
tri-	three	prim-	first	magni-	large
quad-	four	proto-	first	medi-	middle
tetra-	four	sol-	along	mid-	middle
quint-	five	tele-	far	mis-	wrong
penta-	five	under-	below	neo-	new
hexa-	six	ab-	away from	omni-	all
septa-	seven	ad-	to	post-	after
oct-	eight	auto-	self	pre-	before
deca-	ten	bene-	good	pro-	forward
cent-	hundred	circ-	around	re-	again
ambi-	both	con-	with	trans-	across
semi-	half	com-	with	ultra-	beyond
hyper-	over	con-	against		

Common Suffixes and Their Meanings

-less	without	-ness	state of	-ment	state
-er	more	-ous	like	-itis	disease
-est	most	-ish	like	-phobe	one who fears
-ette	small	-logy	study of		
-trix	woman	-ly	like		

Suffixes can be difficult to define. We recommend that suffixes be presented in words, rather than in isolation.

PHONICS

Phonics refers to the ability to use letter–sound correspondences to derive the pronunciation of words. Good phonics assessments are nearly always individually administered, because the application of phonics skills requires that students produce pronunciations. Teachers obviously cannot monitor pronunciations in a group setting. Three phonics assessments are reviewed in this chapter.

Informal Phonics Inventory

The Informal Phonics Inventory (Form 5.3, pp. 125–131) provides a convenient means of monitoring specific skill acquisition. The first three subtests (Consonant Sounds, Consonant Digraphs, and Beginning Consonant Blends) present children with individual letters or two-letter combinations and ask that they provide pronunciations. Some educators may object to such a task on the grounds that individual consonants cannot be pronounced without attaching a vowel sound. This may be true, but it is of very little importance, and taking such an objection too seriously deprives us of a valid means of assessing phonics knowledge. When children see the letter *b*, for example, the teacher should expect them to say something like *buh*.

The next two subtests use real words. On the Final Consonant Blends subtest, the children are scored for their ability to read each blend as part of the real word. On this subtest, children are scored correctly if they pronounce the blend correctly, even if they do not correctly pronounce other parts of the word. Alternatively, in the Short Vowels in CVC Words test the item is scored correctly as long as the correct vowel sound is read. For example, reading *fin* for *tin* is considered correct. The Rule of Silent *e* subtest is more difficult, because it seems to require that the child consciously apply the rule rather than simply read the words. Children who do not master this subtest, but can read vowel digraphs, often can often pick up the silent *e* rule quickly, because they have acquired the long-vowel concept.

We recommend that you use the Informal Phonics Inventory in two steps. Use it first as a screener to determine areas on which to focus instruction. The scoring table will help you determine these areas. You can then use it to track the progress of individual students as they learn specific skills. The chart included in Form 5.3 is designed to help you keep track of skill mastery as you readminister portions of the Informal Phonics Inventory from time to time.

Z-Test

A more advanced phonics assessment targets a child's ability to make analogies to known words based on familiar rimes. The Z-Test (Form 5.4, pp. 132–134) presents the child with the 37 most familiar rimes, using the same onset, in order to focus the child's attention on the rime itself. The result is a series of pseudowords, all beginning with the /z/ sound. Children who are familiar with the compare–contrast method of recognizing the spelling patterns that make up rimes will be able to pronounce most or all of these pseudowords. Students who are not proficient at making such comparisons will experience considerable difficulty. There are no norms or scoring criteria for interpreting the results of this test. Subjective judgment is required. On the other hand, pre- and postadministrations of this simple test will provide an enlightening indicator of improved decoding skills.

Test of Knowledge of Onsets

The Test of Knowledge of Onsets (Form 5.5, pp. 135–141) was developed by James W. Cunningham at the University of North Carolina and is one of the many public-domain instruments included in this book. It consists of three subtests: one targeting initial two-letter consonant blends, one for initial-consonant digraphs, and one for single initial consonants. In the first subtest, the student is shown two words for each item, such as *down* and *crown* (see item 1). The teacher pronounces the first word and asks the child to pronounce the second. The second word always begins with a two-letter consonant blend. By pronouncing the first word, the teacher has provided the child with the rime. It is up to the child to replace the onset of the word the teacher pronounces with the onset of the word the child must pronounce. A check mark is placed in one of the three columns in the right-hand portion of the assessment form, depending on whether the child gives the whole word, just the onset, or just the rime correctly. If none of these is correct, no mark is made. The teacher is interested in those words for which the child has produced the correct onset and/or the entire word. Children who frequently pronounce the onset correctly, but not the whole word, may not understand the format of the test or may have difficulty blending onsets with rimes. Each of the two-letter blends is repeated three times throughout the assessment. You may wish to use the scoring grid to help identify which blends have been mastered and which will require additional work. For example, the blend *bl* occurs in items 11, 29, and 47. At the bottom of each column there is a fraction with a denominator of 3. The idea is to write in the numerator for each fraction—that is, the number of times the child correctly pronounced a specific blend (from 0 to 3).

The second subtest targets consonant digraphs. This is a shorter test because there are fewer digraphs to assess. Only five are targeted, and there are three words for each of them, as is the case in the first subtest. The administration is exactly the same. The chart at the end of this subtest is also used in the same way. Items 8, 9, and 10, for example, all contain the digraph *ch*.

The third subtest targets single consonants. The administration is the same as the first two subtests, and the scoring grid is used in the same way as the ones with the other two subtests.

The three subtests of onset knowledge are ordered from hardest (two-letter blends) to easiest (single consonants). A child who does well on a harder test can probably be expected to do as well or better on the easier one(s).

Students who get most of the whole words correct on any of the three subtests probably know and can blend that particular type of onset well. However, the greater usefulness of the subtests lies in their identification of specific onsets of each type that the child has not yet mastered. The link between assessment and instruction is clear.

SPELLING

Since the pioneering work of Edmund Henderson (1981), Charles Read (1971), and Carol Chomsky (1979), educators have known that the invented spelling of young children follows a clear developmental pattern. As children learn about written words, their attempts at spelling reflect this growing sophistication of their knowledge of orthographic patterns. We will follow the stages outlined by Henderson as we examine this growth. Different authors may use different names to describe the developmental stages. We apply the stage names used by Bear and colleagues (2008).

Emergent Spelling

Children's initial attempts at writing are generally nonalphabetic; sometimes these first attempts are pictures but are called "writing" by the child. Later attempts are scribbles that, although illegible to an observer, can be "read" by the young writer. Harste, Burke, and Woodward (1982), working with children of different cultures in a university day care center, found that their scribbles reflected the print to which they were exposed. Thus children from Arab families produced scribbles that resembled Arabic, children from Chinese families made scribbles that resembled Chinese, and so on. This correspondence suggests that scribbles represent an early understanding of the form of print.

When children learn letters, they incorporate those letters into their spelling. At first, these letter strings have nothing to do with the sounds in the word itself. So *bear* might be represented by MSDF.* The use of letters, rather than scribbles, suggests that the child (1) knows the convention that words must be made up of letters, and (2) knows at least some letters. At this stage, children often begin to write words logographically. That means that they may be spelling a learned word as a unit, such as their names, MOM or STOP.

As children continue to learn letters and develop some phonological awareness, their spellings begin to reflect their emergent analysis of words. Children's spellings may consist only of a letter representing an initial or final sound, such as *J* for *jam* or *S* for *sun*. Sometimes a child at this stage may put down a letter representing a single sound and then add others, such as the girl we worked with who first put down an *f* for *fish* and then added additional letters—FZTHSLT—saying that "*f*-words were always long." Children who can represent a sound in a word with a letter are developing rudimentary phonological awareness. Our research shows that such children nearly always use initial sounds to identify written words (Stahl & McKenna, 2001). Spelling development closely follows the development of word recognition but lags a little behind, because spelling is a pro-

---

*We use all caps to note invented spelling, regardless of how a "word" was written.

duction task, and production tasks are more difficult than recognition tasks. This level, however, seems necessary for children to make sense of the alphabetic system.

As children continue to analyze words in terms of phonological awareness as well as written word recognition, their spellings become increasingly complex. First they add final consonants, so that *bear* becomes BR or *hen* becomes HN. Often their spellings reflect the way they analyze the words as they are saying them. So blends such as *dr*, as in *dragon*, may be represented by JR, because that is how the child may hear it. Other blends may be represented by single consonants.

Letter Name–Alphabetic Spelling

Learning about vowels is the next large conceptual leap for children. Emergent spellings do not include vowels. The inclusion of vowel markers, whether correct or incorrect, represents the child's beginning knowledge of the alphabetic principle. Spoken words fold consonants around the vowel, so that they are copronounced; a consonant is pronounced slightly differently with each vowel, but consonants are difficult to isolate within words. Children can be aware of consonants through sensitivity to articulatory gestures (Byrne, 1998); still, consonants are more difficult to isolate (Shankweiler & Liberman, 1972).

Children generally begin to include vowels in their spellings around first grade. Whether this inclusion is due to instruction or experience with language is not clear, but the shift is an important one for children learning to read and spell. At this point, *bear* may be represented by BAR, with the child using the letter name to represent the long-vowel sound; similarly, *hen* may be spelled HAN.*

At the earlier points of this stage, children may use the letter name to represent a syllable—GRL and LETR are common—but most typical is the emergence of vowels. When a child consistently represents vowels in words, that child can be thought of as understanding the alphabetic principle.

Within Word Pattern Spelling

The letter name spelling stage represents acquisition of the alphabetic principle. The within word pattern stage involves the learning of patterns that occur in written words. At this point, children (1) consistently spell words with short vowels correctly, (2) begin to show sensitivity to patterns in words, (3) make distinctions between long and short vowels, and (4) use long-vowel markers, although not always correctly. Thus *bake* might be BAIK but not BAK; *like* is spelled LIKE, not LEIK; *chart* is not spelled CHRAT. In addition, children use -*ed* and -*ing* endings and add preconsonantal nasals (i.e., the /n/ and /m/ in words such as *jump* and *hand*), which are the latest consonants to emerge. This stage, which is usually achieved by the end of third or fourth grade, is characterized by a growing knowledge about spelling patterns and basic sound–symbol spelling conventions. Children's further growth in spelling moves from the purely sound–symbol level to

---

*The substitution of *a* for short *e* may be due to a letter name. The sound of long *a* is really a diphthong of /ey/. When children want the short *e* sound, they find it in the sound of the letter name "a," which actually begins with a short *e* sound! Although this hypothesis seems to be a stretch, the substitution of short *a* for short *e*, and *i* for short *a* (/ay/), is common enough that it seems a plausible explanation.

the morphological level, as they master the basic orthographic patterns and move on to spelling–meaning relationships.

Syllables and Affixes Spelling

The next stage represents children's knowledge of how syllables fit together. The most obvious marker is the consonant doubling rule; children during this stage develop consistency in spelling words that end with -ing or -ed, and in knowing when the consonants have to be doubled and when they do not (e.g., bat–batted vs. bait–baited). Children learn other conventions at this stage, such as the use of -y or -le at the end of words, but they may not consistently apply them. This stage signals that children are ready to work with strategies for approaching multisyllabic words.

This stage represents children's initial use of morphological knowledge to spell words. During this time period, children master bound morphemes, or morphemes that do not have their own meaning. The morphemes mastered also tend to function as syntactic markers, such as tense or number (e.g., plural formed by adding -s or -es). Children can usually be observed in this stage between grades 3 and 8.

Derivational Relations Spelling

At this stage, children learn to use semantic relationships between words, even words that are pronounced differently. Thus a child may use knowledge that words are derived from a common root to spell them conventionally. For example, children may use the relationships between words like fantasy and fantastic and fantasize or inspire and inspiration to help spell them conventionally. This stage may continue through adulthood as the derivational relationships between words provide a means of connecting spelling and meaning.

We have included three spelling lists. The first one, the Elementary Spelling Inventory and Feature Guide (Bear et al., 2008; Form 5.6, pp. 142–144), is a developmental spelling list to capture children's growth from one stage to the next. Additional developmental tests for a more finely grained analysis can be found in Bear and colleagues (2008) and Ganske (2000). (The Qualitative Spelling Checklist [Form 5.7, p. 145] can be used to interpret the results of the Elementary Spelling Inventory. It can also be used to interpret the results of other spelling inventories as well as children's free-writing samples, as discussed below.) The Morris–McCall Spelling List (Form 5.8, pp. 146–147), provides grade-level norms. All three instruments can be used to track growth over the year, although from somewhat different measurement perspectives.

Using the Qualitative Spelling Checklist to Observe Children's Writing

The Qualitative Spelling Checklist can be used as a general guide for observing children's writing, as well as used to evaluate a spelling inventory. Consider the pieces of children's early writing presented in Figure 5.1. (The first piece was written by Max Stahl; the remainder were taken from Chomsky, 1979.)

DR HP
BR PL
(Caption on Max's drawing)

TARWANSWASALITLGRLE
ANDSHEWOTIDAFRE
ND
OANDAY ALITLBOY
KAMEBIHIIWOTAFREN
UALIWOTIDAFENDTO
UALLESSBEFENDSOKY
(Story from first grader)

IV I CUD WISH ENEASING IT WOD BE TO MC
EVEREBODE LIV FOREVER
(First grader)

THIS IS A ROCKIT. THE LOONER MOJRAI IS ON THE
THERD DECK. IT'S A PEAS OF SIYINTIFIC EQUIPMENT.
THE NEXT PEAS OF SIYINTIFIC EQUIPMENT IS THE CMAND MOJRAI.
(First grader)

FIGURE 5.1. Example of children's early writing.

Max's writing, a caption to a drawing which reads "Danger! Bear! Help, please!" is an example of early letter-name writing. He is marking only the initial and final consonant sounds in his spelling. His writing is not using the left–right convention of English; instead, he is writing his words in vertical columns.

The second piece, from a first grader, uses vowels, although not in every word (LITL, GRLE) and not always correctly.* Consonant blends and digraphs are used inconsistently (TAR, FEND, but SHE, FREN). We estimate that this child is in the middle letter-name stage.

Although the third piece seems more advanced because of the use of spacing and the more sophisticated words (EVERYBODE, ENEASING), we would rate the student as a late-stage letter-name speller. Short vowels are spelled correctly (WISH, IV, LIV), but long vowels are not (MC for *make*). The child is attempting longer words and the attempts are reasonable. This text is easy to read.

The fourth text probably includes spellings that were given to the child (EQUIP-MENT), but shows the sophistication of ideas possible in invented spelling. This child is using but confusing long vowels (LOONER, PEAS, SIYINTIFIC) but generally getting short vowels correct. We would rate this at Stage 7. The ideas, however, go far beyond the child's ability to spell, which is a prime reason for using invented spelling—at least in the draft stages—in the first place.

---

*The text reads, "There once was a little girl / And she wanted a friend. / One day a little boy / Came by. Hi, I want a friend. / Well, I want a friend too. / Well, let's be friends, Okay?"

This discussion is only preliminary; the interested reader is referred to the books by Bear and colleagues (2008) and Ganske (2000) for more in-depth discussions of how spelling analysis can be used for planning instructional programs. Bear and colleagues offer excellent additional instruments for assessing primary- and upper-grade students.

TEACHING WORD RECOGNITION AND SPELLING

There could literally be a book written on techniques for teaching children to recognize words (and several of them have been written, such as those by Bear et al., 2008; Cunningham, 1999; Ganske, 2000). In this section we highlight a few techniques that we use often in the clinic.

The first rule of clinical practice is to "find out what has been done before, and don't do it." This is truer in the area of word recognition than in any other area. A child with whom one of us worked as a teacher had come from another school and read at a pre-primer level. He had worked very diligently and had reached a point where he was ready to use a particular phonics workbook for additional practice. In his then-current development, this would have been an easy review, for he had already mastered the material. However, because he had used that particular book in his previous school and had failed miserably with it, he recoiled and would not touch it. Perhaps this is an extreme example, but the principle holds. Do not use an approach that has failed in the past, whether or not it is appropriate, because it will not work now.

Numerous different approaches to teaching word recognition are currently available. Stahl, Duffy-Hester, and Stahl (1998) divide phonics instruction into traditional, constructivist-based, and spelling-based approaches. Hence, we briefly review synthetic phonics (a traditional approach), compare–contrast (a constructivist approach), and making words (Cunningham & Cunningham, 1992) and word sorts (Bear et al., 2008) (spelling-based approaches). We begin with a description of "Three Strikes and You're Out," a method of building sight vocabulary.

"Three Strikes and You're Out"

Words missed or causing trouble during oral reading should be used to develop a word bank or as an informational source for planning additional instruction. Words can be put on $3'' \times 5''$ index cards and used for practice. Children can practice words from each other's word banks during individual reading time. Words correctly identified by the child on three different occasions are retired from the word bank; a growing number of "retired" words is highly motivating.

Synthetic Phonics

The basic synthetic phonics approach begins with direct instruction of individual letter–sound correspondences. These then are practiced by reading words, first in lists and then in texts, often decodable texts. The hallmark of synthetic phonics is that children are taught to *blend* sounds together to make words, thus the instruction is *synthetic*. An example:

1. If the letter *e*, representing the short sound of *e*, is to be taught, the teacher might present the letter *e* on the blackboard or on a note card. The teacher might say, "This is the letter *e*. It says /e/."

2. Next, the teacher might write the word *pet* on the board or present three note-cards with the letters *p*, *e*, and *t* on them. (The use of notecards allows one to physically demonstrate blending.) The teacher would demonstrate the blending of the letters to make the word *pet* by running his or her finger under the letters (if the blackboard is used) or pushing the cards together.

3. Students would practice blending the word *pet* as a group.

4. The teacher would write or show a list of words, such as:

| pen | bet | deck | mesh | then | peck | let |
| send | less | yet | fed | bent | shed | tell |

The students would blend the words together, at first as a group and then individually.

5. Next, the students would read a decodable text that contains words with the short sound of *e*.

6. We find that an especially effective follow-up, either later in the lesson or immediately following the reading of the decodable text, is to have children write short-*e* words from dictation.

7. Following this lesson, the teacher might further follow up on the short sound of *e* by using a compare–contrast approach, practice on short-*e* words with a partner, or practice with a computer program that provides practice on short-*e* words.

Synthetic phonics is used in a number of commercial programs, but the basic lesson can be done quite easily. This foundational approach can be used to introduce patterns that the child has missed on the Informal Phonics Survey or on one of the other measures presented in this chapter.

Compare–Contrast Approaches to Phonics

In the compare–contrast approach, we are trying to teach children to compare new words to already known words. This method is used at the Benchmark School in Media, Pennsylvania (Gaskins et al., 1988; Gaskins, Ehri, Cress, O'Hara, & Donnelly, 1996). In synthetic phonics, teachers help children learn to sound out words; in the compare–contrast system, teachers help children learn how to use analogies to decode unknown words. Since adult learners use both types of knowledge, these approaches, in our view, are not mutually exclusive. Instead, we feel that once children have acquired some sound–symbol knowledge, possibly through synthetic phonics instruction, they should learn to compare new words to already known words. Compare–contrast approaches are especially useful for decoding polysyllabic words, because that is where we use analogies the most.

The basic compare–contrast lesson consists of a dialogue aimed at helping the child internalize the process of identifying words by (1) identifying known words that resemble an unknown word, (2) seeing what is similar between the two, (3) using what is similar to make a tentative identification of the word, and (4) checking to make sure that the identified word makes sense in context. A simple version of a compare–contrast lesson follows:

1. Give students six index cards. Have them print the following six words on the cards so that you can see them. These words become the students' key words.

> black   hold   kind   play   rain   run

Now display words from the following group. Have each child find the word that looks most like the presented word. At a signal from you, have all the students display their "lookalike" word. Students should respond to questions such as, "Where are the two words alike? Where are they different?" Ask a volunteer to pronounce both words.

mind	crack	blind	hind	fold	lack	runt
pain	smack	hay	main	blast	slack	stack
gold	rind	bind	mold	tack	bay	bun
gain	gray	plain	raid	pray		

2. On the following day (or when you feel the students are ready), add three words to their key word list: *man, less, her*. Match these nine words to the following group.

clay	per	ban	lent	fan	bless	pan
led	press	sun	sold	sack	stain	

You can make up other words (with or without students' help) to add to any of these matching lists.

The compare–contrast approach might be used with the phonograms in the Z-Test, described earlier in this chapter. For words that are not known, a key word can be taught, using the same procedures as above. Additionally, multisyllabic words that contain one or more of the key rimes can be introduced using the procedures suggested in Step 1. These difficult words might be drawn from wide-ranging reading contexts. Whether or not you use the technique with words in context, you should make a significant effort to help students see the relationship between what they do during the exercises and how they can use the new skills during their independent reading.

Making Words

Making words is a spelling-based decoding activity. In this activity, children learn to think about letters in words by manipulating letters in a spelling task. For example:

1. The teacher might take 1-inch-square index cards containing the following letters:

a   i   o   d   n   s   r   u

2. The teacher announces, "I want you to make a two-letter word [signals with two fingers]—*an*." As children move letters to make the word, the teacher checks their efforts and offers praise.
3. After all children have spelled the word, the teacher displays the word on a word card and puts it in a pocket chart.
4. The teacher proceeds through other two-letter words (e.g., *do*, *is*, *in*), three-letter words (e.g., *run*, *sad*, *rid*, *nod*), four-letter words (e.g., *said*, *rods*, *rind*), five-letter words (e.g., *sound*, *round*), and up to an eight-letter word (e.g., *dinosaur*).

Patricia Cunningham and Dorothy Hall have several books with lesson plans for "making words" (short words, appropriate for students through second grade) and "making big words" (appropriate for students in third to sixth grade). These books are available from Good Apple.

Word Sorts

Word sorts are another spelling-based approach to teaching children how to decode. With this method, children are given lists of words and asked to sort them. In *closed sorts*, children are given categories; in *open sorts*, children are asked to come up with their own categories. Open sorts can be difficult for children who have reading problems or if the children have minimal experience working with particular patterns. We recommend beginning with closed sorts, introducing open sorts only after children have had ample practice with the easier task or as a review of several previously taught patterns. When introducing open sorts, the teacher needs to provide needed modeling to the group.

A list of words like the following word group might be used for children who are learning to contrast *sh* and *st*.

rest	stand	last	mush	list	shop
fist	fast	step	just	shut	stamp
fish	shall	shed	rash	past	mist
trash					

In a closed sort these words might be sorted as words with *sh*, as in *she*, and words with *st* as in *stop*. Or they might be sorted as having *st* and *sh* at the beginning or at the end. Bear and colleagues (2008) and Ganske (2000) have many ideas for word sorting that are tied to children's spelling and decoding knowledge.

Fry Sight-Word Inventory

This instrument surveys a child's ability to recognize 300 frequently occurring words, as selected by Edward B. Fry (1980). The words are grouped into three sets of 100 by relative difficulty, and each group of 100 words is, in turn, grouped into sets of 25.

Directions for Administration

Place the student version of the First 100 Words in front of the child. Position the teacher's version so that you can make notations on it. There are three blanks for each word, for repeated administrations. You may want to record the date at the top of each column of blanks. Explain that you will be showing the child some words and that you want the child to say them aloud. Use the window card below to reveal the words one at a time, or make your own from a 3 x 5-inch index card with an X-Acto knife. A window card screens the other words and helps the child focus.

For each word, write a plus (+) in the blank next to it if the child correctly pronounces it in less than 1 second (informally timed). If the child takes more time but eventually pronounces the word accurately, write *D*, for *decoded*. That is to say, the word was not identified automatically and is therefore not yet a sight word. If the child mispronounces the word, try to spell the response phonetically. If there is no response, write *NR*. Move the window card to each word in succession while, with your other hand, you record the response. Proceed through each of the five columns.

Repeat these steps with the Second 100 and the Third 100. Discontinue testing if, in your judgment, the words become too difficult.

If you readminister the inventory, return only to those words not automatically recognized during previous testing.

Scoring and Interpretation

There is no cumulative score. Each word is actually a separate "skill," which means that there is a very direct link between testing and teaching. Any word that is not pronounceable automatically simply requires more practice!

(continued)

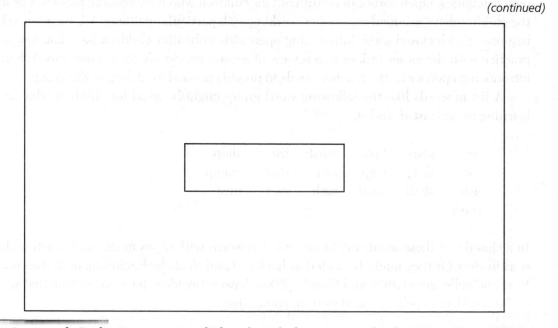

First 100 Words

the	or	will	number
of	one	up	no
and	had	other	way
a	by	about	could
to	word	out	people
in	but	many	my
is	not	then	than
you	what	them	first
that	all	these	water
it	were	so	been
he	we	some	call
was	when	her	who
for	your	would	oil
on	can	make	now
are	said	like	find
as	there	him	long
with	use	into	down
his	an	time	day
they	each	has	did
I	which	look	get
at	she	two	come
be	do	more	made
this	how	write	may
have	their	go	part
from	if	see	over

(continued)

First 100 Words

the	___	or	___	will	___	number	___
of	___	one	___	up	___	no	___
and	___	had	___	other	___	way	___
a	___	by	___	about	___	could	___
to	___	word	___	out	___	people	___
in	___	but	___	many	___	my	___
is	___	not	___	then	___	than	___
you	___	what	___	them	___	first	___
that	___	all	___	these	___	water	___
it	___	were	___	so	___	been	___
he	___	we	___	some	___	call	___
was	___	when	___	her	___	who	___
for	___	your	___	would	___	oil	___
on	___	can	___	make	___	now	___
are	___	said	___	like	___	find	___
as	___	there	___	him	___	long	___
with	___	use	___	into	___	down	___
his	___	an	___	time	___	day	___
they	___	each	___	has	___	did	___
I	___	which	___	look	___	get	___
at	___	she	___	two	___	come	___
be	___	do	___	more	___	made	___
this	___	how	___	write	___	may	___
have	___	their	___	go	___	part	___
from	___	if	___	see	___	over	___

(continued)

Second 100 Words

new	great	put	kind
sound	where	end	hand
take	help	does	picture
only	through	another	again
little	much	well	change
work	before	large	off
know	line	must	play
place	right	big	spell
year	too	even	air
live	mean	such	away
me	old	because	animal
back	any	turn	house
give	same	here	point
most	tell	why	page
very	boy	ask	letter
after	follow	went	mother
thing	came	men	answer
our	went	read	found
just	show	need	study
name	also	land	still
good	around	different	learn
sentence	form	home	should
man	three	us	America
think	small	move	world
say	set	try	high

(continued)

Second 100 Words

new ＿＿＿	great ＿＿＿	put ＿＿＿	kind ＿＿＿
sound ＿＿＿	where ＿＿＿	end ＿＿＿	hand ＿＿＿
take ＿＿＿	help ＿＿＿	does ＿＿＿	picture ＿＿＿
only ＿＿＿	through ＿＿＿	another ＿＿＿	again ＿＿＿
little ＿＿＿	much ＿＿＿	well ＿＿＿	change ＿＿＿
work ＿＿＿	before ＿＿＿	large ＿＿＿	off ＿＿＿
know ＿＿＿	line ＿＿＿	must ＿＿＿	play ＿＿＿
place ＿＿＿	right ＿＿＿	big ＿＿＿	spell ＿＿＿
year ＿＿＿	too ＿＿＿	even ＿＿＿	air ＿＿＿
live ＿＿＿	mean ＿＿＿	such ＿＿＿	away ＿＿＿
me ＿＿＿	old ＿＿＿	because ＿＿＿	animal ＿＿＿
back ＿＿＿	any ＿＿＿	turn ＿＿＿	house ＿＿＿
give ＿＿＿	same ＿＿＿	here ＿＿＿	point ＿＿＿
most ＿＿＿	tell ＿＿＿	why ＿＿＿	page ＿＿＿
very ＿＿＿	boy ＿＿＿	ask ＿＿＿	letter ＿＿＿
after ＿＿＿	follow ＿＿＿	went ＿＿＿	mother ＿＿＿
thing ＿＿＿	came ＿＿＿	men ＿＿＿	answer ＿＿＿
our ＿＿＿	went ＿＿＿	read ＿＿＿	found ＿＿＿
just ＿＿＿	show ＿＿＿	need ＿＿＿	study ＿＿＿
name ＿＿＿	also ＿＿＿	land ＿＿＿	still ＿＿＿
good ＿＿＿	around ＿＿＿	different ＿＿＿	learn ＿＿＿
sentence ＿＿＿	form ＿＿＿	home ＿＿＿	should ＿＿＿
man ＿＿＿	three ＿＿＿	us ＿＿＿	America ＿＿＿
think ＿＿＿	small ＿＿＿	move ＿＿＿	world ＿＿＿
say ＿＿＿	set ＿＿＿	try ＿＿＿	high ＿＿＿

(continued)

Third 100 Words

every	left	until	idea
near	don't	children	enough
add	few	side	eat
food	while	feet	face
between	along	car	watch
own	might	mile	far
below	close	night	Indian
country	something	walk	real
plant	seem	while	almost
last	next	sea	let
school	hard	began	above
father	open	grow	girl
keep	example	took	sometimes
tree	begin	river	mountain
never	life	four	cut
start	always	carry	young
city	those	state	talk
earth	both	once	soon
eye	paper	book	list
light	together	hear	song
thought	got	stop	leave
head	group	without	family
under	often	second	body
story	run	late	music
saw	important	miss	color

(continued)

Third 100 Words

every _____	left _____	until _____	idea _____
near _____	don't _____	children _____	enough _____
add _____	few _____	side _____	eat _____
food _____	while _____	feet _____	face _____
between _____	along _____	car _____	watch _____
own _____	might _____	mile _____	far _____
below _____	close _____	night _____	Indian _____
country _____	something _____	walk _____	real _____
plant _____	seem _____	while _____	almost _____
last _____	next _____	sea _____	let _____
school _____	hard _____	began _____	above _____
father _____	open _____	grow _____	girl _____
keep _____	example _____	took _____	sometimes _____
tree _____	begin _____	river _____	mountain _____
never _____	life _____	four _____	cut _____
start _____	always _____	carry _____	young _____
city _____	those _____	state _____	talk _____
earth _____	both _____	once _____	soon _____
eye _____	paper _____	book _____	list _____
light _____	together _____	hear _____	song _____
thought _____	got _____	stop _____	leave _____
head _____	group _____	without _____	family _____
under _____	often _____	second _____	body _____
story _____	run _____	late _____	music _____
saw _____	important _____	miss _____	color _____

Dolch Words Organized by Level (Teacher Version)

Preprimer		Primer		First grade		Second grade		Third grade	
a		all		after		always		about	
and		am		again		around		better	
away		are		an		because		bring	
big		at		any		been		carry	
blue		ate		as		before		clean	
can		be		ask		best		cut	
come		black		by		both		done	
down		brown		could		buy		draw	
find		but		every		call		drink	
for		came		fly		cold		eight	
funny		did		from		does		fall	
go		do		give		don't		far	
help		eat		going		fast		full	
here		four		had		first		got	
I		get		has		five		grow	
in		good		her		found		hold	
is		have		him		gave		hot	
it		he		his		goes		hurt	
jump		into		how		green		if	
little		like		just		its		keep	
look		must		know		made		kind	
make		new		let		many		laugh	
me		no		live		off		light	
my		now		may		or		long	
not		on		of		pull		much	
one		our		old		read		myself	
play		out		once		right		never	
red		please		open		sing		only	
run		pretty		over		sit		own	
said		ran		put		sleep		pick	
see		ride		round		tell		seven	
the		saw		some		their		shall	
three		say		stop		these		show	
to		she		take		those		six	
two		so		thank		upon		small	
up		soon		them		us		start	
we		that		then		use		ten	
where		there		think		very		today	
yellow		they		walk		wash		together	
you		this		were		which		try	
		too		what		why		warm	
		under		when		wish			
		want				work			
		was				would			
		well				write			
		went				your			
		white							
		who							
		will							
		with							
		yes							

(continued)

a	all	after	always	about
and	am	again	around	better
away	are	an	because	bring
big	at	any	been	carry
blue	ate	as	before	clean
can	be	ask	best	cut
come	black	by	both	done
down	brown	could	buy	draw
find	but	every	call	drink
for	came	fly	cold	eight
funny	did	from	does	fall
go	do	give	don't	far
help	eat	going	fast	full
here	four	had	first	got
I	get	has	five	grow
in	good	her	found	hold
is	have	him	gave	hot
it	he	his	goes	hurt
jump	into	how	green	if
little	like	just	its	keep
look	must	know	made	kind
make	new	let	many	laugh
me	no	live	off	light
my	now	may	or	long
not	on	of	pull	much
one	our	old	read	myself
play	out	once	right	never
red	please	open	sing	only
run	pretty	over	sit	own
said	ran	put	sleep	pick
see	ride	round	tell	seven
the	saw	some	their	shall
three	say	stop	these	show
to	she	take	those	six
two	so	thank	upon	small
up	soon	them	us	start
we	that	then	use	ten
where	there	think	very	today
yellow	they	walk	wash	together
you	this	were	which	try
	too	what	why	warm
	under	when	wish	
	want		work	
	was		would	
	well		write	
	went		your	
	white			
	who			
	will			
	with			
	yes			

Informal Phonics Inventory

Directions for Administration

Consonant Sounds

Point to **S**. Say, "What sound does this letter say?" Go from left to right, repeating this question. It is fine if the child reads across a line without prompting. For **C** and **G**, have the child give both sounds. [**Note**: If the child cannot pass this subtest, consider giving an alphabet inventory.]

Consonant Digraphs

Point to **th**. Say, "What sound do these letters say?" Go from left to right, repeating this instruction. It is fine if the child reads all five without prompting.

Beginning Consonant Blends

Point to **bl**. Say, "What sound do these letters say?" Allow child to proceed with or without prompting.

Final Consonant Blends and ng

Point to **bank**. Say, "What is this word?" Allow child to proceed with or without prompting.

Short Vowels in CVC Words

Point to **fit**. Say, "What is this word?" Allow child to proceed with or without prompting.

The Rule of Silent e

Point to **cap**. Say, "If this is **cap**, what is this?" Point to **cape** as you say the second part of this sentence. Go from left to right, repeating the question for each pair.

Vowel Digraphs, Diphthongs, r-*Controlled Vowels, and* -al

Have the child read each word across each line, from left to right.

Scoring

For all subtests and for the total test, use the following criteria:

Mastery	80%+
Needs Review	60–79%
Needs Systematic Instruction	Below 60%

The table below gives the number of correct answers that roughly correspond to these percentages.

Subtest	Total possible	Mastery	Review	Systematic instruction
Consonant Sounds	20	16–20	12–15	0–11
Consonant Digraphs	5	4–5	3	0–2
Beginning Consonant Blends	20	16–20	12–15	0–11
Final Consonant Blends and *ng*	12	10–12	8–9	0–7
Short Vowels in CVC Words	10	8–10	6–7	0–5
The Rule of Silent *e*	4	4	2–3	0–1
Long Vowel Digraphs	10	8–10	6–7	0–5
Diphthongs	6	5–6	4	0–3
r-Controlled Vowels and *-al*	6	5–6	4	0–3
Total	**93**	**75–93**	**56–74**	**0–55**

(continued)

Phonics Skills Record

Use a check mark to note specific skills that still require instruction.

Phonics Skills		Date						
Consonant Sounds	S							
	D							
	F							
	G							
	H							
	J							
	K							
	L							
	Z							
	P							
	C							
	V							
	B							
	N							
	M							
	Qu							
	W							
	R							
	T							
	Y							
Consonant Digraphs	th							
	sh							
	ch							
	wh							
	ph							

(continued)

Beginning Consonant Blends	bl								
	fl								
	fr								
	gl								
	br								
	gr								
	pl								
	pr								
	cl								
	sk								
	sl								
	sm								
	cr								
	sn								
	sp								
	tr								
	dr								
	st								
	str								
	sw								
Final Consonant Blends and *ng*	nk								
	pt								
	mp								
	nd								
	ct								
	lt								
	ng								
	ft								
	sp								
	sk								
	nt								
	st								

(continued)

Short Vowels	a								
	e								
	i								
	o								
	u								
Rule of Silent *e*	a								
	o								
	u								
	i								
Long Vowel Digraphs	oa								
	ea								
	ai								
	ee								
	ay								
	ue								
Diphthongs	ow								
	ou								
	oy								
	ew								
	oi								
	aw								
r-Controlled Vowels	ar								
	ir								
	or								
	ur								
	er								
-al	al								

(continued)

128

Informal Phonics Inventory

Name _____   Date _____

____/20   Consonant Sounds

           S   D   F   G   H   J

           K   L   Z   P   C   V

           B   N   M   Qu   W   R

           T   Y

____/5   Consonant Digraphs

           th   sh   ch   wh   ph

____/20   Beginning Consonant Blends

           bl   fl   fr   gl

           br   gr   pl   pr

           cl   sk   sl   sm

           cr   sn   sp   tr

           dr   st   str   sw

____/12   Final Consonant Blends and *ng*

bank	apt	limp
band	pact	lilt
bang	lift	lisp
bask	lint	list

____/10   Short Vowels in CVC Words

           fit   led   sup   lap   hug

           rot   tin   rag   wet   job

____/4   The Rule of Silent *e*

cap	tot	cub	kit
cape	tote	cube	kite

____/10   Long Vowel Digraphs

loaf	heat	aim	weed	ray
gain	fee	coal	leaf	due

____/6   Diphthongs

           town   loud   joy   threw   oil   law

____/6   *r*-Controlled Vowels and *-al*

           tar   hall   sir   port   hurt   fern

____/93   **Total**

(continued)

S	D	F	G	H	J
K	L	Z	P	C	V
B	N	M	Qu	W	R
T	Y				

th	sh	ch	wh	ph

bl	fl	fr	gl
br	gr	pl	pr
cl	sk	sl	sm
cr	sn	sp	tr
dr	st	str	sw

(continued)

bank   apt   limp
band   pact   lilt
bang   lift   lisp
bask   lint   list

fit   led   sup   lap   hug
rot   tin   rag   wet   job

cap   tot   cub   kit
cape   tote   cube   kite

loaf   heat   aim   weed   ray
gain   fee   coal   leaf   due

town   loud   joy   threw   oil   law

tar   hall   sir   port   hurt   fern

Z-Test

Name _____   Teacher/Clinician _____

Directions. Tell the student you are going to show him/her some pretend words and that you would like for him/her to pronounce each one. Say that all of the words begin with "/z/, like *zebra.*" Then expose the words on the student form, one a time. Place a check in the blank under the date of testing if the child pronounces a pseudoword accurately.

Date of Testing   ___ ___ ___ ___

zit	___	___	___	___
zay	___	___	___	___
zin	___	___	___	___
zap	___	___	___	___
zan	___	___	___	___
zill	___	___	___	___
zack	___	___	___	___
zing	___	___	___	___
zip	___	___	___	___
zat	___	___	___	___
zore	___	___	___	___
zug	___	___	___	___
zell	___	___	___	___
zink	___	___	___	___
zump	___	___	___	___
zash	___	___	___	___
zank	___	___	___	___
zice	___	___	___	___
zoke	___	___	___	___
zick	___	___	___	___
zock	___	___	___	___
zunk	___	___	___	___

(continued)

zake   __   __   __   __

zame   __   __   __   __

zaw   __   __   __   __

zide   __   __   __   __

zeat   __   __   __   __

zop   __   __   __   __

zot   __   __   __   __

zuck   __   __   __   __

zight   __   __   __   __

zale   __   __   __   __

zest   __   __   __   __

zail   __   __   __   __

zain   __   __   __   __

zate   __   __   __   __

zine   __   __   __   __

These words are arranged in order of increasing difficulty, as determined empirically. See J. W. Cunningham et al. (1999).

(continued)

133

zit	zell	zaw
zay	zink	zide
zin	zump	zeat
zap	zash	zop
zan	zank	zot
zill	zice	zuck
zack	zoke	zight
zing	zick	zale
zip	zock	zest
zat	zunk	zail
zore	zake	zain
zug	zame	zate
		zine

Test of Knowledge of Onsets

Subtest for Initial Consonant Blends (Two-Letter)

Format: "This word is *(say word from first column)*. What is this word: *(point to word from second column)*'?

			WHOLE WORD CORRECT	ONSET CORRECT	RIME CORRECT
	hall	call			
	way	day			
Examples:	go	no			
1.	down	crown			
2.	look	brook			
3.	did	grid			
4.	tell	swell			
5.	did	slid			
6.	not	trot			
7.	will	spill			
8.	just	crust			
9.	can	clan			
10.	him	skim			
11.	made	blade			
12.	more	snore			
13.	my	spy			
14.	ball	stall			
15.	way	pray			
16.	best	crest			
17.	rain	brain			
18.	back	track			
19.	sing	swing			
20.	make	flake			
21.	time	slime			
22.	make	brake			
23.	did	skid			
24.	way	tray			
25.	back	smack			
26.	set	fret			
27.	down	drown			
28.	cat	flat			

(continued)

			WHOLE WORD CORRECT	ONSET CORRECT	RIME CORRECT
29.	best	blest			
30.	down	frown			
31.	way	clay			
32.	my	dry			
33.	will	drill			
34.	way	sway			
35.	now	plow			
36.	hat	scat			
37.	made	glade			
38.	make	snake			
39.	made	grade			
40.	not	slot			
41.	will	grill			
42.	not	plot			
43.	see	free			
44.	rain	plain			
45.	had	glad			
46.	will	skill			
47.	find	blind			
48.	top	prop			
49.	like	spike			
50.	man	scan			
51.	back	snack			
52.	more	score			
53.	tell	smell			
54.	good	stood			
55.	same	flame			
56.	ride	glide			
57.	not	clot			
58.	time	prime			
59.	part	smart			
60.	back	stack			

(continued)

Scoring Grid

bl	br	cl	cr	dr	fl	fr	gl	gr	pl	pr	sc	sk	sl	sm	sn	sp	st	sw	tr
			1																
	2							3										4	
													5						6
																7			
			8																
		9										10							
11															12	13	14		
			16							15									
	17																		
																			18
																		19	
				20									21						
	22											23							24
														25					
						26													
			27	28															
29						30													
		31	32																
			33															34	
								35			36								
					37										38				
							39						40						
							41	42											
						43		44											
						45						46							
47										48						49			
											50				51				
											52			53				54	
				55		56													
		57								58				59			60		
$\overline{3}$	$\overline{3}$	$\overline{3}$	$\overline{3}$	$\overline{3}$	$\overline{3}$	$\overline{3}$	$\overline{3}$	$\overline{3}$	$\overline{3}$	$\overline{3}$	$\overline{3}$	$\overline{3}$	$\overline{3}$	$\overline{3}$	$\overline{3}$	$\overline{3}$	$\overline{3}$	$\overline{3}$	$\overline{3}$

(continued)

Subtest for Initial Consonant Digraphs

Examples:	ball way go	call day no	WHOLE WORD CORRECT	ONSET CORRECT	RIME CORRECT
1.	feel	wheel			
2.	tell	shell			
3.	meat	wheat			
4.	saw	thaw			
5.	more	shore			
6.	tale	whale			
7.	bone	phone			
8.	best	chest			
9.	rain	chain			
10.	more	chore			
11.	see	thee			
12.	bird	third			
13.	make	shake			
14.	bony	phony			
15.	gooey	phooey			

Scoring Grid

ch	ph	sh	th	wh
				1
		2		
				3
			4	
		5		
				6
	7			
8				
9				
10			11	
			12	
		13		
	14			
	15			
$\overline{3}$	$\overline{3}$	$\overline{3}$	$\overline{3}$	$\overline{3}$

(continued)

138

Subtest for Single Initial Consonants

Format: "This word is *(say word from first column)*. What is this word: *(point to word from second column)*?"

			WHOLE WORD CORRECT	ONSET CORRECT	RIME CORRECT
	ball	call			
	way	day			
Examples:	go	no			
1.	down	gown			
2.	look	nook			
3.	did	bid			
4.	tell	yell			
5.	did	rid			
6.	not	cot			
7.	will	mill			
8.	just	dust			
9.	can	van			
10.	him	dim			
11.	made	fade			
12.	more	core			
13.	like	hike			
14.	ball	mall			
15.	way	nay			
16.	best	vest			
17.	rain	vain			
18.	back	sack			
19.	sing	zing			
20.	make	wake			
21.	time	lime			
22.	make	fake			
23.	did	lid			
24.	way	gay			
25.	back	lack			
26.	set	yet			
27.	seen	keen			
28.	did	kid			
29.	best	nest			
30.	did	hid			
31.	way	bay			
32.	big	jig			
33.	will	sill			

(continued)

139

			WHOLE WORD CORRECT	ONSET CORRECT	RIME CORRECT
34.	way	jay			
35.	now	wow			
36.	can	tan			
37.	best	zest			
38.	make	sake			
39.	too	zoo			
40.	not	rot			
41.	will	kill			
42.	not	jot			
43.	see	fee			
44.	make	rake			
45.	had	pad			
46.	will	dill			
47.	find	mind			
48.	but	cut			
49.	like	pike			
50.	will	pill			
51.	back	tack			
52.	more	bore			
53.	will	gill			
54.	hard	yard			
55.	look	hook			
56.	big	wig			
57.	not	tot			

(continued)

Scoring Grid

b	c	d	f	g	h	j	k	l	m	n	p	r	s	t	v	w	y	z
				1						2								
3																	4	
												5						
	6								7									
		8													9			
		10	11															
	12				13			14	15						16			
															17			
													18					19
																20		
						21												
			22				23											
				24			25										26	
						27												
						28				29								
					30													
31						32							33					
						34										35		
														36				37
														38				39
											40							
						41												
						42												
			43									44						
											45							
	46							47										
	48										49							
											50			51				
52				53													54	
					55											56		
														57				
3̄	3̄	3̄	3̄	3̄	3̄	3̄	3̄	3̄	3̄	3̄	3̄	3̄	3̄	3̄	3̄	3̄	3̄	3̄

141

Elementary Spelling Inventory and Feature Guide

General Instructions for Administering the Inventories

Students should not study the words in advance of testing. Assure the students that this is not for a grade but to help you plan for their needs. *Possible script:* "I am going to ask you to spell some words. Spell them the best you can. Some of the words will be easy to spell; some may be difficult. When you do not know how to spell a word, spell it the best you can."

    Ask students to number their paper (or prepare a numbered paper for kindergarten or early first grade). Call each word aloud and repeat it. Say each word naturally, without emphasizing phonemes or syllables. Use it in a sentence, if necessary, to be sure students know the exact word. Sample sentences are provided along with the words. After administering the inventory use the Feature Guide, Class Composite Form and, if desired, a Spelling-by-Stage Classroom Organization Chart to complete your assessment.

Scoring the Inventory Using the Feature Guide

1. Make a copy of the appropriate Feature Guide for each student. Draw a line under the last word called if you called less than the total number, and adjust the possible total points at the bottom of each feature column.
2. Score the words by checking off the features spelled correctly that are listed in the cells to the left of each word. For example, if a student spells *bed* as BAD, he or she gets a check in the initial *b* cell, and the final *d* cell, but not for the short vowel. Write in the vowel used (A in this case) but do not give any points for it. If a student spells *train* as TRANE he or she gets a check in the initial *tr* cell, and the final *n* cell, but not for the long vowel pattern. Write in the vowel pattern used (A-E in this case) but do not give any points for it. Put a check in the "correct" column if the word is spelled correctly. Do not count reversed letters as errors, but note them in the cells. If unnecessary letters are added, give the speller credit for what is correct (e.g., If *bed* is spelled BEDE, the student still gets credit for representing the short vowel), but do not check correct spelling.
3. Add the number of checks under each feature and across each word, allowing you to double-check the total score recorded in the last cell. Modify the ratios in the last row, depending on the number of words called aloud.

Interpreting the Results of the Spelling Inventory

4. Look down each feature column to determine instructional needs. A student who misses only one (or two if the features sample 8 to 10 words) can go on to other features. A student who misses two or three needs some review work, but students who miss more than three need careful instruction on this feature. If a student did not get any points for a feature, then earlier features need to be studied first.
5. To determine a stage of development, note where student first made more than one error under the stages listed in the shaded box at the top of the Feature Guide.

Spelling Stage Expectations by Grade

Grade level	Typical spelling stage ranges within grade	End-of-year spelling stage goal
K	Emergent–Letter Name–Alphabetic	Middle Letter Name–Alphabetic
1	Late Emergent–Within Word Pattern	Early Within Word Pattern
2	Late Letter Name–Early Syllables and Affixes	Late Within Word Pattern
3	Within Word Pattern–Syllables and Affixes	Early Syllables and Affixes
4	Within Word Pattern–Syllables and Affixes	Middle Syllables and Affixes
5	Syllables and Affixes–Derivational Relations	Late Syllables and Affixes
6+	Syllables and Affixes– Derivational Relations	Derivational Relations

(continued)

Elementary Spelling Inventory (ESI)

The Elementary Spelling Inventory can be used as early as first grade, particularly if a school system wants to use the same inventory across the elementary grades. The 25 words are ordered by difficulty to sample features from the letter name–alphabetic stage to derivational relations stage. Call out enough words so that you have at least five or six misspelled words to analyze. The book *Words Their Way: Word Study for Phonics, Vocabulary, and Spelling Instruction* has additional inventories for more detailed analysis (Bear et al., 2008). We highly recommend this resource. For students in the primary grades, you may prefer the Primary Spelling Inventory. If any students spell more than 20 words correctly, use the Upper Level Spelling Inventory.

1. bed   I hopped out of bed this morning. *bed*
2. ship   The ship sailed around the island. *ship*
3. when   When will you come back? *when*
4. lump   He had a lump on his head after he fell. *lump*
5. float   I can float on the water with my new raft. *float*
6. train   I rode the train to the next town. *train*
7. place   I found a new place to put my books. *place*
8. drive   I learned to drive a car. *drive*
9. bright   The light is very bright. *bright*
10. shopping   She went shopping for new shoes. *shopping*
11. spoil   The food will spoil if it is not kept cool. *spoil*
12. serving   The restaurant is serving dinner tonight. *serving*
13. chewed   The dog chewed up my favorite sweater yesterday. *chewed*
14. carries   She carries apples in her basket. *carries*
15. marched   We marched in the parade. *marched*
16. shower   The shower in the bathroom was very hot. *shower*
17. bottle   The bottle broke into pieces on the tile floor. *bottle*
18. favor   He did his brother a favor by taking out the trash. *favor*
19. ripen   The fruit will ripen over the next few days. *ripen*
20. cellar   I went down to the cellar for the can of paint. *cellar*
21. pleasure   It was a pleasure to listen to the choir sing. *pleasure*
22. fortunate   It was fortunate that the driver had snow tires. *fortunate*
23. confident   I am confident that we can win the game. *confident*
24. civilize   They wanted to civilize the forest people. *civilize*
25. opposition   The coach said the opposition would be tough. *opposition*

(continued)

Elementary Spelling Inventory and Feature Guide *(page 3 of 3)*

Words Their Way Elementary Spelling Inventory Feature Guide

Student _____ Teacher _____ Grade _____ Date _____

Words Spelled Correctly: _____ / 25   Feature Points: _____ / 62   Total _____ / 87   Spelling Stage _____

Stages and gradations →	Emergent — Late / Early		Letter Name — Middle / Late			Within Word Pattern — Middle / Late		Syllables and Affixes — Early / Middle / Late			Derivational Relations — Early / Middle		Feature Points	Words Spelled Correctly
Features → ↓ Words	Consonants Begin.	Final	Short Vowels	Digraphs	Blends	Long Vowels	Other Vowels	Inflected Endings	Syllable Junctures	Unaccented Final Syllables	Harder Suffixes	Bases or Roots		
1. bed	b	d	e											
2. ship		p	i	sh										
3. when			e	wh										
4. lump	l		u		mp									
5. float		t			fl	oa								
6. train		n			tr	ai								
7. place					pl	a-e								
8. drive		v			dr	i-e								
9. bright					br	igh								
10. shopping			o	sh				pping						
11. spoil					sp		oi							
12. serving							er	ving						
13. chewed				ch			ew	ed						
14. carries							ar	ies	rr					
15. marched				ch			ar	ed						
16. shower				sh			ow			er				
17. bottle									tt	le				
18. favor									v	or				
19. ripen									p	en				
20. cellar									ll	ar				
21. pleasure											ure	pleas		
22. fortunate											ate	fortun		
23. confident											ent	confid		
24. civilize											ize	civil		
25. opposition											tion	pos		
Totals	/7		/5	/6	/7	/5	/7	/5	/5	/5	/5	/5	/62	/25

Qualitative Spelling Checklist

Student _____ Observer _____

Use this checklist to analyze students' uncorrected writing and to locate their appropriate stages of spelling development. There are three gradations within each stage—early, middle, and late. Examples in parentheses are from the Elementary Spelling Inventory 1 and the Intermediate list.

The spaces for dates at the top of the checklist are used to follow students' progress. Check when certain features are observed in students' spelling. When a feature is always present check "Yes." The last place where you check "Often" corresponds to the student's stage of spelling development.

Emergent Stage   Dates: _____ _____ _____

Early
• Does the child scribble on the page?   Yes _____   Often _____   No _____
• Do the scribbles follow the conventional direction? (left to right in English)   Yes _____   Often _____   No _____

Middle
• Are there random letters and numbers used in pretend writing? (4BT for *ship*)   Yes _____   Often _____   No _____

Late
• Are key sounds used in syllabic writing? (/s/ or /p/ for *ship*)   Yes _____   Often _____   No _____

Letter Name–Alphabetic

Early
• Are beginning consonants included? (*b* for *bed*, *s* for *ship*)   Yes _____   Often _____   No _____
• Is there a vowel in each word?   Yes _____   Often _____   No _____

Middle
• Are some consonant digraphs and blends spelled correctly? (*ship, when, float*)   Yes _____   Often _____   No _____
• Are there logical vowel substitutions with a letter name strategy?
  (FLOT for *float*, BAD for *bed*)   Yes _____   Often _____   No _____

Late
• Are short vowels spelled correctly? (*bed, ship, when, lump*)   Yes _____   Often _____   No _____
• Is the *m* or *n* included in front of other consonants? (*lump, stand*)   Yes _____   Often _____   No _____

Within Word Pattern

Early
• Are long vowels in single-syllable words used but confused?
  (FLOTE for *float*, TRANE for *train*)   Yes _____   Often _____   No _____

Middle
• Are most long vowel words spelled correctly, but some long vowel
  spelling and other vowel patterns used but confused? (DRIEV for *drive*)   Yes _____   Often _____   No _____
• Are the most common consonant digraphs and blends spelled correctly?
  (**sled, dream, fright**)   Yes _____   Often _____   No _____

Late
• Are the harder consonant digraphs and blends spelled correctly?
  (*speck, switch, smudge*)   Yes _____   Often _____   No _____
• Are most other vowel patterns spelled correctly? (*spoil, chewed, serving*)   Yes _____   Often _____   No _____

Syllables and Affixes

Early
• Are inflectional endings added correctly to base vowel patterns with
  short-vowel patterns? (*shopping, marched*)   Yes _____   Often _____   No _____
• Are junctures between syllables spelled correctly? (*cattle, cellar, carries, bottle*)   Yes _____   Often _____   No _____

Middle
• Are inflectional endings added correctly to base words? (*chewed, marched, shower*)   Yes _____   Often _____   No _____

Late
• Are unaccented final syllables spelled correctly? (*bottle, fortunate, civilize*)   Yes _____   Often _____   No _____
• Are less frequent prefixes and suffixes spelled correctly? (**confident**, *favor,*
  ripen, cellar, pleasure)   Yes _____   Often _____   No _____

Derivational Relations

Early
• Are most polysyllabic words spelled correctly? (*fortunate, confident*)   Yes _____   Often _____   No _____

Middle
• Are unaccented vowels in derived words spelled correctly? (*confident, civilize,*
  category)   Yes _____   Often _____   No _____

Late
• Are words from derived forms spelled correctly? (**pleasure**, *opposition, criticize*)   Yes _____   Often _____   No _____

Morris–McCall Spelling List (Grades 2–9)

Directions: "I am going to say some words that I want you to spell for me. Some of the words will be easy to spell, and some will be more difficult. When you don't know how to spell a word, just do the best you can. Each time, I will say the word, then use it in a sentence, and then I will say the word again." Start at the beginning of the list and continue testing until child makes five consecutive errors.

1.	run	The boy can *run*.
2.	top	The *top* will spin.
3.	red	My apple is *red*.
4.	book	I lost my *book*.
5.	sea	The *sea* is rough.
6.	play	I will *play* with you.
7.	lay	*Lay* the book down.
8.	led	He *led* the horses to the town.
9.	add	*Add* those numbers.
10.	alike	These books are *alike*.
11.	mine	That bicycle is *mine*.
12.	with	Mary will go *with* you.
13.	easy	Our lessons are not *easy*.
14.	shut	Please *shut* the door.
15.	done	Has he *done* the work?
16.	body	The chest is part of the *body*.
17.	anyway	I will go *anyway*.
18.	omit	Please *omit* the next verse.
19.	fifth	This is my *fifth* trip.
20.	reason	Give me a *reason* for being late.
21.	perfect	This is a *perfect* day.
22.	friend	She is my *friend*.
23.	getting	I am *getting* tired.
24.	nearly	*Nearly* all the candy is gone.
25.	desire	I have no *desire* to go.
26.	arrange	Please *arrange* a meeting for me.
27.	written	I have *written* four letters.
28.	search	*Search* for your book.
29.	popular	He is a *popular* boy.
30.	interest	Show some *interest* in your work.

(continued)

31. pleasant   She is very *pleasant*.
32. therefore   *Therefore*, I cannot go.
33. folks   My *folks* have gone away.
34. celebration   There will be a *celebration* today.
35. minute   Wait a *minute*.
36. divide   *Divide* this number by ten.
37. necessary   It is *necessary* for you to study.
38. height   What is your *height*?
39. reference   He made *reference* to the lesson.
40. career   The future holds a bright *career* for you.
41. character   He has a good *character*.
42. separate   *Separate* these papers.
43. committee   The *committee* is small.
44. annual   This is the *annual* meeting.
45. principle   The theory is wrong in *principle*.
46. immense   The man is carrying an *immense* load.
47. judgment   The teacher's *judgment* is good.
48. acquaintance   He is an *acquaintance* of mine.
49. discipline   The army *discipline* is strict.
50. lieutenant   He is a *lieutenant* in the Army.

Grade norms are based on of the average number of words spelled correctly. Use these as guides.

Grade	No. of Words
2	11
3	18
4	24
5	30
6	35
7	39
8	42
9	44

CHAPTER SIX

Fluency

If fluency was once the "neglected reading goal" (Allington, 1983), it is no longer. There has been an increased interest in developing fluency, as indicated by the findings of the National Reading Panel on the effectiveness of guided oral reading approaches to developing comprehension (National Reading Panel, 2000) and by research (e.g., Kuhn & Stahl, 2003).

There are three components to fluency: Fluent reading should involve *accurate* and *automatic* word recognition, with appropriate *prosody*, or inflection. Each component affects comprehension in its own way.

Obviously, if children cannot read the text relatively accurately, their comprehension will suffer. As noted in Chapter 3, the reading does not have to be word-perfect. A child can misread five words out of 100 (or 95% accuracy) and still be within the instructional range. With more instructional support, such as that found in some of the fluency-oriented approaches discussed at the end of this chapter, the child can read initially with less accuracy. However, word-recognition accuracy will continue to affect comprehension.

Automaticity is also important for comprehension. By *automaticity* we mean the ability to read words without conscious effort, as you are doing now. Unless we throw in a word in a crazy font, like 𝕂𝔼𝕋ℂℍ𝕌ℙ, your reading proceeds without your having to think about the words; instead, you continue to focus on comprehension. If a child reads accurately but has to sound out or stumble over every word, his or her comprehension also will suffer. People have just so much mental energy to devote to a cognitive task such as comprehension. If they have to put extra mental energy into decoding the words, that energy or focus will not be available for comprehension. We find that many struggling readers who have experienced successful remediation of their word-recognition skills often have difficulty with automaticity.

Prosody is the ability to read with some sort of inflection. When we read aloud, our voice goes up and down, depending on the part of the sentence we are reading. We tend to drop our voice (slightly, but perceptively) at the ends of sentences and raise our inflection at the end of questions. We see prosody as an indicator that children are understanding the parts of speech in a sentence—in essence, a low-level type of comprehension.

JUDGING ORAL FLUENCY

When we consider fluency, we are interested in all three components: accuracy, automaticity, and prosody. We can judge accuracy by applying the procedures of informal reading inventories, as discussed in Chapter 3. Automaticity is usually assessed using rate of reading. We provide guides for reading rates later in this chapter. Prosody is the most difficult of these components to assess. For example, in IRIs we have found that it is difficult to get agreement on whether readers left out periods or ran sentences together when reading. Judging whether a child uses inflection well can be even more difficult. The NAEP rubric is a simple 4-point scale that can only give the broadest indication of a child's fluency, but it can be used easily. This scale can be used on any oral reading sample, either from an IRI or classroom reading. You can tape-record individual students to observe growth over time. Taped reading samples can be used for parent–teacher conferences and can be a powerful demonstration of a child's progress over time.

NAEP Rubric

Table 6.1 shows the fluency scale used in the National Assessment of Educational Progress oral reading study, given as part of the 1992 and 2002 NAEP.

We have found this scale to be fairly easy to apply to a child's oral reading sample. To do so, tape a sample of the child's oral reading. Listen to the entire selection and give an overall rating, using the four levels described in Table 6.1. We strongly recommend that you meet with another person who is doing the same thing and that you try to establish interrater agreement before doing this on your own. Our experience is that interrater reliability is easy to establish on this scale, because it is straightforward—and it is an

TABLE 6.1. The NAEP Oral Reading Fluency Scale

Level 4	Reads primarily in larger, meaningful phrase groups. Although some regressions, repetitions, and deviations from text may be present, these do not appear to detract from the overall structure of the story. Preservation of the author's syntax is consistent. Some or most of the story is read with expressive interpretation.
Level 3	Reads primarily in three- or four-word phrase groups. Some smaller groupings may be present. However, the majority of phrasing seems appropriate and preserves the syntax of the author. Little or no expressive interpretation is present.
Level 2	Reads primarily in two-word phrases with some three- or four-word groupings. Some word-by-word reading may be present. Word groupings may seem awkward and unrelated to larger context of sentence or passage.
Level 1	Reads primarily word-by-word. Occasional two-word or three-word phrases may occur, but these are infrequent and/or they do not preserve meaningful syntax.

Note. From U.S. Department of Education, National Center for Education Statistics (1995, p. 15).

important part of the process. School teams may wish to create tape recordings to use as examples of each level to insure consistency.

Multidimensional Scale

The Multidimensional Scale (Zutell & Rasinski, 1991) in Table 6.2 provides a more refined measure of fluency than the NAEP rubric does. It provides a summative quantitative score for multiple dimensions of prosodic reading. However, the individual dimensions provide formative information that may be used to guide instruction. In addition, teachers can use the scale to help students increase self-awareness of specific aspects of their

TABLE 6.2. Multidimensional Fluency Scale

Use the following scales to rate reader fluency (expression and volume, phrasing, smoothness, and pace). Scores range from 4 to 16. Generally, scores below 8 indicate that fluency may be a concern. Scores of 8 or above indicate that the student is making good progress in fluency.

Dimension	1	2	3	4
A. Expression and volume	Reads with little expression or enthusiasm in voice. Reads words as if simply to get them out. Little sense of trying to make text sound like natural language. Tends to read in a quiet voice.	Some expression. Begins to use voice to make text sound like natural language in some areas of the text, but not others. Focus remains largely on saying the words. Still reads in a quiet voice.	Sounds like natural language throughout the better part of the passage. Occasionally slips into expressionless reading. Voice volume is generally appropriate throughout the text.	Reads with good expression and enthusiasm throughout the text. Sounds like natural language. The reader is able to vary expression and volume to match his or her interpretation of the passage.
B. Phrasing	Monotonic with little sense of phrase boundaries, frequent word-by-word reading.	Frequent two- and three-word phrases giving the impression of choppy reading; improper stress and intonation that fail to mark ends of sentences and clauses.	Mixture of run-ons, midsentence pauses for breath, and possibly some choppiness; reasonable stress/ intonation.	Generally well phrased, mostly in clause and sentence units, with adequate attention to expression.
C. Smoothness	Frequent extended pauses, hesitations, false starts, sound-outs, repetitions, and/or multiple attempts.	Several "rough spots" in text where extended pauses, hesitations, etc., are more frequent and disruptive.	Occasional breaks in smoothness caused by difficulties with specific words and/ or structures.	Generally smooth reading with some breaks, but word and structure difficulties are resolved quickly, usually through self-correction.
D. Pace (during sections of minimal disruption)	Slow and laborious.	Moderately slow	Uneven mixture of fast and slow reading.	Consistently conversational.

Note. From Zutell and Rasinski (1991). Copyright 1991 by The Ohio State University College of Education and Human Ecology. Adapted by permission.

own reading fluency. Eventually students may use the scale in self-evaluations of their own reading fluency.

CURRICULUM-BASED MEASUREMENTS

Another way of using oral reading to determine a child's achievement is through curriculum-based measurements (CBMs). This approach uses short passages, usually 100 words, taken from texts that are used in the child's class. The child is asked to read the passage and is judged on the basis of rate and accuracy. The procedures for developing and administering CBMs are presented in Table 6.3.

Hasbrouck and Tindal (2006) developed norms for CBMs that can be used for judging fluent oral reading using other materials. To use the norms found in Table 6.4, calculate the number of words correctly read per minute: (% accuracy × number of words × 60)/reading time in seconds. Hasbrouck and Tindal give the median score at the 10th, 25th, 50th, 75th, and 90th percentile rank at three testing times (fall, winter, and spring). Compare the score you obtained to the scores in Table 6.4. Scores between the 25th and 75th percentiles would be considered roughly average; scores above or below would be considered above or below average.

TABLE 6.3. Curriculum-Based Measurement Procedures for Assessing and Scoring Oral Reading Fluency

Say to the student: *"When I say 'start,' begin reading aloud at the top of this page. Read across the page* [demonstrate by pointing]. *Try to read each word. If you come to a word you don't know, I'll tell it to you. Be sure to do your best reading. Are there any questions?"*
Say, *"Start."*
Follow along on your copy of the story, marking the words that are read incorrectly. If a student stops or struggles with a word for 3 seconds, tell the student the word and mark it as incorrect.
Place a vertical line after the last word read and thank the student.

The following guidelines determine which words are counted as correct:

1. *Words read correctly.* Words read correctly are those words that are pronounced correctly, given the reading context.
   a. The word *read* must be pronounced *reed*, not as *red*, when presented in the context of "He will read the book."
   b. Repetitions are not counted as incorrect.
   c. Self-corrections within 3 seconds are counted as correctly read words.
2. *Words read incorrectly.* The following types of errors are counted: (a) mispronunciations, (b) substitutions, and (c) omissions. Furthermore, words not read within 3 seconds are counted as errors.
   a. *Mispronunciations* are words that are misread: *dog* for *dig.*
   b. *Substitutions* are words that are substituted for the stimulus word; this is often inferred by a one-to-one correspondence between word orders: *dog* for *cat.*
   c. *Omissions* are words skipped or not read; if a student skips an entire line, each word is counted as an error.
3. *Three-second rule.* If a student is struggling to pronounce a word or hesitates for 3 seconds, the student is told the word, and it is counted as an error.

Note. From Shinn (1989, pp. 239–240). Copyright 1989 by The Guilford Press. Adapted by permission.

TABLE 6.4. Hasbrouck and Tindal's (2006) Oral Reading Fluency Data

Grade	Percentile	Fall WCPM[a]	Winter WCPM[a]	Spring WCPM[a]	Avg. weekly improvement[b]
1	90		81	111	1.9
	75		47	82	2.2
	50		23	53	1.9
	25		12	28	1.0
	10		6	15	0.6
2	90	106	125	142	1.1
	75	79	100	117	1.2
	50	51	72	89	1.2
	25	25	42	61	1.1
	10	11	18	31	0.6
3	90	128	146	162	1.1
	75	99	120	137	1.2
	50	71	92	107	1.1
	25	44	62	78	1.1
	10	21	36	48	0.8
4	90	145	166	180	1.1
	75	119	139	152	1.0
	50	94	112	123	0.9
	25	68	87	98	0.9
	10	45	61	72	0.8
5	90	166	182	194	0.9
	75	139	156	168	0.9
	50	110	127	139	0.9
	25	85	99	109	0.8
	10	61	74	83	0.7
6	90	177	195	204	0.8
	75	153	167	177	0.8
	50	127	140	150	0.7
	25	98	111	122	0.8
	10	68	82	93	0.8
7	90	180	192	202	0.7
	75	156	165	177	0.7
	50	128	136	150	0.7
	25	102	109	123	0.7
	10	79	88	98	0.6
8	90	185	199	199	0.4
	75	161	173	177	0.5
	50	133	146	151	0.6
	25	106	115	124	0.6
	10	77	84	97	0.6

Note. Jan Hasbrouck and Gerald Tindal completed an extensive study of oral reading fluency, the results of which were published in a technical report that is available on the University of Oregon's website, *burt.uoregon.edu/tech_reports.htm,* and in Hasbrouck and Tindal (2006). The table shows the mean oral reading fluency of students in grades 1 through 8, as determined by Hasbrouck and Tindal's data.

You can use the information in this table to draw conclusions and make decisions about the oral reading fluency of your students. *Students scoring 10 or more words below the 50th percentile using the average score of two unpracticed readings from grade-level materials need a fluency-building program.* In addition, teachers can use the table to set the long-term fluency goals for their struggling readers.

Average weekly improvement is the average words per week growth you can expect from a student. It was calculated by subtracting the fall score from the spring score and dividing the difference by 32, the typical number of weeks between the fall and spring assessments. For grade 1, since there is no fall assessment, the average weekly improvement was calculated by subtracting the winter score from the spring score and dividing the difference by 16, the typical number of weeks between the winter and spring assessments.
aWCPM, words correct per minute.
bAverage words per week growth.

DIBELS

Another approach to fluency assessment is the Dynamic Indicators of Basic Early Literacy Skills (DIBELS), developed at the University of Oregon. These assessments can be used to assess progress over time, since they can be given at different points in the school year. Since DIBELS was developed by a federal grant, the use of both benchmark assessments and additional tests for progress monitoring are available for free on their website (*dibels.uoregon.edu*).

The DIBELS assessments begin in kindergarten and progress to sixth grade. Figure 6.1 displays the schedule of DIBELS assessments. It is important to note that DIBELS uses the term *fluency* to mean automaticity and proficiency. Thus they speak of "phoneme segmentation fluency," and so forth. DIBELS measures have been widely used in classrooms around the country. Consequently, the website is able to provide benchmark goals and an estimated risk status for each assessment administration. The website (*dibels.uoregon.edu/techreports/index.php*) also provides information that describes the research supporting and extending this assessment system. This set of tools is an inexpensive, convenient, and time-efficient means of monitoring many early literacy skills.

Recent evidence indicates that DIBELS Oral Reading Fluency (ORF) is a better predictor of reading comprehension than other DIBELS subtests, including a retell fluency subtest designed to explicitly measure comprehension (Riedel, 2007). In addition, combining other subtests with the ORF did not significantly improve the predictive power beyond that provided by ORF alone. Our topic in this chapter is oral reading fluency in context, and so we focus on the DIBELS ORF task that is administered beginning in the middle of first grade.

For each of three passages, the child is asked to read the passage aloud and is stopped after a minute. The score is calculated as the number of words correct per minute. Of the three scores, the median or middle number is used to determine whether the child is "at risk" for reading difficulties, might be at "some risk," or is at "low risk." Three benchmark passages are administered individually in a single sitting three times a year. Additional passages are available for progress monitoring. The DIBELS manual suggests that

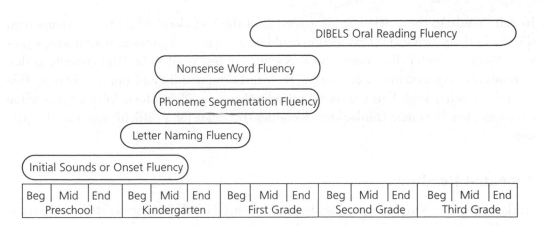

FIGURE 6.1. DIBELS measures.

a retelling be conducted immediately after reading using a count of the number of words retold in 1 minute. It's possible that this accountability for a retelling may encourage the child to read for meaning, not just speed, but we question the construct as a measure of comprehension.

FLUENCY-ORIENTED APPROACHES

A rule in our clinical work is that children need to spend the majority of the time during tutoring reading connected text aloud; if it helps, the tutor can read one page and the student the next page, in alternating fashion. Repeated readings or any variation of fluency-oriented instruction can be employed. We find that repeated or assisted reading gives children the support they need to read increasingly difficult texts. Our research (Kuhn & Stahl, 2003) suggests that assigning children a passage to read repeatedly is not as effective as assisted reading, in which an adult actively models reading. In a clinic, repeated reading can be monitored closely. In the classroom, we prefer a more assisted reading model.

Several approaches to fluency development are described below. These approaches are most useful for children who already have good oral language comprehension but either poor or slow word-recognition abilities.

We suggest that you choose material that is relatively difficult for the child, although not beyond his or her level of comprehension—perhaps one level above his or her instructional level, but not so far above it that the child cannot cope. We have found that children can benefit from reading material with as low as 85% accuracy, if they are given adequate support.

A desired criterion for fluency is (1) reading a passage at 100 words per minute, with (2) zero or one insignificant errors and (3) adequate inflection.

Some suggested activities follow.

Echo Reading

In echo reading, the teacher reads a section of the text aloud while the students read silently in their own texts. This section could be a sentence, a paragraph, or a longer passage. Students "echo" the section back. Sections of text need to be long enough so that students are required to rely on reading their texts and prohibited from simply repeating what the teacher said. This is a useful introduction to a difficult text. After echo reading a passage, teachers may think-aloud decoding strategies for a difficult word in the passage.

Repeated Readings

Students read the same text repeatedly, until a desired level of fluency is attained. We use a specific procedure in the reading clinic, as follows:

1. Choose a passage to read that is slightly above the child's instructional level, but one that the child might be interested in reading. (This method may be used, with grade-level materials, for a child who is reading significantly below grade level.)
2. Take a 100-word excerpt from this passage. (You may use different lengths, but the math is more difficult!)
3. Have the child read the passage aloud, marking all his or her miscues. Tape-record and time the reading (using a stopwatch or watch with a sweep second hand). Mark the child's speed and error rate on a chart.
4. Review the child's miscues with him or her, using the tape or through discussion.
5. Have the child reread the passage, and mark his or her errors and time on the chart.
6. Have the child continue until a speed of 100 words per minute, with zero or one miscue, is achieved. If achieving this goal takes more than seven tries, you might want to try an easier passage. This process usually takes more than one session; chart each attempt.
7. Proceed to another section at the same level. When the child can read relatively fluently for the first time, select a more difficult passage.

An Alternate Approach

This instructional method can be used with small groups or an entire class, as well as with an individual child. Take a book or passage and have the child(ren) read orally for 3 minutes. At the end of 3 minutes, have the child(ren) mark the last word read with a pencil. You might discuss words with which the child had problems. Then have the child(ren) reread the passage, again for 3 minutes. Have the child(ren) mark the last word read. He or she should have been able to read more in the second attempt. This procedure can be repeated a third time.

Tape Reading

The teacher records a longer passage or uses a commercially available tape. The student reads along with the tape until he or she can read the story comfortably and fluently. Then the student reads to the teacher, who judges whether or not the reading is adequate. Make sure that students are responsible for reading the text themselves. Too often these "read-along" opportunities turn into listening opportunities. Children who need fluency practice generally have good language abilities and do not benefit as much from listening as they do from reading practice. We cannot stress too strongly that *unless students are responsible for reading what they have practiced to an adult, taped reading is a waste of time.*

Partner Reading

Students choose partners and read an entire story, taking turns. Usually turn taking proceeds page by page, but partners can negotiate differently. During reading, one partner reads while the other monitors the reading and helps, if needed.

A related alternative to partner reading is paired repeated readings. Students pair up, and the teacher selects short, interesting passages at the students' instructional or independent (98%+ accuracy) level. Each student reads his or her passage three times. The other student in the pair comments on how well it was read.

Still another alternative is a team effort in which partners or a group work together as problem solvers. The children work on a difficult text, sentence by sentence, striving together to understand the meaning of the text. In such a group, you might have three older children with reading problems working with a text that might be far too difficult for any one of them to work on alone. One child would read a sentence of the text, and the group would discuss any difficulties they might have with that sentence, such as difficulties with words, with the meaning, or with specific vocabulary. After the sentence is discussed, the student who read it now paraphrases the sentence. The next student reads the next sentence, and so it goes.

Choral Reading

Choral reading, which involves the simultaneous reading of a passage, can be done individually or in groups. In classes, it is often fun to use the choral reading format with poems. Anthologies of poems by authors such as Shel Silverstein and Jack Prelutsky are popular choices. In a choral reading session it is important to monitor children's reading to ensure that *all* children are participating.

For individual work, choral reading can be applied to any passage and can be done repeatedly. In repeated choral reading, the tutor might lower his or her voice with each repeated reading, thus phasing him- or herself out. (This approach used to be called the "neurological impress method" for reasons best forgotten.)

Plays, Reader's Theater, and Famous Speeches

Plays and famous speeches are two effective approaches for engaging children in reading practice. Having children practice parts is an excellent way of getting them to read text repeatedly, until they reach a desired level of fluency. Speeches work well for older students; several websites serve as good sources (*www.famousquotes.me.uk/speeches* or *www.americanrhetoric.com/top100speechesall.html*). One guideline: It may be the weakest readers who benefit from this activity the most. Give them substantial roles, and then make sure they have adequate practice prior to performance.

Oral Recitation

The oral recitation lesson (Hoffman, 1987) format is an approach that combines a number of these procedures into a single lesson plan. An oral recitation lesson has two parts: A direct teaching phase and a mastery phase.

Direct Teaching

1. For a regular-length story, the teacher begins by reading the entire story to the group. Then the teacher discusses the story as a whole, either using questions or developing a group story map.

2. Then the teacher rereads the story, either sentence by sentence or paragraph by paragraph (use your judgment), as students follow along in their books, after which students echo back the portion read. Teacher and students proceed through the story in this way.

3. The teacher divides the story into parts and assigns a section to each student. Students practice their assigned section and perform it for the group. As an alternative, students can choose their parts, based on interest.

4. Teacher and students proceed to the next story. You may assign worksheets, work on skills, and so on here.

Mastery Phase

Students practice stories covered in the direct teaching phase until they are able to read them with 99%+ accuracy and at a rate of at least 85 words per minute (or another acceptable level of fluency). This practice is done on their own. The teacher works with them when they feel they are ready.

Students progress more quickly through the direct teaching phase than the mastery phase, so that a child may be on a fifth story in the direct teaching phase but only have mastered the first three stories. Students engage in mastery work during independent work time, in place of some seat work.

Paired Reading

Paired reading, a program developed by Keith Topping (1987) in Scotland, is widely used in the United Kingdom and Canada. In paired reading, a more capable reader, usually an adult, works one-on-one with a struggling reader. A paired reading session begins with the tutor and child choosing a book together. The only selection requirement is that the book be of interest to the child. There should be no readability limits (although our experience is that children rarely choose material that is far too difficult). They begin by reading in unison, until the child signals the tutor, by touching the tutor or raising a hand or some other prearranged signal, when he or she wants to read solo. The solo reading continues until the child makes an error. The tutor provides the word, they repeat the sentence in unison, and the procedure begins again. (See Topping, 1987, for more details. A video is available from Filmwest Associates, *www.filmwest.com*.)

Buddy Reading

Children with reading problems benefit from working with younger children as readers or tutors. Reading to younger students is a good way for children to practice their own reading in a natural setting. Pick a book that might be interesting to younger children. It should be short, colorful, with few sentences on each page. The student practices the book until he or she feels comfortable. Then he or she reads the book to a younger child or to the class, to the benefit of both. In the case of older children who read at a very low level (e.g., a sixth grader reading at a first-grade level), allowing them to select books to read to kindergartners, say, is a practical way of allowing them to practice appropriate material while maintaining their self-esteem.

Tutoring a younger child is potentially a richer experience. As opposed to merely reading to a child, tutoring involves instructional interactions that can lead the tutor to greater awareness of the processes involved in learning to read. In a tutoring situation, we recommend the following steps:

1. *Choose a book at an appropriate level.* Prior to the tutoring session, the tutor (the older child with reading problems) chooses a book at an appropriate level for the tutee to read. Initially, this selection might be made with the help of the younger child's teacher. The tutor should read and practice the book to be used prior to the tutoring session.
2. *Make lesson plans and review them with the teacher.* The tutor should make lesson plans, including words that he or she needs to preteach. The teacher can review a rationale for teaching words. The lesson plans also might include a comprehension activity, writing activity, and so on.
3. *Tutor the child.*
4. *Keep a journal about the tutoring experience.* A reflective journal can be used to discuss with the teacher how the session went, what worked, what did not work, and so forth.

In preparation for tutoring, students should be taught procedures for responding to oral reading errors, such as: If the tutee misreads a sentence, ask "Does that make sense?" If the child says no, then ask him or her to make a correction so that it does make sense. Every so often, also ask whether the sentence makes sense when, in fact, it does. Otherwise, your question becomes a statement. If the child is unable to correct him- or herself or hesitates at a word (for more than 5 seconds), just give the word to the child then have him or her reread the entire sentence. Note the word that was missed and, *after the reading lesson is over,* provide extra help with that word. For example, the word can be added to a set of word cards and used in a paired drill.

Tutoring and reading to children can be done with middle school and high school children as well, provided transportation can be arranged. We suggest contacting an elementary school with an after-school program and working 1 or 2 days a week.

Closed-Captioned Television

According to research, children's word identification improves from watching closed-captioned television (Koskinen, Wilson, & Jensema, 1985). We are not sure how effective this "method" is, but it is relatively easy to suggest that children with reading problems watch TV with the captions on at home. It does not hurt and might help.

CHAPTER SEVEN

Comprehension

There has always been an intense interest in reading comprehension assessment. After all, comprehension could be called the "bottom line" of reading. Measuring it provides an indicator of how well all of the subprocesses of reading are working together. Comprehension assessment is a somewhat controversial topic, in that no general agreement exists on how best to do it. An extreme point of view was voiced by Frank Smith (1988) in the fourth edition of his book *Understanding Reading*. In it he says, "Comprehension cannot be measured at all . . . because it is not a quantity of anything" (p. 53). Most reading experts would certainly acknowledge that comprehension assessment raises important issues, but most would also agree that useful estimates can be reached of (1) a child's overall ability to comprehend, and (2) how well a child has comprehended a particular selection.

TWO REASONS TO ASSESS COMPREHENSION

There are two principal reasons for assessing comprehension. The first reason for assessing reading comprehension is to gauge the degree to which a student has comprehended a particular selection. Chapter tests and other postreading assessments often serve this function. The second reason is to estimate general level of proficiency. The result of this kind of assessment might be an estimate of the instructional reading level by means of an informal reading inventory or a normative judgment by means of an achievement test. Mastery tests of specific comprehension skills also correspond to this purpose.

APPROACHES TO COMPREHENSION ASSESSMENT

Let's consider the major approaches to assessing comprehension and examine the strengths and limitations of each.

Questions

The most traditional method of testing reading comprehension is by asking questions. The use of questions offers great administrative flexibility, ranging from formal testing situations to class discussions. Questions allow teachers to focus on particular facts, conclusions, and judgments in which the teachers have an interest. By posing questions at various levels of thinking, a teacher can get a glimpse of how the child has processed a reading selection.

Types of Questions

There are many ways of categorizing questions. Bloom's (1969) taxonomy is sometimes used, for example. A far simpler approach is to think of questions in terms of levels of comprehension. We conventionally speak of three levels.

1. *Literal questions* require a student to recall a specific fact that has been explicitly stated in the reading selection. Such questions are easy to ask and answer, but they may reflect a very superficial understanding of content. Edgar Dale (1946), an eminent reading authority during the first half of the 20th century, once referred to literal comprehension as "reading the lines" (p. 1).

2. *Inferential questions*, like literal questions, have factual answers. However, the answers cannot be located in the selection. Instead, the reader must make logical connections among facts in order to arrive at an answer. The answer to a question calling for a prediction, for example, is always inferential in nature even though we are uncertain of the answer, for the reader must nevertheless use available facts in an effort to arrive at a fact that is not stated.

Answers to inferential questions are sometimes beyond dispute and sometimes quite speculative. Let's say that a class has just read a selection on New Zealand. They have read that New Zealand is south of the equator and was colonized by Great Britain. If a teacher were to ask whether Auckland, New Zealand's capital, is south of the equator, the answer would require inferential thinking. There is no dispute about the answer, but the selection does not specifically mention Auckland, and the students must infer its location in relation to the equator.

On the other hand, were the teacher to ask the students if English is spoken in New Zealand, the answer would be inferential as well as speculative. The mere fact that Britain colonized New Zealand does not guarantee that English is spoken there today. For all inferential questions, the reader must use facts that are stated to reach a conclusion about a fact that is not stated. For this reason, Dale (1946) described inferential comprehension as "reading between the lines" (p. 1).

3. *Critical questions* call upon students to form value judgments about the selection. Such judgments can never be characterized as right or wrong, because these types of answers are not facts. They are evaluations arrived at on the basis of an individual's value system. Critical questions might target whether the selection is well written, whether certain topics should have been included, whether the arguments an author

makes are valid, and whether the writing is biased or objective. Understandably, Dale (1946) equated critical comprehension with "reading beyond the lines" (p. 1). (Hint: A shortcut to asking a critical-level question is to insert the word *should*. Doing so always elevates the question to the critical level. Of course, there are other ways to pose critical questions, but this method is surefire.)

A teacher's judgment of how well a child comprehends may depend in part on the types of questions asked. Thus the choice of question type can affect a child's performance during a postreading assessment. A student may well do better if asked questions that are entirely literal than if asked questions at a variety of levels. The issue of which type(s) of questions to include in any postreading assessment is therefore an important one. Perhaps the best advice is to ask the type(s) of questions that you would expect a child to be able to answer during the course of day-to-day classroom instruction.

A final issue concerning types of comprehension questions is whether to subdivide each of the three levels into specific skills. For example, the literal level is often seen as composed of skills involving sequences, cause-and-effect relationships, comparisons, character traits, and the like. Does it make sense to ask questions corresponding to each of these skills? Yes, as long as very little is made of the results. Skill-related questions can assure us that a range of comprehension skills is being developed, but when we attempt to compute scores for each skill, we often run into trouble. The problem is twofold. First, there are seldom enough questions for reliable measurement. Second, scores on specific skill tests tend to be almost perfectly correlated, suggesting that the skills are difficult to separate for assessment. In other words, a student who scores high on a test of literal sequences almost always scores high on a test of literal cause-and-effect relationships. It's hardly worth the effort to splinter comprehension to this extent.

Questions Based on Reading Dependency

Reading dependency (also called *passage dependency*) is the need to have read a selection in order to answer a particular comprehension question. Consider the following example. The children have just read a story about a girl who brings a frog to school for Show and Tell. The frog jumps out of her hands and causes merry havoc in the classroom. The teacher then asks two comprehension questions:

1. "What did the girl bring to Show and Tell?"
2. "What color was the frog?"

These two questions are both literal. That is, they both require the students to respond with facts explicitly stated in the story. They differ considerably, however, in terms of their reading dependency. Even children with extensive experience participating in Show and Tell would be unlikely to predict the answer to the first question simply on the basis of experience. In short, it is necessary to have read the story in order to answer the question. The second question is another matter. Most children know that nearly all

American frogs are green, and the children would not need to have read the passage in order to respond correctly. On the other hand, if the girl had brought some rare South American species that was, say, red and yellow, the same question would have been reading dependent.

Which of these two questions tells the teacher more about whether the students comprehended the text? Clearly, questions that can be answered without having adequately comprehended a selection fail to assess reading comprehension. They may well be justified in the interest of conducting a worthwhile discussion, but teachers should not be misled into assuming that such questions would help them monitor their students' comprehension.

We have noted that even the questions in commercial test instruments tend to have problems regarding reading dependency. Many studies (e.g., Tuinman, 1971) have shown that when given only the questions and *not* the selections on which they are based, students do far better than chance would have predicted. This outcome implies that they are using prior knowledge to correctly answer some of the questions. The challenge in devising assessment instruments, or even informal approaches, is that it is difficult to determine what children are likely to know before they read a selection. This problem is especially troublesome with nonfiction text because of its factual content. Children already familiar with the content may find themselves with an unintended advantage in responding to postreading questions.

To better understand the concept of reading dependency, read the simple nonfiction example, "Crows," in Figure 7.1. The four comprehension questions that follow the passage represent four basic possibilities in regard to the degree of reading dependence reflected in the question. For most adults, the answer to question 1 lies not only in the passage but in their prior knowledge. This means that the question is not reading dependent and is not a good indicator of reading comprehension. The answer to question 2, on the other hand, lies entirely within the adult's prior knowledge (in this case, prior experi-

Crows

Crows are large black birds that pose a threat to farmers. They belong to the genus *Corvus*.

1. What color are crows?
2. Have you ever had a pet crow?
3. To what genus do crows belong?
4. How long do crows usually live?

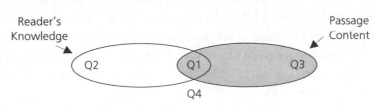
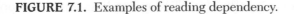

FIGURE 7.1. Examples of reading dependency.

ence), but not within the passage. The answer to question 3 lies in the passage, but not in a typical adult's prior knowledge. This makes question 3 a reading-dependent one—and a much better indicator of comprehension. Finally, the answer to question 4 lies neither in prior knowledge (typically) nor in the passage. The issue of reading dependence boils down to a single guideline: If your intent is to assess reading comprehension, then your comprehension questions should target information that lies within the passage but that is not likely to lie within the student's prior knowledge. The Venn diagram used in Figure 7.1 may help conceptualize the four types of questions in relation to effective comprehension assessment.

Keep in mind that reading dependence is related to how much the reader knows in advance. What if question 3 were addressed to an ornithologist? Because an expert on birds could probably answer the question without needing to read the passage, the very same question is no longer a reading-dependent one. It all depends on whom you're asking. This is why the problem of reading dependence sometimes gets the better of commercial test developers. It's hard to predict what students, in general, may or may not know!

Readability of Questions

A third aspect of reading comprehension questions involves their readability. It is possible for the question itself to be harder to comprehend than the selection on which it is based. Written questions should be kept as simple as possible. Their difficulty level should certainly be no higher than that of the selections on which they are based, and ideally should be simpler. Consider, in particular, the vocabulary you use in framing a question and also the complexity of your sentence structures. The KISS method (Keep It Simple, Sweetheart!) has much to recommend it when formulating comprehension questions.

Cloze Assessment

Cloze testing involves deleting words from a prose selection and asking students to replace them on the basis of the remaining context. The ability to provide logical replacement words is thought to indicate the extent to which a student is able to comprehend the material. Cloze testing has several important advantages. First, it can be administered in a group setting, once students have been introduced to its rather unusual format. Second, it does not require comprehension questions. This means that issues such as reading dependence and question readability do not arise. Third, cloze scores correlate highly with more conventional methods of assessing comprehension, such as asking questions. Finally, cloze and modifications of cloze have been successfully used as a form of ESL and bilingual assessment. The cloze method allows the ESL reader to devote processing resources to comprehension (Francis, 1999).

On the other hand, cloze testing has significant limitations. Its strange format can confuse some students. Spelling and fine-motor limitations can prevent students from displaying what they actually comprehended. (In fact, cloze testing is rarely administered below fourth grade for this reason.) Finally, research indicates that cloze assessments, as unusual as the format may appear, tend to assess comprehension at only a very low level. A student's ability to integrate information across sentences and paragraphs is not readily tapped by cloze items.

Figure 7.2 provides streamlined suggestions for constructing, administering, and scoring a cloze test. The sample cloze test in Form 7.1 (p. 179) serves as a model of what a cloze test should look like in its conventional format. You might try your hand at taking this test and then scoring it using the answer key in Figure 7.3. In scoring the test, make sure to give yourself credit for only verbatim responses—that is, for the exact word that was deleted in each case. You may be tempted to award credit for synonyms and other

Construction

- Start with a passage of about 300 words. Shorter passages may be used, but reliability could be jeopardized.
- Choose any word as the first to be deleted, but leave a sentence or so intact at the beginning of the test.
- Thereafter, mark every fifth word, until there are 50 in all.
- Word process the test so that the words you've marked are replaced by blanks.
- The blanks must be of equal length.
- For younger students, leave blanks of around 15 spaces to give them room to write.
- For older students, you may wish to number the blanks so that students can write their answers on a separate sheet.

Administration

- It is generally unwise to administer cloze tests prior to grade 4.
- Make certain students know that each blank represents only one word.
- Explain that this is more like a guessing game than a test. Even the best readers will not be able to guess many of the words.
- Encourage them to try to guess the word that was actually there—the word the author used.
- There is no time limit.

Scoring and Interpretation

- Give credit for verbatim answers only. Synonyms and other semantically acceptable responses are considered incorrect.
- Minor misspellings are counted as correct. However, spellings that indicate that the child might have been thinking of another word are counted as incorrect. Examples:

Original word	Child's answer	Scoring
Mississippi	Missisippi	Correct
scarlet	crimson	Incorrect

- Compute the percentage of correct answers and use the following scoring guide:

Independent level:	above 60%
Instructional level:	40–60%
Frustration level:	below 40%

FIGURE 7.2. Guidelines for cloze testing.

From *The Telltale Heart*
Edgar Allan Poe

True!—nervous—very, very dreadfully nervous I had been and am; but why *will* you say that I am mad? The disease had sharpened my senses—not destroyed, not dulled them. Above __all__ was the sense of __hearing__ acute. I heard all __things__ in the heaven and __in__ the earth. I heard __many__ things in hell. How, __then__, am I mad? Hearken! __and__ observe how healthily, how __calmly__ I can tell you __the__ whole story.

It is __impossible__ to say how first __the__ idea entered my brain; __but__ once conceived, it haunted __me__ day and night. Object __there__ was none. Passion there __was__ none. I loved the __old__ man. He had never __wronged__ me. He had never __given__ me insult. For his __gold__ I had no desire. __I__ think it was his __eye__! Yes, it was this! __He__ had the eye of __a__ vulture—a pale blue __eye__, with a film over __it__. Whenever it fell upon __me__, my blood ran cold; __and__ so by degrees—very __gradually__—I made up my __mind__ to take the life __of__ the old man, and __thus__ rid myself of the __eye__ forever.

Now this is __the__ point. You fancy me __mad__. Madmen know nothing. But __you__ should have seen *me*. __You__ should have seen how __wisely__ I proceeded—with what __caution__, with what foresight, with __what__ dissimulation I went to __work__! I was never kinder __to__ the old man than __during__ the whole week before __I__ killed him. And every __night__, about midnight, I turned __the__ latch of his door __and__ opened it—oh, so __gently__! And then, when I __had__ made an opening sufficient __for__ my head, I put __in__ a dark lantern, all closed, closed, so that no light shone out, and then I thrust in my head. Oh, you would have laughed to see how cunningly I thrust it in! I moved it slowly—very, very slowly, so that I might not disturb the old man's sleep. It took me an hour to place my whole head within the opening so far that I could see him as he lay upon his bed. Ha!—would a madman have been so wise as this?

FIGURE 7.3. Answers to sample cloze test.

reasonable responses, but this temptation must be resisted. There are four reasons for accepting only verbatim replacements:

1. Verbatim scoring is more objective than the policy of awarding credit for synonyms. Otherwise, different scorers would tend to produce different scores.
2. Verbatim scoring leads to tests that are far easier to grade. Imagine how long it would take if you had to stop and carefully consider the semantic acceptability of every wrong answer.
3. Research has shown convincingly that verbatim scoring correlates very highly with scores based on accepting synonyms and other reasonable responses. The only thing accomplished by awarding credit for synonyms is to inflate scores. The rank ordering of students in a classroom is not likely to change.
4. Scoring criteria are based on verbatim scoring. If you give credit for synonyms and other logical responses, it will be nearly impossible to interpret the results. This reason alone is sufficient to justify giving credit for verbatim replacements only. The multitude of studies establishing the scoring criteria given in Figure 7.2 has assessed a variety of populations, including elementary students, middle and secondary students, college students, vocational–technical students, and even various special-education categories. If your score on the sample cloze test was 60% or higher, it is reasonable to conclude that the passage is at your independent reading level.

Maze

The maze task, introduced by Guthrie, Seifert, Burnham, and Caplan (1974), is a multiple-choice variation of the cloze task. The maze task is appealing because of its ease of administration and scoring. It can be administered in an individual or group setting, manually or through a computer program. The multiple-choice format makes it easy to score. Maze items can be presented in various ways. For example, the options can be stacked vertically or arranged horizontally:

The boy climbed the $\left\{\begin{array}{l}\text{tree}\\\text{story}\\\text{of}\end{array}\right\}$ in his backyard.

The boy climbed the [tree, story, of] in his backyard.

The student circles or underlines the correct choice while reading. Taking a maze test is like making one's way through a maze. The greatest source of psychometric concern is the selection of distractors (Parker & Hasbrouck, 1992). The number, quality, and lexical characteristics of distractors can vary greatly. Guthrie recommended that three options be presented, and that one of the distractors be the same part of speech as the answer and that the other represent a different part of speech. The example above represents this approach. McKenna (1981), in discussing how maze might be used with poetry, recommended that all distractors make sense but that only one have the proper poetic qualities. For example:

The iron [tone, tongue, bell] of midnight hath told twelve.[*]

Parker and Hasbrouck (1992) recommend that test designers choose four distractors that are (1) the same part of speech as the deleted word, (2) meaningful and plausible within one sentence, (3) related in content to the passage (when possible), (4) as familiar to the reader as the deleted word, and (5) either clearly wrong or less appropriate, given broader passage content (p. 216).

Evidence indicates that maze tests are sensitive to the reading comprehension development of novice readers (Francis, 1999; Shin, Deno, & Espin, 2000). The minimal demand placed on working memory, spelling, and fine-motor development is advantageous for younger students.

Oral Retellings

Comprehension is sometimes assessed by asking a student to retell orally the content of the reading selection. The degree of detail provided and the general coherence of the retelling are used to gauge comprehension. A checklist of details is used to record which points the student includes in the retelling. That is, when the student mentions a particular detail, a check is placed next to it for later reference by the teacher. Facts that go

---

[*] This line is from Shakespeare. Can you match wits with the Bard?

unmentioned in a student's retelling may be assessed by probe questions that are posed following the retelling. Retellings have the advantage of (1) being naturalistic, (2) avoiding many of the pitfalls of questioning, and (3) gauging how well the child internalized the content of a selection. The openness of the retelling task allows for observation of the child's thought processes, what the child values as important, and cultural influences in story interpretation. Story retellings have been used successfully with children as early as kindergarten and first grade.

Retellings demonstrate consequential validity. Consequential validity results in positive consequences for the examinee as a result of the experience. Studies have demonstrated that just the practice of retelling narrative and expository texts results in improvements in adherence to story grammar, selection of high-level propositions, and cued recall. In other words, we use retellings for assessment purposes, but they have an instructional benefit as a by-product.

But retellings have major limitations as well. They rely very heavily on the student's oral expressive ability, and a deficiency in this area could lead to an inaccurate judgment about how well the student has understood the selection. One should always prompt students to retell the story (or informational text) as though they were telling it to a classmate who had not read it. Because orchestrating the retelling task is cognitively demanding for students, one must always supplement a retelling task with questions about the story to ensure a comprehensive measure of the student's text comprehension.

WORD LISTS
FOR GENERAL COMPREHENSION ASSESSMENT

A shortcut to assessing general comprehension ability is to examine a student's ability to pronounce words, presented in the form of graded lists. Scoring criteria are then used to estimate a student's instructional level, based on how far the student can progress through these lists of increasing difficulty. Offsetting the obvious efficiency of this approach to comprehension assessment lies an important challenge to validity: It seems dubious to estimate a child's instructional reading level through an assessment that involves no actual reading and no measure of comprehension. On the other hand, research indicates that the correlation between word-list performance and more conventional approaches to reading comprehension assessment is high. Graded word lists are probably best thought of as a shortcut to estimating a child's overall proficiency as a reader. They can be used to determine a text-level starting point for a more elaborated measure of reading comprehension. They are, however, no substitute for the "real thing."

One of the most popular graded word lists in the public domain is the San Diego Quick Assessment (SDQA). Form 7.2 (pp. 180–185) presents the SDQA in its entirety, including the student version of the word cards. You are free to reproduce the SDQA if you feel this particular test meets your needs. The scoring protocol will help you organize all of the results of a single testing. The protocol might be included in a student's portfolio and updated through subsequent testing from time to time.

Other Assessment Formats

Questions, cloze, and retellings are the three most popular approaches to comprehension assessments. These three by no means exhaust the possibilities, however. Other comprehension assessment formats include:

- Written responses to a selection
- Oral miscue analysis
- Sentence verification
- Student-generated questions
- Performance tasks based on the selection
- Evaluations of student participation in high-level discussions or book clubs

You may have used still other formats for assessing your students' comprehension. The relative merits of the various formats used to assess reading comprehension vary considerably in their advantages and drawbacks. The debate over which is best is not likely to be resolved in the near future.

ASSESSING THE READABILITY OF MATERIALS

Whenever we assess comprehension, it is essential to know and report the text genre and readability level. If we know the level of difficulty of the materials we ask our students to read, we are in a better position to ensure the likelihood of success and to identify specific challenges. The term *readability* refers to the difficulty level of prose, expressed as a grade level. It can be estimated by several means. You might:

- Use your subjective judgment
- Create a short test out of the selection and see how well your students do
- Apply a readability formula

Readability formulas are quantitative procedures that yield an estimated grade level based on surface features of text. These features are typically limited to the length of sentences and words, although some computerized formulas are much more sophisticated and tap other characteristics as well. Two of the most common formulas, developed by Edward Fry (1977) and Alton Raygor (1977), respectively, appear in Figures 7.4 and 7.5. Try applying them to the following passage, which we used in Chapter 3 (Forms 3.1 and 3.2). (In this case, ignore the direction to sample three passages from the beginning, middle, and end of a book.) Before you apply the formulas, read the passage and make your own best estimate of its readability! Then compare your estimate with those produced by the two formulas and the results of the two formulas with each other.

Togo

Togo is a small country in Africa, just north of the Equator. In area, it is about the same size as West Virginia. The people who live there produce coffee, cocoa, cotton, and other crops. The capital of Togo is called Lomé, a city of about a half million.

Togo has three neighbors. To the east is the country of Benin, to the west is Ghana, and to the north is Burkina Faso. Togo's fourth border is the Atlantic Ocean.

The main language of Togo is French, but four African languages are also spoken. Most of the people in Togo belong to one of 37 tribes. Togo is an interesting place, filled with variety and life.

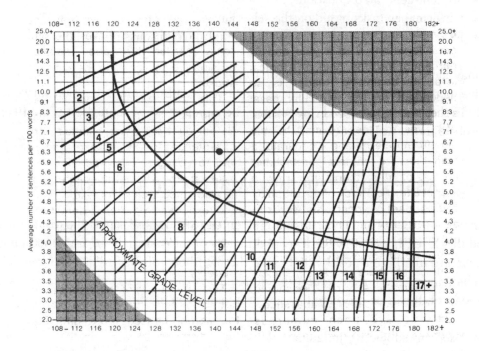

DIRECTIONS: Randomly select three 100-word passages from a book or an article. Plot average number of syllables and average number of sentences per 100 words on graph to determine the grade level of the material. Choose more passages per book if great variability is observed and conclude that the book has uneven readability. Few books will fall in gray area, but when they do grade-level scores are invalid.

Count proper nouns, numerals, and initializations as words. Count a syllable for each symbol. For example, "1945" is one word and five syllables, and "IRA" is one word and three syllables.

EXAMPLE:

	SYLLABLES	SENTENCES
1st Hundred Words	124	6.6
2nd Hundred Words	141	5.5
3rd Hundred Words	158	6.8
AVERAGE	141	6.3

READABILITY 7th GRADE (see dot plotted on graph)

FIGURE 7.4. Graph for Estimating Readability—Extended, by Edward Fry, Rutgers University Reading Center, New Brunswick, NJ 08904. Reprinted by permission of Edward Fry.

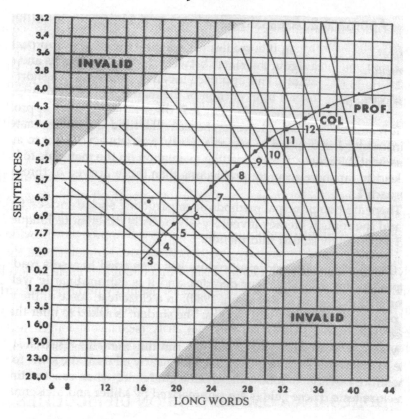

DIRECTIONS: Count out three 100-word passages at the beginning, middle, and end of a selection or book. Count out proper nouns, but not numerals.
1. Count sentences in each passage, estimating to nearest tenth.
2. Count words with six or more letters.
3. Average the sentence length and word length over the three samples and plot the average on the graph.

EXAMPLE:

	Sentences	6+ Words
A	6.0	15
B	6.8	19
C	6.4	17
Total	19.2	51
Average	6.4	17

FIGURE 7.5. The Raygor Readability Estimate, by Alton L. Raygor, University of Minnesota. From Raygor (1977). Reprinted by permission of the National Reading Conference.

Another approach to readability is the Lexile framework. Lexiles are complex metrics that bypass the need to apply formulas. There are two ways to use them and both are free, although you must register at the Lexile website (*www.lexile.com*). The first is to locate a book title in the database. The odds are good that it has already been analyzed. The second is to upload a file in plain text format (i.e., with the extension *.txt*). You can easily change a Word file to plain text simply by saving it in this format. To interpret the Lexile score, you must use a table that converts it to an approximate grade level. This table is also available online.

Remember that quantitative approaches to readability can lead to results that are at odds with one another. (For example, the Lexile rating of the Togo passage is grade 12. How does this compare with your computations of the Fry and Raygor formulas?) Although we believe that they can give useful guidance, numerical approaches provide estimates only. Today there are several qualitative systems being used to determine the difficulty level of early reading materials. The Fountas and Pinnell (2005) criteria for leveling text is one of the more popular qualitative leveling systems, but many publishers of early reading texts are currently using similar systems. Qualitative leveling systems typically consider a text's predictability, content density, content familiarity, page layout, length, text structure, language characteristics, and decodability in determining the readability level.

ADDRESSING COMPREHENSION DIFFICULTIES

It is not enough to determine that a child has a problem with comprehension. It is essential to ask why. The answer to this question will help us sharpen our instructional response. We suggest three questions that can help clarify the issue.

Is Comprehension Hindered by Poor Decoding?

Students who spend too much time and mental energy figuring out words have little of either to devote to comprehension. If comprehension improves when the child listens as a selection is read aloud, this improvement would be evidence of inadequate decoding ability as the fundamental problem. However, it is easy to be deceived into believing that if we improve decoding, comprehension will automatically improve. Often the child may need instruction in both decoding *and* comprehension strategies.

Is Comprehension Hindered by Limited Prior Knowledge and Vocabulary?

We have mentioned the strong relationship between one's knowledge base, including knowledge of word meanings, and one's ability to comprehend. Building knowledge and vocabulary are long term school goals, of course, and their effects on comprehension ability will be gradual and cumulative. Teachers can facilitate comprehension of particular selections, however, by providing thorough background information in advance, including preteaching key vocabulary. A conventional way of doing so is the directed reading activity, which begins with background-building activities. This lesson format is useful for students whose prior knowledge is not greatly deficient, but what about children who need more help before they can begin to comprehend what they read? A promising alternative is the listen–read–discuss technique.

Listen–Read–Discuss

Manzo and Casale (1985) introduced a technique for improving comprehension that assumes little or no background for a nonfiction reading selection. Rather than creating a foundation of knowledge that will be useful for comprehending the additional knowledge presented in the selection, the teacher actually *covers* the content of the selection. That is, the teacher presents, in advance, everything the students will read about, almost as if there were no reading to be done. There is no guesswork or preassessment about what information the students may already know. The teacher assumes they know little or nothing.

The question many teachers raise when they learn about the listen–read–discuss method is, Why bother to read, then? If the teacher presents—via lecture, discussion, demonstration, and the like—the entire contents of the selection, then what is the point of asking students to read it? The answer is that their reading will be greatly facilitated. Listen–read–discuss may not be the most exciting technique ever devised, but it permits children of limited knowledge to experience proficient comprehension, often for the first time. The studies conducted by Manzo and Casale (1985) and later by Watkins, McKenna, Manzo, and Manzo (1994) have established the listen–read–discuss procedure as a viable approach to the problem of limited knowledge and vocabulary.

Is Comprehension Hindered by Poorly Developed Strategies?

We use the word *strategies* to refer to methods proficient readers deliberately employ to facilitate their own comprehension. *Skills*, on the other hand, enable a reader to employ strategies, but are used automatically. Afflerbach, Pearson, and Paris (2008) have offered a distinction that may help clarify the confusion that has long surrounded these terms:

> Reading strategies are deliberate, goal-directed attempts to control and modify the reader's efforts to decode text, understand words, and construct meanings of text. Reading skills are automatic actions that result in decoding and comprehension with speed, efficiency, and fluency and usually occur without awareness of the components or control involved. The reader's deliberate control, goal-directedness, and awareness define a strategic action. (p. 368)

The National Reading Panel (2000) has determined that instructing students to monitor their reading, answer high-level comprehension questions, generate questions about the text, identify and organize ideas based on the text's structure, and summarize the text increases reading comprehension. There is also some support for teaching students to apply their prior knowledge and to create mental images during text reading. Our experience and research support indicate that struggling readers almost invariably profit from strategy instruction. Not surprisingly, a number of evidence-based approaches has been introduced in recent years. We summarize a few of these in the following pages.

Explicit Instruction

Explicit strategy instruction incorporates instruction in declarative knowledge, procedural knowledge, and conditional knowledge (Paris, Lipson, & Wixson, 1983). Declarative knowledge involves teaching the children what the strategy is. Instruction in how to use the strategy develops procedural knowledge, and the instruction in when and why the strategy is most useful (or not applicable) constitutes conditional knowledge.

Effective strategy instruction also utilizes a gradual release of responsibility instructional model (Pearson & Gallagher, 1983). Teachers begin instruction with explicit teaching, model the application of the strategy, perhaps with a think-aloud, and provide guided practice before asking the students to apply the strategy independently. Over time the responsibility for cognitive decision making and putting strategies into practice is released to the students. For a practical discussion of explicit strategy instruction, see Duffy (2003).

Many of the evidence-based approaches described in the following pages can be used during these phases of instruction.

Think-Alouds

In a think-aloud, the teacher models how to flexibly use cognitive strategies or handle a comprehension problem that may arise during reading. Proficient readers continually find themselves in minor comprehension predicaments. What distinguishes them from struggling readers, however, is the fact that good readers can apply strategies for "fixing" such problems. These "fix-up" strategies include (McKenna, 2002):

1. Reading ahead to see whether the problem can be resolved.
2. Rereading to see whether something has been misunderstood.
3. Reflecting on what has been read to see whether some alternative explanation can be inferred.
4. Seeking information beyond the text (from an individual or a second print source) in order to resolve the dilemma.

In a think-aloud, a teacher models this "fix-up" process or strategy use by articulating it. In the words of Scott Paris, the teacher "makes thinking public" so that students are privy to how a proficient reader contends with problem situations. For example, suppose a teacher is reading the following sentence aloud in science class:

Of the more than 20,000 types of spiders in the world, all are poisonous.

The teacher pauses at this point and says aloud to the students, "Wait a minute. How can there be so many poisonous spiders? Did I read that wrong? I'd better go back and check." The teacher then rereads the sentence. "Yeah, that's what it says. I thought there were only a few poisonous spiders. Maybe it'll explain if we keep reading." Sure enough, the passage continues:

> However, very few spiders are dangerous to humans.

"I think I get it now," the teacher observes. "The dangerous ones are the ones I was thinking of. I didn't think the others were poisonous at all, but I guess they are."

Student-Generated Questions

Self-questioning helps students appraise their understanding of the important ideas in a text. Students may find that self-questioning helps them clarify and resolve challenging text. In a review of 26 intervention studies investigating student-generated questions, Rosenshine, Meister, and Chapman (1996) determined that the most effective heuristics seem to be those that are most concrete and easy to use. Studies that taught students the use of signal words (*who, where, when, why,* and *how*) or generic question stems (How are . . . and . . . alike? What is the main idea of . . . ? How is . . . related to . . . ? Why is it important that . . . ?) yielded the most success, especially with the youngest students. Using a story grammar model to develop questions was also fairly effective.

Reciprocal Questioning (ReQuest)

Manzo's (1969) technique of reciprocal questioning (ReQuest) has been effectively used for four decades. It involves students actively in asking questions of the teacher (or one another) during a discussion. The basic idea is that in order to ask good questions, a reader must understand the content reasonably well. If a student reads with the aim of asking questions, then comprehension is apt to be good. In the years following its introduction, research has continually validated ReQuest, and many variations of the technique have been developed. This approach works well after some preliminary explicit instruction on how to ask a good question. It is considered guided practice.

In one approach, the teacher introduces the reading selection and asks the students to begin reading. At a predetermined point, the students stop reading and one student is called on to ask questions of the teacher. The teacher must answer as many questions as the student can think to ask. When the student can think of no more questions, the teacher asks the student additional questions. Another student is called on for the next segment of the reading selection.

An alternative technique is for the teacher to call on a student at random after the selection has been completed. The student asks the teacher one question and the teacher asks the student a question. The teacher then calls on another student, and so forth.

In still another variation, the teacher begins the postreading discussion by calling on a student. The student asks a question, but instead of answering it, the teacher reflects it to another student, who must try to answer. This second student may then ask a question, which the teacher reflects to a third student, and so forth. The teacher may use his or her knowledge of students' abilities to decide which questions to reflect to which students.

Summary Writing

Studies have clearly shown that writing summaries improves comprehension of the material that has been read and enhances comprehension ability generally (see Pressley & Woloshyn, 1995). These are impressive claims! One reason summary writing is so effective is that it compels students to transform content into their own words and expressions; doing so requires active thought. Another reason is that students must make repeated judgments about the relative importance of ideas. Instruction in summarization teaches students to select important ideas, eliminate details, eliminate redundancies, and integrate the ideas in a synthesized and organized manner. We briefly describe three evidence-based, step-by-step approaches to summary writing.

Barbara Taylor (1986) developed a five-step method of assisting middle schoolers in writing coherent hierarchical summaries:

1. Read only the subheadings of a chapter.
2. List the subheadings on paper.
3. Read the material.
4. Convert each subheading into a main-idea sentence.
5. For each main-idea sentence, add one to three sentences containing supporting details.

Contrast her approach with that of David (Jack) Hayes (1989), who developed an effective group strategy for teaching summary writing. He called it the guided reading and summarizing procedure (GRASP). GRASP also has five steps:

1. After the students have read a section of text, ask them to turn their books face down. Ask them to recall whatever they can from the material. Record their input in a list on the board or on a transparency.
2. Allow the students to return to the text and to locate more information and to make corrections.
3. With student participation, rearrange the information into categories.
4. Help the students write a topic sentence for each category and detail sentences that support it.
5. Engage the students in revising the summary to make it more coherent.

A strategy that has been used successfully with older students and might be useful with younger students is the Generating Interactions between Schemata and Text (GIST) procedure (Cunningham, 1982). In GIST, students begin creating summaries for sentences using 15 spaces. The teacher gradually increases the amount of text being summarized in the 15 spaces. GIST is conducted as a whole-class procedure first, then in small groups, and finally, individually. This concrete visual procedure may hold potential as a summarization strategy for younger children.

Graphic Organizers

A large body of evidence supports the use of graphic organizers to help students organize their ideas. The use of graphic organizers, including story maps, can help students recall the most important story elements. Graphic organizers that reflect the text structures of expository text can help students recall and organize the ideas in informational texts.

Reading Guides

A reading guide is "a list of questions and other tasks to which a child must respond while reading" (McKenna, 2002, p. 132). Reading guides focus a child's attention on the key ideas of the reading selection, and in so doing, model the process of strategic reading. Reading guides are not the same as postreading questions, because students complete the guides *while* they read, not afterward.

Each guide is unique in that a teacher must first decide what is important for students to grasp and then construct tasks for helping them do so. These tasks might include (McKenna & Robinson, 2009):

- Questions to be answered
- Charts to be completed
- Diagrams to be constructed
- Pictures to be drawn
- Responses to be written

There is really no limit to the ways such tasks can be created and interwoven, and there is certainly an element of creativity in constructing a good reading guide! The following steps might be helpful:

- Read the selection carefully.
- Decide which ideas and facts are important to know.
- Create tasks that help students attain this knowledge.
- Include a variety of tasks, not just questions.
- Aim for simple wording.
- Leave plenty of space for children to write.
- Arrange the tasks sequentially.
- Include page numbers and/or subheads.
- Where appropriate, include comprehension aids.

Using reading guides can be effective, but only with adequate preparation. Teachers sometimes balk at the work involved in developing a good guide, but because they are to be completed in class, as the teacher circulates and assists, there is no need to create a conventional lesson. If you teach students at grade 3 or higher, we urge you to try reading guides.

Reciprocal Teaching

Proficient readers apply multiple strategies flexibly as needed to make sense of text. An overarching teaching approach that encompasses several effective strategies is that of reciprocal teaching. Modeled after ReQuest, this approach was introduced by Palincsar and Brown in 1984. According to Duke (2002), reciprocal teaching is among the most thoroughly validated of comprehension strategies, and it deserves careful consideration.

Students work in small groups, applying comprehension strategies to a new reading selection during reading. The teacher and students engage in a discussion about a segment of text structured by four strategies: summarizing, questioning, clarifying, and predicting (Palincsar & Brown, 1984). Initially the teacher explicitly teaches and models each of these strategies for the students. After the strategies have been modeled, the students take turns leading the discussion about each segment of text.

The students begin by examining the reading selection and *predicting* the topic it seems likely to cover. To do so they consider subtitles, pictures, bold-face terminology, and graphic aids. Then the students read a segment of text. A student leader facilitates a dialogue that focuses on the four strategies. The student leader generates a group discussion to clarify any impediments to comprehension. New content may well contain concepts and ideas that are not entirely clear while students are reading. In *clarifying*, they focus on words, ideas, and even pronunciations that may require further explanation. Others in the group may be able to help, as can the teacher. The important point is that they realize where their problems lie.

Students are asked to engage in *questioning* once they have read each portion of a selection. The student discussion leader asks a question about the important information in the text; the other students answer the question and might suggest others. They are encouraged to ask questions at a variety of comprehension levels. Then the student leader *summarizes* the text and predicts what is likely to come next, including a justification for the prediction. The process continues with the students reading the next section of text followed by the discussion led by a different student.

For the proficient reader, all of these strategies are applied internally and independently. The strategies form a kind of dialogue through which good readers attempt to monitor their own comprehension in order to ensure understanding. Struggling readers frequently lack this internal "conversation," and their comprehension suffers as a result. Reciprocal teaching is a means of fostering these healthy mental habits.

Reciprocal teaching can be employed effectively at grades 4 and higher. Evidence indicates that with modifications it also works with students in primary grades. For more on specific steps for implementing this important technique, see McKenna (2002).

Sample Cloze Test

From *The Telltale Heart*
by Edgar Allan Poe

True!—nervous—very, very dreadfully nervous I had been and am; but why *will* you say that I am mad? The disease had sharpened my senses—not destroyed, not dulled them. Above _____ was the sense of _____ acute. I heard all _____ in the heaven and _____ the earth. I heard _____ things in hell. How, _____, am I mad? Hearken! _____observe how healthily, how _____ I can tell you _____ whole story.

It is _____ to say how first _____ idea entered my brain; _____ once conceived, it haunted _____ day and night. Object _____ was none. Passion there _____ none. I loved the _____ man. He had never _____ me. He had never _____ me insult. For his _____ I had no desire. _____ think it was his _____! Yes, it was this! _____ had the eye of _____ vulture—a pale blue _____, with a film over _____. Whenever it fell upon _____, my blood ran cold; _____ so by degrees— very _____—I made up my _____ to take the life _____ the old man, and _____ rid myself of the _____ forever.

Now this is _____ point. You fancy me _____. Madmen know nothing. But _____should have seen *me*. _____ should have seen how _____ I proceeded—with what _____, with what foresight, with _____ dissimulation I went to _____! I was never kinder _____ the old man than _____ the whole week before _____ killed him. And every _____, about midnight, I turned _____ latch of his door _____ opened it—oh, so _____! And then, when I _____ made an opening sufficient _____ my head, I put _____ a dark lantern, all closed, closed, so that no light shone out, and then I thrust in my head. Oh, you would have laughed to see how cunningly I thrust it in! I moved it slowly—very, very slowly, so that I might not disturb the old man's sleep. It took me an hour to place my whole head within the opening so far that I could see him as he lay upon his bed. Ha!—would a madman have been so wise as this?

San Diego Quick Assessment, Form I

Description: Beginning with the three readiness levels (RR[1], RR[2], RR[3]) of recognizing letters as similar, saying letter names, and matching sounds to letters, this test proceeds to recognition of words. Level 1 is representative of PP, Level 2—Primer, Level 3—Grade 1, and to Level 13, which is representative of Grade 11.

Appropriate for: Students at the end of summer vacation or new students entering the classroom without recent or detailed records.

Ages: 5–16, or older students with learning disabilities.

Testing Time: 2 minutes.

Directions for Use: *Preparation:* For this test you will need copies of the 13 SDQA assessment cards. Sequence the cards in ascending order of difficulty.

   You will also need copies of the attached SDQA record sheet.

Administration: Administer each form of the SDQA individually, as follows:

1. Begin with a card that is at least 2 years below the student's grade-level assignment.
2. Ask the student to read the words aloud to you. If he or she misreads any on the list, drop to easier lists until the student makes no errors. This indicates the base level.
3. Place a checkmark (✓) at the appropriate entry on the record sheet for each correct response. This indicates the base level.
4. Direct the child as follows:

   RR[1]: "Which letters are alike?"
   RR[2]: "Name these letters."
   RR[3]: "Circle the letter you think this word begins with."
   1–13: "Read as many of the words on this list as you can."
        "Try to sound out words that are new to you."
        "Don't be afraid to tell me ANY part of a word that you recognize."
   1–13: "Each list gets harder. You won't be able to recognize all of the words,
        but do the best you can."

5. Encourage the student to read words he or she does not know so that you can identify the techniques the student uses for word identification.

Scoring: The list in which a student misses no more than one of the 10 words is the level at which he or she can read independently. Two errors indicate his or her instructional level. Three or more errors identify the level at which reading material will be too difficult for the student.

The type of errors noted in the word substitutions dictates the remediation to be used. For example, students who consistently miss words by starting the word incorrectly:

   toad for *road*
   give for *live*
   digger for *bigger*
   right for *night*

need exercises stressing initial consonants. This is equally true of medial and final errors.

(continued)

B	B		
A	C		
M	M		
C	C		
S	Q		
J	J		
T	T		
H	H		
D	L		
W	M		I–RR[1]

B			
A			
M			
C			
S			
J			
T			
H			
D			
W			I–RR[2]

D	B	A	
A	E	K	
L	F	M	
B	C	G	
O	S	P	
A	B	J	
D	G	T	
A	H	B	
D	I	M	
W	G	J	I–RR[3]

see	
play	
me	
at	
run	
go	
and	
look	
can	
here	I–1

(continued)

you	road
come	live
not	thank
with	when
jump	bigger
help	how
is	always
work	night
are	spring
this I–2	today I–3
our	city
please	middle
myself	moment
town	frightened
early	exclaimed
send	several
wide	lonely
believe	drew
quietly	since
carefully I–4	straight I–5

(continued)

decided		scanty	
served		business	
amazed		develop	
silent		considered	
wrecked		discussed	
improve		behaved	
certainly		splendid	
entered		acquainted	
realized		escape	
interrupted	I–6	grim	I–7
bridge		amber	
commercial		dominion	
abolish		sundry	
trucker		capillary	
apparatus		impetuous	
elementary		blight	
comment		wrest	
necessity		enumerate	
gallery		daunted	
relativity	I–8	condescend	I–9

(continued)

capacious	conscientious
limitations	isolation
pretext	molecule
intrigue	ritual
delusions	momentous
immaculate	vulnerable
ascent	kinship
acrid	conservatism
binoculars	jaunty
embankment I–10	inventive I–11
zany	galore
jerkin	rotunda
nausea	capitalism
gratuitous	prevaricate
linear	risible
inept	exonerate
legality	superannuate
aspen	luxuriate
amnesty	piebald
barometer I–12	crunch I–13

(continued)

SAN DIEGO QUICK ASSESSMENT   Student _____

I-1 (Preprimer)	I-2 (Primer)	I-3 (1st reader)	I-4 (Grade 2)
_____ see	_____ you	_____ road	_____ our
_____ play	_____ come	_____ live	_____ please
_____ me	_____ not	_____ thank	_____ myself
_____ at	_____ with	_____ when	_____ town
_____ run	_____ jump	_____ bigger	_____ early
_____ go	_____ help	_____ how	_____ send
_____ and	_____ is	_____ always	_____ wide
_____ look	_____ work	_____ night	_____ believe
_____ can	_____ are	_____ spring	_____ quietly
_____ here	_____ this	_____ today	_____ carefully

I-5 (Grade 3)	I-6 (Grade 4)	I-7 (Grade 5)	I-8 (Grade 6)
_____ city	_____ decided	_____ scanty	_____ bridge
_____ middle	_____ served	_____ business	_____ commercial
_____ moment	_____ amazed	_____ develop	_____ abolish
_____ frightened	_____ silent	_____ considered	_____ trucker
_____ exclaimed	_____ wrecked	_____ discussed	_____ apparatus
_____ several	_____ improve	_____ behaved	_____ elementary
_____ lonely	_____ certainly	_____ splendid	_____ comment
_____ drew	_____ entered	_____ acquainted	_____ necessity
_____ since	_____ realized	_____ escape	_____ gallery
_____ straight	_____ interrupted	_____ grim	_____ relativity

I-9 (Grade 7)	I-10 (Grade 8)	I-11 (Grade 9)	I-12 (Grade 10)
_____ amber	_____ capacious	_____ conscientious	_____ zany
_____ dominion	_____ limitations	_____ isolation	_____ jerkin
_____ sundry	_____ pretext	_____ molecule	_____ nausea
_____ capillary	_____ intrigue	_____ ritual	_____ gratuitous
_____ impetuous	_____ delusions	_____ momentous	_____ linear
_____ blight	_____ immaculate	_____ vulnerable	_____ inept
_____ wrest	_____ ascent	_____ kinship	_____ leaglity
_____ enumerate	_____ acrid	_____ conservatism	_____ aspen
_____ daunted	_____ binoculars	_____ jaunty	_____ amnesty
_____ condescend	_____ embankment	_____ inventive	_____ barometer

I-13 (Grade 11)

_____ galore
_____ rotunda
_____ capitalism
_____ prevaricate
_____ risible
_____ exonerate
_____ superannuate
_____ luxuriate
_____ piebald
_____ crunch

DATE: _____
ESTIMATED READING LEVELS:
   INDEPENDENT _____
   INSTRUCTIONAL _____
   FRUSTRATION _____

CHAPTER EIGHT

Strategic Knowledge

When you picked this book up, you had a purpose. You knew what you wanted to get out of it and had some tentative strategies that you intended to use to achieve your purpose. If you intended to use this book to find measures that you might use for an individual assessment of a child with reading difficulties, then you have probably skipped over this introduction, since it did not match your purpose. If you are reading this book for a college course, then you might spend a little more time, possibly taking notes. Odds are good that you are in a place that you ordinarily use for studying. Some people like quiet when they study; others like music. You are probably in an environment of your choice. You might be using a highlighter or notecards. Again, different people prefer to use different study techniques. Chances are that you will flip through the material to find out how long it is and how difficult you think it will be. You will estimate the amount of time you will need and compare it with the amount of time that you have before dinner or bed or some other point in the future. You are also likely to be asking yourself what information your college instructor will think is important, as well as what information you feel that you need to get out of the reading. If you are reading this book for a course, you will want to earn as good a grade as possible, which requires figuring out what the teacher will want you to know and making sure you know it.

A second situation is reading a book for pleasure. Here you will sit in a comfortable chair, on a couch, or even lie in bed. You might read before you go to sleep, or outdoors on a sunny weekend. You will not be concerned with how much you remember or what a teacher would ask, nor would you plan to use cards, a highlighter, or any study aids.

These two situations differ in terms of the text used and the purpose for reading, leading to the use of different strategies while reading. As an accomplished reader, you have a broad range of strategies that you can apply to a number of different purposes and texts. In addition, if you are not achieving your purpose during reading, because the text is more difficult than you thought or for some other reason, you can adjust your strategies so that you do achieve those purposes. You would probably allocate different amounts of time for different purposes, according more time for reading a text in detail, for example, in the knowledge that you might be tested.

In the work we have done with children who have reading problems, we find that they often have no idea how to deploy different strategies to achieve different purposes. Often, they are even unaware of their purpose for reading. Children with reading problems tend to focus on the basic decoding of a text, rather than on what they need to get out of it, a habit that persists even after they become competent at decoding and word recognition.

Consider a particular child from one of our clinics. When he was asked how he would study a textbook, he said that he would "start at the beginning and read through to the end." Since he had previously said that he read very slowly, he was asked whether he often made it to the end. He said that he didn't. When asked whether he paid any special notice to bold-faced words or any features of the text, like a summary or headings, he said that he did not. Finally, when asked what kind of grades he received while reading in this way, he replied, "D's and F's." It was unclear from this interview whether he knew that his system of studying was not working, or, if he did, whether he felt there was any other way of doing it.

Given the paucity of strategy instruction in schools, it is likely that no one taught you to be as flexible in your strategy use as we are assuming that you are. Instead, you developed these abilities through trial and error, probably in high school and college. Research has found that teaching children strategies can improve their reading and studying abilities (Afflerbach & Cho, in press; Pressley & Woloshyn, 1995). This instruction can help diminish some of the differences between proficient and struggling readers.

We have found that interviews or self-reports are the best way of ascertaining how strategic children are in their reading. An alternative is to have children think aloud during reading or studying. If children are comfortable with thinking aloud, this approach can supply a very valuable form of data. But most children are not comfortable thinking aloud, so if you do not get useful information, it could be because the child is not able to think about reading strategies, or it could simply be that the child does not know how to handle thinking aloud. The textbook interview is a structured way of having children demonstrate their thinking during reading, which might suffice for this purpose.

GENERAL PURPOSES FOR READING

Proficient and struggling readers differ in their knowledge of general reading purposes. If I asked a proficient reader in fifth grade or above a question such as "What makes someone a good reader?" or "If I gave you something to read, how would you know you were reading it well?" the answer would probably focus on comprehension. For example, the student might reply that good readers understand what they read, or that people are reading well if they understand what they read, if they get the main ideas from their reading, and so on. Struggling readers, even into middle school, tend to focus on decoding. To a struggling reader, good readers are those who say the words correctly, and people who are reading well pronounce all the words correctly in a story. For a question such as "What makes something difficult to read?" proficient readers tend to focus on the ideas or the difficult vocabulary, whereas struggling readers cite "big words."

These differences are likely to be significant; after all, if one does not know the desired end of reading instruction, it is difficult to get there. Differences in the instruction given to children of different reading abilities certainly affect the way they view reading. Allington (1983), reviewing a number of observational studies, identified the following differences:

- Proficient readers tend to have a greater focus on comprehension in their lessons; struggling readers are focused more on word recognition.
- When they miss a word during reading, proficient readers are more likely to be given meaning cues than struggling readers, who tend to receive more decoding cues.
- Proficient readers are interrupted fewer times during their lessons than struggling readers.
- Proficient readers are more likely to read a whole story during a reading period; struggling readers are more likely to read a portion of a story.
- Proficient readers are more likely to read silently; struggling readers are more likely to read aloud.
- Proficient readers cover more material in the course of the school year than struggling readers (Allington, 1984). Moreover, because practice in reading is related to progress, the gap between struggling and proficient readers appears to widen as children move through school (Stanovich, 1986).

The different cues that readers receive, the different focus of instruction, whether students read a story as a whole or not, and how much they are interrupted during reading all seem to lead to different orientations toward reading. These orientations can be turned around relatively easily through comprehension-oriented reading instruction. Even if one's immediate instructional goals are decoding and fluency, a teacher should make sure that the child understands that the purpose of reading is comprehension.

We include several interviews in this chapter. Good general protocols are the Burke Reading Interview (Burke, 1987; Form 8.1, p. 190) and the Awareness of Purposes of Reading Interview (Garner & Kraus, 1981; Form 8.2, p. 191). The Burke Reading Interview is especially suited to younger children, in grades 1 and 2. The Awareness of Purposes Reading Interview can be used with older children.

SPECIFIC PURPOSES AND STRATEGY KNOWLEDGE

As we noted earlier, proficient readers can differentiate among different purposes for reading and can adapt their strategies to accomplish those purposes. Two interviews that can help you ascertain how children adapt their reading for different purposes are provided: the Index of Reading Awareness (Jacobs & Paris, 1987; Form 8.3, pp. 192–197) and a Textbook Interview (Form 8.4, pp. 198–199).

We find that for older children, including the college students we see occasionally, an interview is the most useful means for helping us understand how they approach text and how to change that approach. Older children are very aware of their deficiencies, even if they do not act upon that awareness. A dialogue around a textbook can be useful not only for the examiner but also for the child. This dialogue can include discussion of study strategies, so that the child can learn as much as the examiner. After you have conducted the Burke Reading Interview, note that questions 2 and 4 set up the questions that follow. Questions 3, 5, 6, and 7 elicit the child's orientation toward reading. Note whether the orientation is toward meaning, decoding, or something else. Look for a pattern across these questions. Question 1 elicits the strategies that the child might use during reading. Note whether the child uses one strategy or can provide multiple strategies. We find that struggling readers tend to say they would "sound words out" but cannot give any other strategy. It is important to look for evidence of flexible strategy use, even with young children.

As you interpret the Awareness of Purposes of Reading Interview, note first that questions 1 and 5 are set-up questions. Ignore them. Questions 2, 3, and 4 elicit the child's orientation toward reading. Evaluate them as in the Burke Reading Interview. Question 6 elicits strategies. Again, you are interested in whether a child can list multiple strategies. You are also interested in any independent strategies. Children often say they would "ask my teacher" or "ask my mother." There is nothing wrong with this as a response, but you would prefer the child to suggest some independent strategies.

Finally, the Internet has created the need to be strategic when navigating in hypermedia environments. Its use requires readers to apply strategies that have little or no counterpart in print settings (Duke, Schmar-Dobler, & Zhang, 2006). Unless we are merely "surfing" with no particular goal in mind, it is important to choose among the many available options those that are most likely to get us the results we desire. How well can children pursue purposes when the information they encounter is not arranged as linear text, but is presented as an assortment of text segments, graphics, video, and other features? The interviews we have discussed so far are intended for print environments. They do not get at strategic questions associated with hypermedia settings that children encounter online. To fill this gap, Don Leu and his colleagues (2008) have created an observation instrument to help teachers gauge the proficiencies of their students. Teachers can use various types of data to form their judgments, such as observations made while students work and conversations with individual students. The instrument appears in Form 8.5 (pp. 200–203).

FORM 8.1

Burke Reading Interview

Name _____   Class _____

Date _____   Interviewer _____

1. When you are reading and you come to something you don't know, what do you do?

    Do you ever do anything else?

2. Who is a good reader that you know?

3. What makes him/her a good reader?

4. Do you think that she/he ever comes to something she/he doesn't know when she's/he's reading?

5. (If yes)   When she/he does come to something she/he doesn't know, what do you think she/he does about it?

    (If no)   *Pretend* that she/he does come to something that she/he doesn't know. What do you think she/he does about it?

6. If you knew that someone was having difficulty reading, how would you help them?

7. What would your teacher do to help that person?

8. How did you learn to read?

    What do (they/you) do to help you learn?

9. What would you like to do better as a reader?

10. Do you think that you are a good reader? Why?

FORM 8.2

Awareness of Purposes of Reading Interview

Name _____ Date of Interview _____

1. What kind of reader are you?

2. What makes someone a good reader?

3. If I gave you something to read right now, how would you know you were reading it well?

4. What makes something hard to read?

5. Do you understand everything you read?

6. What do you do if you don't understand something?

191

Index of Reading Awareness

Administration and Scoring

Because of its multiple-choice format, the Index of Reading Awareness may be administered in a group setting. If significant decoding deficits are suspected, it may be wise to read each item aloud to the students (both stem and choices).

The instrument comprises four subtests of five items each. These are Evaluation, Planning, Regulation, and Conditional Knowledge. Each student earns a score for each of these subtests. No composite score is computed. The subtest scores are computed by using the following key. The response to each item receives 0, 1, or 2 points. The subtest score is simply the sum of these points for the five items of that subtest.

Once the subtest scores are determined, the following scale can be used to interpret them:

Subtest score	Interpretation
8–10	No significant weakness.
6–7	Some instructional support needed.
0–5	Serious need for instruction in this area.

Name _____

1. What is the hardest part about reading for you?

   a. Sounding out the hard words.

   b. When you don't understand the story.

   c. Nothing is hard about reading for you.

2. What would help you become a better reader?

   a. If more people would help you when you read.

   b. Reading easier books with shorter words.

   c. Checking to make sure you understand what you read.

3. What is special about the first sentence or two in a story?

   a. They always begin with "Once upon a time . . . "

   b. The first sentences are the most interesting.

   c. They often tell what the story is about.

4. How are the last sentences of a story special?

   a. They are the exciting action sentences.

   b. They tell you what happened.

   c. They are harder to read.

(continued)

_____

From Jacobs and Paris (1987). Copyright 1987 by Taylor & Francis. Reprinted by permission.

5. How can you tell which sentences are the most important ones in a story?

    a. They're the ones that tell the most about the characters and what happens.

    b. They're the most interesting ones.

    c. All of them are important.

6. If you could only read some of the sentences in the story because you were in a hurry, which ones would you read?

    a. Read the sentences in the middle of the story.

    b. Read the sentences that tell you the most about the story.

    c. Read the interesting, exciting sentences.

7. When you tell other people about what you read, what do you tell them?

    a. What happened in the story.

    b. The number of pages in the book.

    c. Who the characters are.

8. If the teacher told you to read a story to remember the general meaning, what would you do?

    a. Skim through the story to find the main parts.

    b. Read all of the story and try to remember everything.

    c. Read the story and remember all of the words.

9. Before you start to read, what kind of plans do you make to help you read better?

    a. You don't make any plans. You just start reading.

    b. You choose a comfortable place.

    c. You think about why you are reading.

10. If you had to read very fast and could only read some words, which ones would you try to read?

    a. Read the new vocabulary words because they are important.

    b. Read the words that you could pronounce.

    c. Read the words that tell the most about the story.

11. What things do you read faster than others?

    a. Books that are easy to read.

    b. When you've read the story before.

    c. Books that have a lot of pictures.

12. Why do you go back and read things over again?

    a. Because it is good practice.

    b. Because you didn't understand it.

    c. Because you forgot some words.

(continued)

13. What do you do if you come to a word and you don't know what it means?

    a.   Use the words around it to figure it out.

    b.   Ask someone else.

    c.   Go on to the next word.

14. What do you do if you don't know what a whole sentence means?

    a.   Read it again.

    b.   Sound out all the words.

    c.   Think about the other sentences in the paragraph.

15. What parts of the story do you skip as you read?

    a.   The hard words and parts you don't understand.

    b.   The unimportant parts that don't mean anything for the story.

    c.   You never skip anything.

16. If you are reading a story for fun, what would you do?

    a.   Look at the pictures to get the meaning.

    b.   Read the story as fast as you can.

    c.   Imagine the story like a movie in your mind.

17. If you are reading for science or social studies, what would you do to remember the information?

    a.   Ask yourself questions about the important ideas.

    b.   Skip the parts you don't understand.

    c.   Concentrate and try hard to remember it.

18. If you are reading for a test, which would help the most?

    a.   Read the story as many times as possible.

    b.   Talk about it with somebody to make sure you understand it.

    c.   Say the sentences over and over.

19. If you are reading a library book to write a report, which would help you the most?

    a.   Sound out words you don't know.

    b.   Write it down in your own words.

    c.   Skip the parts you don't understand.

20. Which of these is the best way to remember a story?

    a.   Say every word over and over.

    h   Think about remembering it.

    c.   Write it down in your own words.

(continued)

SCORING GUIDE

EVALUATION

1.   What is the hardest part about reading for you?

1   a.   Sounding out the hard words.

2   b.   When you don't understand the story.

0   c.   Nothing is hard about reading for you.

2.   What would help you become a better reader?

1   a.   If more people would help you when you read.

0   b.   Reading easier books with shorter words.

2   c.   Checking to make sure you understand what you read.

3.   What is special about the first sentence or two in a story?

1   a.   They always begin with "Once upon a time . . . "

0   b.   The first sentences are the most interesting.

2   c.   They often tell what the story is about.

4.   How are the last sentences of a story special?

1   a.   They are the exciting action sentences.

2   b.   They tell you what happened.

0   c.   They are harder to read.

5.   How can you tell which sentences are the most important ones in a story?

2   a.   They're the ones that tell the most about the characters and what happens.

1   b.   They're the most interesting ones.

0   c.   All of them are important.

PLANNING

6.   If you could only read some of the sentences in the story because you were in a hurry, which ones would you read?

0   a.   Read the sentences in the middle of the story.

2   b.   Read the sentences that tell you the most about the story.

1   c.   Read the interesting, exciting sentences.

(continued)

7. When you tell other people about what you read, what do you tell them?

2   a.   What happened in the story.

0   b.   The number of pages in the book.

1   c.   Who the characters are.

8. If the teacher told you to read a story to remember the general meaning, what would you do?

2   a.   Skim through the story to find the main parts.

1   b.   Read all of the story and try to remember everything.

0   c.   Read the story and remember all of the words.

9. Before you start to read, what kind of plans do you make to help you read better?

0   a.   You don't make any plans. You just start reading.

1   b.   You choose a comfortable place.

2   c.   You think about why you are reading.

10. If you had to read very fast and could only read some words, which ones would you try to read?

1   a.   Read the new vocabulary words because they are important.

0   b.   Read the words that you could pronounce.

2   c.   Read the words that tell the most about the story.

REGULATION

11. What things do you read faster than others?

1   a.   Books that are easy to read.

2   b.   When you've read the story before.

0   c.   Books that have a lot of pictures.

12. Why do you go back and read things over again?

1   a.   Because it is good practice.

2   b.   Because you didn't understand it.

0   c.   Because you forgot some words.

13. What do you do if you come to a word and you don't know what it means?

2   a.   Use the words around it to figure it out.

1   b.   Ask someone else.

0   c.   Go on to the next word.

(continued)

14.   What do you do if you don't know what a whole sentence means?

1   a.   Read it again.

0   b.   Sound out all the words.

2   c.   Think about the other sentences in the paragraph.

15.   What parts of the story do you skip as you read?

1   a.   The hard words and parts you don't understand.

2   b.   The unimportant parts that don't mean anything for the story.

0   c.   You never skip anything.

CONDITIONAL KNOWLEDGE

16.   If you are reading a story for fun, what would you do?

1   a.   Look at the pictures to get the meaning.

0   b.   Read the story as fast as you can.

2   c.   Imagine the story like a movie in your mind.

17.   If you are reading for science or social studies, what would you do to remember the information?

2   a.   Ask yourself questions about the important ideas.

0   b.   Skip the parts you don't understand.

1   c.   Concentrate and try hard to remember it.

18.   If you are reading for a test, which would help the most?

1   a.   Read the story as many times as possible.

2   b.   Talk about it with somebody to make sure you understand it.

0   c.   Say the sentences over and over.

19.   If you are reading a library book to write a report, which would help you the most?

1   a.   Sound out words you don't know.

2   b.   Write it down in your own words.

0   c.   Skip the parts you don't understand.

20.   Which of these is the best way to remember a story?

0   a.   Say every word over and over.

1   b.   Think about remembering it.

2   c.   Write it down in your own words.

Textbook Interview

Name _____   Date _____
Grade _____

Directions: For this section, use the student's classroom basal reader. If no basal is used in the classroom, select a piece of literature that is representative of classroom reading materials. Place the text in front of the student. As each question is asked, open the appropriate text in front of the student to help provide a point of reference for the question.

Basal Reader or Literature

Open to a story that the student has not yet read.

1. Why do we read this kind of book? [*Note*: Possible answers might be "to learn to read" or "enjoyment."]

2. Why do you think your teacher wants you to read this book?

3. Describe how you might read this story in class?

4. Do you enjoy reading this type of material? [Probe for a fuller answer than "yes" or "no"]

5. What do you need to do to get a good grade in reading?

Directions: For this section, use a content area text, preferably the one the student uses in the classroom. Choose a text that has a great many features, such as bold-faced words, headings, a summary, etc. Place the text in front of the student. As each question is asked, open the appropriate text in front of the student to help provide a point of reference for the question. This is an informal interview. You can integrate questions 8–12 into a natural conversation.

6. Why do we read this kind of book? [*Note*: Possible answers might be "to learn from" or "to learn to read from."]

7. Why do you think your teacher wants you to read this book?

(continued)

8. [Open to a chapter somewhat beyond where the child has already covered.] Suppose you were to be given a test on this chapter. How would you read it? [Have the child model his or her reading, showing you the things that he or she would do.]

9. Would you pay attention to any particular parts of the text? [Possible answers: bold-faced words, chapter summary, headings, etc.]

10. [If not included in the answer to #9] Would you pay attention to these? [Point to bold-faced words.] What are these for?

11. [If not included in the answer to #9] Would you pay attention to these? [Point to headings.] What are these for?

12. [If not included in the answer to #9] Would you pay attention to this? [Point to summary at the end of the chapter.] What is this for?

13. [If not included in the answer to #9] Would you pay attention to these? [Point to questions at the end of the chapter.] What are these for?

14. Does the teacher do anything additional to help you study? [Probe for study guides, prequestioning, and so on.]

15. How well do you do on tests on this type of material?

16. What do you have to do to get a good grade in _____?

17. What do you think you need to do in order to do better?

18. Have you ever tried skimming before you read a chapter to get an idea of what it is about?

19. Have you ever tried summarizing or making notes to remember what you've read?

20. Have you ever tried asking yourself questions to remember what you've read?

TICA Phase 2 Checklist

Most of the students and all of the groups in my class know how to:	
Understand and Develop Questions	Lesson Evidence and Comments
Teacher-Generated Questions	
☐ Use strategies to ensure initial understanding of the question such as: • Rereading the question to make sure they understand it. • Paraphrasing the question. • Taking notes on the question. • Thinking about the needs of the person who asked the question.	
☐ Use strategies to monitor an understanding of the question such as: • Knowing when to review the question. • Checking an answer in relation to the question to ensure it is complete.	
Student-Generated Questions	
☐ Determine what a useful initial question is, based on a variety of factors that include interest, audience, purpose, and the nature of the inquiry activity.	
☐ Determine a clear topic and focus for questions to guide the search for information.	
☐ Modify questions, when appropriate, using strategies such as the following: • Narrowing the focus of the question. • Expanding the focus of the question. • Developing a new or revised question that is more appropriate after gathering information.	
Locate Information	Lesson Evidence and Comments
Locating Information by Using a Search Engine and Its Results Page	
☐ Locate at least one search engine.	
☐ Use key words in a search window on a browser that has this or on a separate search engine.	
☐ Use several of the following general search engine strategies during key word entry: • Topic and focus • Single and multiple key word entries • Phrases for key word entry	
☐ Use several of the following more specialized search engine strategies during key word entry: • Quotation marks • Paraphrases and synonyms • Boolean • Advanced search tool use	

Note. These skills and strategies inform and guide instruction during Phase 1, but they are not intended to limit instruction. New skill and strategy needs will emerge within each classroom. Each teacher must respond to (and document) those additional skill and strategy needs during the year. When most students and all groups can accomplish this list, the move to Phase 2 will take place

☐	Copy and paste keywords and phases into the search engine window while searching for information.	
☐	Read search engine results effectively to determine the most useful resource for a task using strategies such as: • Knowing which portions of a search results page are sponsored, containing commercially placed links, and which are not. • Skimming the main results before reading more narrowly. • Reading summaries carefully and inferring meaning in the search engine results page to determine the best possible site to visit. • Understanding the meaning of bold face terms in the results. • Understanding the meaning of URLs in search results (.com, .org, .edu, .net). • Knowing when the first item is not the best item for a question. • Monitoring the extent to which a search results page matches the information needs. • Knowing how to use the history pull-down menu.	
☐	Monitor the multiple aspects of search engine use and make appropriate revisions and changes throughout the process.	
☐	Select from a variety of search engine strategies to locate useful resources when an initial search is unsuccessful: • Knows the use and meaning of the "Did you mean . . . ?" feature in Google. • Adjusts search engine keywords according to the results of a search. • Narrows the search. • Expands the search. • Reads search results to discover the correct vocabulary and then use this more appropriate vocabulary in a new search. • Shifts to another search engine.	
☐	Bookmark a site and access it later.	
☐	Use specialized search engines for images, videos, and other media sources.	
Locating Information within a Website		
☐	Quickly determine whether a site is potentially useful and worth more careful reading.	
☐	Read more carefully at a site to determine whether the required information is located there.	
☐	Predict information behind a link accurately to make efficient choices about where information is located.	
☐	Use structural knowledge of a Web page to help locate information, including the use of directories.	
☐	Recognize when you have left a site and know how to return back to the original site.	
☐	Know how to open a second browser window to locate information, without losing the initial Web page.	
☐	Know how to use an internal search engine to locate information at a site.	
☐	Monitor the reading of a Web page and knows when it contains useful information and when it does not.	

(continued)

Critically Evaluate Information	Lesson Evidence and Comments
Bias and Stance	
☐ Identify, evaluate, and recognize that all websites have an agenda, perspective, or bias.	
☐ Identify and evaluate bias, given a website with a clear bias.	
☐ Identify and evaluate the author of a website whenever visiting an important new site.	
☐ Use information about the author of a site to evaluate how information will be biased at that site.	
Reliability	
☐ Investigate multiple sources to compare and contrast the reliability of information.	
☐ Identify several markers that may affect reliability such as: • Is this a commercial site? • Is the author an authoritative source (e.g., professor, scientist, librarian, etc.)? • Does the website have links that are broken? • Does the information make sense? • Does the author include links to other reliable websites? • Does the website contain numerous typos? • Does the URL provide any clues to reliability? • Do the images or videos appear to be altered?	
☐ Understand that Wikipedia is a reasonable, but imperfect, portal of information.	
☐ Identify the general purpose of a website (entertainment, educational, commercial, persuasive, exchange of information, social, etc.).	
☐ Identify the form of a website (e.g., blog, forum, advertisement, informational website, commercial website, government website, etc.) and use this information when considering reliability.	
Accuracy	
☐ Evaluate information based on the degree to which it is likely to be accurate by verifying and consulting alternative and/or especially reliable sources.	

Synthesize Information	Lesson Evidence and Comments
☐ Understand both the specific information related to the task as well as the broader context within which that information is located.	
☐ Synthesize information from multiple media sources including written prose, audio, visual, video, and/or tables and graphs.	
☐ Separate relevant information from irrelevant information.	
☐ Organize information effectively.	
☐ Manage multiple sources both on- and offline, including: • Choose tools to meet the needs of managing information (file folders, electronic file folders, notebooks, e-mail, etc.). • Cite sources. • Take notes with paper and pencil, when appropriate. • Take notes with a word processor, when appropriate. • Type notes using short cut strokes such as highlight/cut/copy/paste.	

(continued)

Communicate Information	Lesson Evidence and Comments
☐ Understand that messages have consequences and will influence how others react.	
☐ Use a variety of offline writing/editing tools, such as a word processor spell-checker, dictionary, thesaurus, pdf, etc.	
☐ Copy/paste text or URL to use in the message	
☐ Know how to use e-mail, including attaching and downloading attachments, logging in, sending messages, and opening messages.	
☐ Know how to use instant messaging.	
☐ Know how to use blogs, including reading and posting information.	
☐ Monitor communication of information for audience or voice (i.e., formal vs. informal writing styles).	
☐ Use a wide array of Internet-based forms of communication, such as: • E-mail and attachments • Blogs • Wikis • Google Docs • Instant messaging • Websites • Presentation software	
☐ Are aware of the audience and the relationship between audience, purpose, medium, and message.	
☐ Know how to include multiple-media sources within messages.	
☐ Use formatting such as headings and subheadings to communicate the organization of information within informational text.	

CHAPTER NINE

Affective Factors

If you hope to influence students' attitudes toward reading in a truly substantial way, you must first know something about your children. How positive are their attitudes? What are their likes and dislikes? How do their friends and family feel about reading? A good starting point is to familiarize yourself with the basics concerning reading attitudes—how they're formed, the chief trends you can expect, and the interest areas on which you might be able to capitalize.

ORIGINS OF ATTITUDES

Attitudes are learned. They are not innate but develop over time as the result of cultural forces and our own day-to-day experiences with reading and books. The more positive these forces are, the more likely it is that a child will become a lifelong reader. We can summarize these forces quite simply. Our attitudes toward reading are shaped by:

1. Each and every reading experience.
2. Our beliefs about what will happen when we open a book.
3. Our beliefs about how those we hold in high regard feel about reading.

All three of these forces are subject to teacher intervention—even the last! Effective attitude-building strategies, such as those described here, target one or more of the factors.

WHAT DO WE KNOW ABOUT CHILDREN'S ATTITUDES?

Studies have led to several important conclusions that are useful in understanding what we, as teachers, can expect (McKenna, 2001; McKenna, Kear, & Ellsworth, 1995). Here, in brief, are the major findings of reading attitude research:

1. Reading attitudes tend to worsen over time.
2. Reading attitudes worsen more rapidly for poor readers.
3. Girls tend to possess more positive reading attitudes than boys
4. Ethnic group membership is not, in itself, strongly related to reading attitudes.
5. Instructional methods can have a positive influence on attitudes.

WHAT DO WE KNOW ABOUT CHILDREN'S INTERESTS?

An interest area is really an attitude toward reading about a particular topic. In other words, we have a general attitude toward reading, and we have specific attitudes toward reading about certain subjects. For instance, you may love to read but hate the thought of reading science-fiction books. Knowing about children's interest areas arms teachers with the know-how they need to recommend books that match existing enthusiasms. Through these positive experiences, children come to realize that books afford a means of satisfying and furthering the interests they already have.

Studies of children's reading interests offer useful generalizations that may confirm your own instincts and classroom observations (e.g., McKenna, 1986, 2001). Here are some of the most important findings:

1. The number of interests declines with age.
2. The influence of gender increases with age.
3. Girls are more likely to read "boys' books" than are boys to read "girls' books."
4. Typical male interests include science, machines, sports, and action/adventure.
5. Typical female interests include interpersonal relationships and romance.
6. Three interest areas of strong appeal, regardless of gender or reading ability, are humor, animals, and the unusual.

ASSESSING ATTITUDES AND INTERESTS

It is vital to keep in mind that conclusions based on research are simply generalizations. Although they adequately describe large populations of children and can guide our thinking as we plan instruction and form broad expectations, the attitudes and interests of an individual child may differ sharply from the norm. This is why it is always important to assess children and not merely to assume that they conform to stereotypical patterns. Some useful ways of gathering information about your students include the following:

- Classroom observation
- Tracking entries in students' reading journals
- Administering open-ended questionnaires
- Administering interest inventories
- Administering attitude surveys

These activities complement each other nicely. The information offered by each is unique and contributes to a complete picture of the child as a developing reader. Let's look briefly at each.

Classroom Observation

Observing children as they take part in classroom activities can provide you with valuable information about their likes and dislikes. One way to systematize these observations is to jot them briefly into a log, which can be kept in a child's portfolio. Entries might include notations such as these:

9/25	Beth told me she really liked the Critter books.
10/14	Beth's mom said she wants to be a scientist.
11/2	Beth checked out two books about snakes.

Reading Journals

Another means of gathering data about students' attitudes and interests is by reading the entries in their reading journals. Some teachers require students to make regular entries in such journals. These typically include the title of each book they complete, the date, and a brief response to the material. Journals also might contain general commentaries about reading. An advantage of reading journals is that they compel students to reflect upon their feelings toward reading and about their emerging identities as readers. Journaling also encourages students to form critical judgments about what they've read and conveys the message that their opinions count. This significance becomes especially evident to students when teachers add written responses to their entries. Reading journals also offer a good opportunity for writing development and provide a meaningful context in which to apply writing skills.

An important cautionary note about reading journals: Do not allow them to turn into a series of book reports. You do not want to create the expectation that every book your students read for "pleasure" will inevitably be followed by a laborious writing exercise. Setting some guidelines at the beginning regarding your expectations—and making sure those expectations are modest—can prevent this undesirable shift from occurring.

Open-Ended Questionnaires

A good get-acquainted activity involves asking students to respond to incomplete sentences designed to elicit personal beliefs about reading as well as existing interests. These need not be long and involved—a few statements can go a long way. These statements can be used as a written activity in a group setting (in which case they also reveal information about writing development) or individually as an interview guide, in which you provide each sentence starter orally and jot down the student's response. Try using the questionnaire in Form 9.1 (p. 213) as a starting point and modify it as appropriate.

Interest Inventories

An interest inventory is a list of topics used to identify those that individual students find most appealing. They're easy to make and simple to give, and the results can be very helpful in recommending books that are likely to engage students' interest. In other words, interest inventories can make you a better book broker! They can be given to your class as a group as long as you read the choices aloud, so that poor decoding does not prevent children from making informed choices.

Form 9.2 (p. 214) is a sample interest inventory that you are free to duplicate or modify. Or you can start from scratch. Whichever route you take, here are some guidelines that might help:

- Save your inventory in a computer file so that you can add or delete topics after you've used it a few times.
- Make sure you can deliver the goods—don't include topics for which you have no materials.
- Include a wide range of topics, including those typically of interest to boys and to girls.
- Include topics that might suggest nonfiction titles as well as fiction.
- Add a few blank lines at the end. An interest inventory is like a ballot, and a place for write-ins should be provided! (Trying to fully anticipate kids' interests can be frustrating.)
- Don't mention reading when you give the directions. A negative attitude may lead to negative responses even for true interests.
- Make it easy to respond. Try asking kids to "grade" each topic, just as a teacher might, using whatever grading system they know (such as *A*, *B*, *C*, *D*, *F*). This method provides more detailed information than a checklist, because it indicates the *strength* of the interest.
- Keep completed inventories where you can find them, perhaps in portfolios.
- Use the topics that receive the highest "grades" to recommend books to individual students.

Attitude Surveys

Rating scales are available for assessing the general reading attitudes of your students. The results can be easily quantified and will provide an accurate barometer of how positive (or negative) attitudes may be. They also can be used on a pre–post basis to document progress over the course of a year.

Elementary Reading Attitude Survey

The Elementary Reading Attitude Survey (ERAS) (Form 9.3, pp. 215–223) is based on the cartoon character Garfield. It is reprinted together with directions for administering, scoring, and interpreting it (McKenna & Kear, 1990). Permission has been granted from cartoonist Jim Davis, creator of Garfield and codeveloper of the ERAS, to duplicate the survey for classroom use. You'll even find a table of percentile ranks, so you can see how your students compare to a national sample of more than 17,000 children. A one-page version is provided for older students, and a downloadable version is available on the Professor Garfield website (*www.professorgarfield.org/pgf_Intro.html*).

Motivations for Reading Questionnaire

The Motivations for Reading Questionnaire (MRQ) (Form 9.4, pp. 224–230), designed by Gambrell, Palmer, Codling, and Mazzoni (1995), can be used in grades 3 and above to gauge a range of affective dimensions. This instrument was developed at the National Reading Research Center.

Reader Self-Perception Scale

This group instrument (Form 9.5, pp. 231–234), designed by Henk and Melnick (1995), provides a window onto how students see themselves as readers. Its domain overlaps slightly with that of the MRQ.

Reading Activity Inventory

The Reading Activity Inventory (RAI) (Form 9.6, pp. 235–240), an instrument developed by Guthrie, McGough, and Wigfield (1994), is designed to reveal the amount and types of reading your students do. Like the ERAS and MRQ, it can be administered on a group basis.

Title Recognition Test

This clever group survey (Form 9.7, pp. 241–242) by Cunningham and Stanovich (1991) indirectly measures attitude by assessing students' knowledge of well-known titles—well known to literacy educators and well-read children, that is. In theory, the more reading students have done, the more titles they should be able to select from a list that includes fictitious distractors.

Adolescent Reading Attitudes Survey

This new instrument, designed by McKenna, Nagel, Conradi, and Lawrence (2008), is intended to complement the ERAS by targeting students in the middle and secondary grades. It contains four subscales: (1) recreational reading in print settings, (2) academic reading in print settings, (3) recreational reading in digital settings, and (4) academic reading in digital settings. Student responses enable teachers to tease out important attitude profiles that might offer clues about how best to reach older students. The survey appears in Form 9.8 (pp. 243–245).

ADDRESSING NEGATIVE ATTITUDES

To make progress with children who are not predisposed to read, it is important to ask why they do not enjoy this crucial activity. The answers are not always clear, but a few basic questions can help clarify the situation.

Is the Attitude Problem the Result of Poor Decoding?

No one voluntarily engages in an activity that is frustrating. Dysfluent reading, with all of its natural frustrations, can be a barrier to positive attitudes. Apart from fostering proficiency, teachers can initiate the following actions:

- *Read aloud to children.* Doing so relieves students of the burden of decoding while acquainting them with interesting books and giving them a clearer vision of the benefits of proficient reading.
- *Make materials of appropriate difficulty available.* Sometimes called "hi–lo" books, these materials aim to interest older children but place few demands on their limited decoding and vocabulary. An excellent source of these books is Phelan (1996).
- *Use electronic supports.* E-books with pronunciation supports can make it possible for students to read independently, because they remove the decoding barrier without the need for constant teacher presence. Somewhat less desirable are audiotapes of books—although these can bring literature to life, they do little to further word recognition development.

Is the Attitude Problem the Result of Uninteresting Materials?

Teachers must become "brokers," using their knowledge of books on the one hand and children's interests on the other to recommend appropriate matches. This is why interest inventories can be so important. Teachers must still "deliver the goods," however. Specifically, we recommend the following possibilities:

- *Establish an extensive classroom library.* Don't worry about the condition of the materials—aim for quality and variety. Include back copies of magazines that you can get from the media specialist. Visit garage sales and flea markets. Don't forget the free books you can earn by having your children participate in book clubs. House the books in plastic tubs or baskets.
- *Don't forget nonfiction.* Teachers often forget that nonfiction can be just as appealing to children as literature. In fact, many find it more engaging. Moreover, the ability

to read nonfiction is vital to eventual success in the workplace, so there is a powerful educational rationale for including nonfiction titles in your classroom library. Strive for an effective balance.

• *Note the Children's Choice Awards.* Research shows that award-winning books are not always popular with children, at least when the awards are decided on by adults. This conclusion makes sense when we stop to consider that children's sensibilities and worldviews differ substantially from ours and that it is often difficult to put ourselves in their place. Awards are frequently given to the kinds of books we, as teachers, would like to see our students reading, rather than what children might prefer to read. The fact that a particular book attains critical appeal should not be regarded as unerring testimony about how well kids will like it. One means of contending with this dilemma is to rely on polls conducted among children and teens. Each year the International Reading Association conducts two such polls, one among children ages 5–13, and the other among students in grades 7–12. The books evaluated in these polls are submitted by publishers and must meet certain criteria before they are distributed to classrooms around the country for rating. For example, each book submitted for consideration as a Young Adults' Choice must have received two positive published reviews. In reality, then, adults do have a say about which books qualify, but the final ratings are rendered by students—a vital difference.

• *Include series books.* These can be sequential books (e.g., the Laura Ingalls Wilder series) or books that simply reuse characters (e.g., *Curious George, Clifford*). One advantage of series books is that if a child becomes interested in one, then an entire line of additional books suddenly attains high appeal. A second advantage is that such books are easier to comprehend, because so much of the prior knowledge needed to understand them (information about characters, setting, and typical plot structures) is already present as a result of having read other books in the series.

• *Include illustrated books.* Research shows that older struggling readers often lack the ability to visualize the events about which they read. Illustrated books can support them by providing visual images. This support will lead to a greater willingness to read. The *Illustrated Classics*, for example, provide one drawing on every other page; they are "naturals" for coaxing reluctant readers into extended reading by providing them with the support they need.

What Instructional Techniques Are Effective in Fostering Positive Attitudes?

Although there is no magic bullet, some techniques and activities have yielded good results:

• *Bring in adult models.* Try inviting a variety of adults over the course of a year to speak to your class about their own reading. Individuals such as the principal, the custodian, or the school nurse can convey the message that *everybody* reads; of course, outside visitors can bring the same message. Consider extending invitations to those who reflect the cultural backgrounds of your class.

- *Be a good model yourself.* If reading is worth doing, you must be seen doing it yourself. Children must observe that you, in fact, practice what you preach. Bring and talk about what you've read, whether it's a bestseller, a teacher resource book, or an article from a magazine or newspaper. You will be modeling not only the value of reading as a part of life outside school but the social process of sharing what we read with one another.

- *Provide time for recreational reading.* This protected block of time has been called Drop Everything and Read (DEAR), Uninterrupted Sustained Silent Reading (U.S.S.R.), and Self-Selected Reading (SSR). Regardless of the name, it is a method of scheduling time during the school day for recreational reading by providing the opportunity to explore books in a relaxed atmosphere, without the threat of accountability. It also affords students another means of becoming more proficient by reading in pleasant, authentic contexts.

- *Be cautious of incentive programs.* Outside incentive programs designed to encourage children's reading are a matter of ongoing debate. The Accelerated Reader, Pizza Hut's Book-It program, Scholastic's Reading Counts, and various schoolwide goals (such as the principal or library media specialist kissing a pig, jumping into a tub of Jell-O, etc.) are now commonplace in elementary and middle schools. There is no debate about the fact that these programs can increase the amount of reading children do. Whether they lead to lifelong reading habits is far less certain, although two facts argue that some children may indeed come to value reading more highly. First, the increased amount of reading undoubtedly makes some children more proficient, and having to contend with poor proficiency is a sure way *not* to become an avid reader. Second, by reading in quantity, children are inadvertently exposed to a variety of books, and their perspectives on what is available are broadened. One clever modification is to use *books* as an incentive!

- *Consider cross-age tutoring.* Placing older and younger children together for tutoring can bolster the attitudes of the older students, particularly if they themselves are experiencing problems. The logistics of coordinating your efforts with another teacher are worth the effort. The tutoring need not be technical and is perhaps best when limited to the sharing of books chosen by the older partner.

- *Employ literature circles.* Literature circles, also called literature response groups and literature study groups, are student discussion groups in which risk-free exchanges about mutually read books are invited. In these circles, students interact with other members of the same age and similar cultural background—which, research suggests, can lead to improved attitudes toward reading (e.g., Leal, 1993). The rationale of literature circles is persuasive. Literature groups offer one way to model the sort of behavior that teachers should seek to foster in children if they are to participate in a literate culture. Although reading is typically a solitary activity, it is also an inherently social act involving at least two individuals: reader and writer. In the case of published works, multiple readers afford the opportunity of introducing a second social dimension among readers of the same work. Exposure to peers with positive reading attitudes may improve a struggling reader's perception of reading. Moreover, discussion among readers has the potential to broaden children's critical perspectives on what reading is.

• *Try idea circles.* Literature groups typically bring students together to discuss the *fiction* book(s) they have all read. Guthrie and McCann (1996) discovered that using *nonfiction* as the basis of these discussions can be highly motivating as well. Best of all, kids need not have read the same selection. Rather, the common element is the topic. Guthrie and McCann define an idea circle as a "peer-led, small-group discussion of concepts fueled by multiple text sources" (p. 88). In an idea circle, everyone has something unique to contribute to the discussion by virtue of having read a different source. You can differentiate these assignments deftly, ensuring that abler readers undertake more challenging materials. You may need to take precautions, however, to guard against one or two students' taking over the discussion and eclipsing others. Spelling out some simple ground rules in advance can foster balanced discussions. For example, the discussion might begin with each student sharing one fact he or she discovered. A moderator also might be appointed, whose duty is to solicit input from all participants.

FORM 9.1

Here's How I Feel about Reading

Name _____

1. I like to read about _____ _____ .

2. My friends think reading is _____ _____ .

3. My favorite book is _____ .

4. At home, reading is _____ .

5. On weekends, my favorite thing to do is _____ .

6. When I get older, I'll read _____ .

7. I like books about _____ .

8. When we read library books at school, I _____ .

9. The best thing about reading is _____ .

10. The worst thing about reading is _____ .

Tell Me What You Like!

Name _____

Which topics do you like the most? Pretend you're a teacher and give each one of these a grade. Give it an *A* if you really like it, a *B* if you like it pretty well, a *C* if it's just OK, a *D* if you don't like it, and an *F* if you can't stand it! If I've missed some topics you really like, please write them on the lines at the bottom of the page.

_____	sports	_____	monsters
_____	animals	_____	horses
_____	magic	_____	detectives
_____	jokes	_____	love
_____	exploring the unknown	_____	famous scientists
_____	sharks	_____	ghosts
_____	camping	_____	other countries
_____	UFOs	_____	dogs
_____	spiders	_____	cooking
_____	the jungle	_____	the ocean
_____	drawing, painting	_____	music
_____	riddles	_____	science fiction
_____	friendship	_____	cats
_____	snakes	_____	families
_____	the wilderness	_____	the desert
_____	fishing	_____	computers

What other topics do you really like? Write them here:

_____

_____

_____

FORM 9.3

Elementary Reading Attitude Survey

Directions for Use

The Elementary Reading Attitude Survey provides a quick indication of student attitudes toward reading. It consists of 20 items and can be administered to an entire classroom in about 10 minutes. Each item presents a brief, simply-worded statement about reading, followed by four pictures of Garfield. Each pose is designed to depict a different emotional state, ranging from very positive to very negative.

Administration

Begin by telling students that you wish to find out how they feel about reading. Emphasize that this is not a test and that there are no "right" answers. Encourage sincerity.

Distribute the survey forms and, if you wish to monitor the attitudes of specific students, ask them to write their names in the space at the top. Hold up a copy of the survey so that the students can see the first page. Point to the picture of Garfield at the far left of the first item. Ask the students to look at this same picture on their own survey form. Discuss with them the mood Garfield seems to be in (very happy). Then move to the next picture and again discuss Garfield's mood (this time, a little happy). In the same way, move to the third and fourth pictures and talk about Garfield's moods—a little upset and very upset. It is helpful to point out the position of Garfield's mouth, especially in the middle two figures.

Explain that together you will read some statements about reading and that the students should think about how they feel about each statement. They should then circle the picture of Garfield that is closest to their own feelings. (Emphasize that the students should respond according to their own feelings, not as Garfield might respond!) Read each item aloud slowly and distinctly; then read it a second time while students are thinking. Be sure to read the item number and to remind students of page numbers when new pages are reached.

Scoring

To score the survey, count 4 points for each leftmost (happiest) Garfield circled, 3 for each slightly smiling Garfield, 2 for each mildly upset Garfield, and 1 point for each very upset (rightmost) Garfield. Three scores for each student can be obtained: the total for the first 10 items, the total for the second 10, and a composite total. The first half of the survey relates to attitude toward recreational reading; the second half relates to attitude toward academic aspects of reading.

Interpretation

You can interpret scores in two ways. One is to note informally where the score falls in regard to the four nodes of the scale. A total score of 50, for example, would fall about midway on the scale, between the slightly happy and slightly upset figures, therefore indicating a relatively indifferent overall attitude toward reading. The other approach is more formal. It involves converting the raw scores into percentile ranks by means of Table 1. Be sure to use the norms for the right grade level and to note the column headings (Rec = recreational reading, Aca = academic reading, Tot = total score). If you wish to determine the average percentile rank for your class, average the raw scores first; then use the table to locate the percentile rank corresponding to the raw score mean. Percentile ranks cannot be averaged directly.

(continued)

Midyear percentile ranks by grade and scale

Raw Scr	Grade 1			Grade 2			Grade 3			Grade 4			Grade 5			Grade 6		
	Rec	Aca	Tot	Rec	Aca	Tot	Rec	Aca	Tot	Rec	Aca	Tot	Rec	Aca	Tot	Rec	Aca	Tot
80			99			99			99			99			99			99
79			95			96			98			99			99			99
78			93			95			97			98			99			99
77			92			94			97			98			99			99
76			90			93			96			97			98			99
75			88			92			95			96			98			99
74			86			90			94			95			97			99
73			84			88			92			94			97			98
72			82			86			91			93			96			98
71			80			84			89			91			95			97
70			78			82			86			89			94			96
69			75			79			84			88			92			95
68			72			77			81			86			91			93
67			69			74			79			83			89			92
66			66			71			76			80			87			90
65			62			69			73			78			84			88
64			59			66			70			75			82			86
63			55			63			67			72			79			84
62			52			60			64			69			76			82
61			49			57			61			66			73			79
60			46			54			58			62			70			76
59			43			51			55			59			67			73
58			40			47			51			56			64			69
57			37			45			48			53			61			66
56			34			41			44			48			57			62
55			31			38			41			45			53			58
54			28			35			38			41			50			55
53			25			32			34			38			46			52
52			22			29			31			35			42			48
51			20			26			28			32			39			44
50			18			23			25			28			36			40
49			15			20			23			26			33			37
48			13			18			20			23			29			33
47			12			15			17			20			26			30
46			10			13			15			18			23			27
45			8			11			13			16			20			25
44			7			9			11			13			17			22
43			6			8			9			12			15			20
42			5			7			8			10			13			17
41			5			6			7			9			12			15
40	99	99	4	99	99	5	99	99	6	99	99	7	99	99	10	99	99	13
39	92	91	3	94	94	4	96	97	5	97	98	6	98	99	9	98	99	12
38	89	88	3	92	92	3	94	95	4	95	97	5	96	98	8	97	99	10
37	86	85	2	88	89	2	90	93	3	92	95	4	94	98	7	95	99	8
36	81	79	2	84	85	2	87	91	2	88	93	3	91	96	6	92	98	7
35	77	75	1	79	81	1	81	88	2	84	90	3	87	95	4	88	97	6
34	72	69	1	74	78	1	75	83	2	78	87	2	82	93	4	83	95	5
33	65	63	1	68	73	1	69	79	1	72	83	2	77	90	3	79	93	4
32	58	58	1	62	67	1	63	74	1	66	79	1	71	86	3	74	91	3
31	52	53	1	56	62	1	57	69	0	60	75	1	65	82	2	69	87	2
30	44	49	1	50	57	0	51	63	0	54	70	1	59	77	1	63	82	2
29	38	44	0	44	51	0	45	58	0	47	64	1	53	71	1	58	78	1
28	32	39	0	37	46	0	38	52	0	41	58	1	48	66	1	51	73	1
27	26	34	0	31	41	0	33	47	0	35	52	1	42	60	1	46	67	1
26	21	30	0	25	37	0	26	41	0	29	46	0	36	54	0	39	60	1
25	17	25	0	20	32	0	21	36	0	23	40	0	30	49	0	34	54	0
24	12	21	0	15	27	0	17	31	0	19	35	0	25	42	0	29	49	0
23	9	18	0	11	23	0	13	26	0	14	29	0	20	37	0	24	42	0
22	7	14	0	8	18	0	9	22	0	11	25	0	16	31	0	19	36	0
21	5	11	0	6	15	0	6	18	0	9	20	0	13	26	0	15	30	0
20	4	9	0	4	11	0	5	14	0	6	16	0	10	21	0	12	24	0
19	2	7		2	8		3	11		5	13		7	17		10	20	
18	2	5		2	6		2	8		3	9		6	13		8	15	
17	1	4		1	5		1	5		2	7		4	9		6	11	
16	1	3		1	3		1	4		2	5		3	6		4	8	
15	0	2		0	2		0	3		1	3		2	4		3	6	
14	0	2		0	1		0	1		1	1		1	2		1	3	
13	0	1		0	1		0	1		0	1		1	2		1	2	
12	0	1		0	0		0	0		0	1		0	1		0	1	
11	0	0		0	0		0	0		0	0		0	0		0	0	
10	0	0		0	0		0	0		0	0		0	0		0	0	

(continued)

Elementary Reading Attitude Survey
Scoring sheet

Student name _____

Teacher _____

Grade _____ Administration date _____

```
┌─────────────────────────────────────────┐
│              Scoring guide                │
│                                           │
│   4  points    Happiest Garfield          │
│   3  points    Slightly smiling Garfield  │
│   2  points    Mildly upset Garfield      │
│   1  point     Very upset Garfield        │
└─────────────────────────────────────────┘
```

Recreational reading   Academic reading

1. _____   11. _____
2. _____   12. _____
3. _____   13. _____
4. _____   14. _____
5. _____   15. _____
6. _____   16. _____
7. _____   17. _____
8. _____   18. _____
9. _____   19. _____
10. _____   20. _____

Raw score: _____   Raw score: _____

Full scale raw score (Recreational + Academic): _____

Percentile ranks   Recreational

                        Academic

                        Full scale

(continued)

217

ELEMENTARY READING ATTITUDE SURVEY

School_____ Grade___ Name_____

1. How do you feel when you read a book on a rainy Saturday?

2. How do you feel when you read a book in school during free time?

3. How do you feel about reading for fun at home?

4. How do you feel about getting a book for a present?

(continued)

218

(continued)

9. How do you feel about going to a bookstore?

10. How do you feel about reading different kinds of books?

11. How do you feel when the teacher asks you questions about what you read?

12. How do you feel about doing reading workbook pages and worksheets?

(continued)

(continued)

17. How do you feel about the stories you read in reading class?

18. How do you feel when you read out loud in class?

19. How do you feel about using a dictionary?

20. How do you feel about taking a reading test?

(continued)

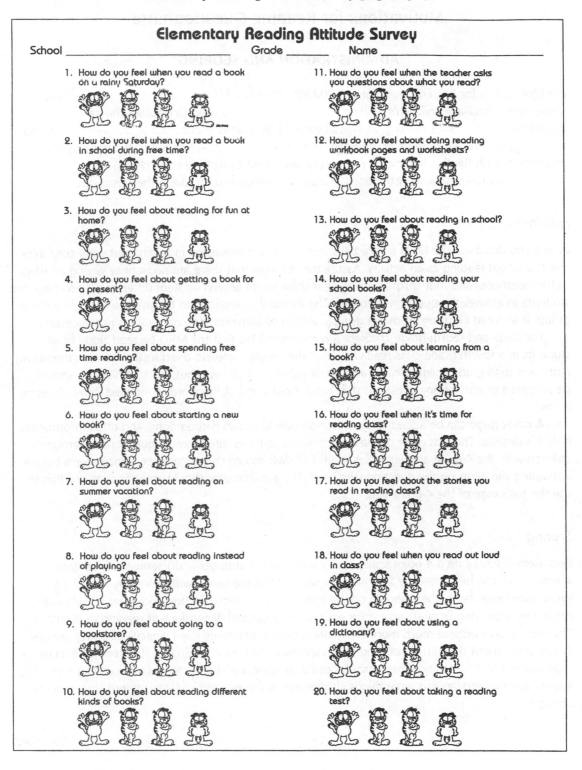

Motivations for Reading Questionnaire

ADMINISTRATION AND SCORING

The Motivations for Reading Questionnaire (MRQ) measures different dimensions or aspects of elementary school-age children's reading motivations. It can be used to discover the nature of children's motivations for reading, as well as some of the things about reading children do not find motivating. It consists of 54 items, and can be administered in 20–25 minutes. It can be used in conjunction with the Reading Activity Inventory developed by Guthrie et al. (1994).

The MRQ follows these instructions. It may be photocopied for use in the classroom.

Administration

Before you distribute the MRQ forms, tell students you are interested in finding out what they think and feel about reading as an activity. Assure the students that there are no right or wrong answers to the questions, and that children sitting near them might answer an item differently. Encourage the students to answer the questions honestly. The measure is designed to be given to a classroom-size group; it also can be given in smaller groups. Individual administration generally is not necessary.

For third- and fourth-grade children, it is recommended that the MRQ be read aloud (if all students in a fourth-grade class read well, then they could complete the questionnaire on their own). Fifth- and sixth-grade children can read the questions on their own, but the administrator should be prepared to answer any questions they have about some of the words contained in the different items.

A cover page can be added to the questionnaire to obtain demographic and other information, if that is desired. The first page of the questionnaire contains three sample questions to familiarize children with the 4-point answer scales used. The class should complete these sample items before answering the items on the questionnaire itself. The administrator should emphasize to children to use the full range of the 4-point scale.

Scoring

Each item is scored on a 4-point scale; higher scores mean stronger endorsement of the item. A total score can be derived by summing the scores of all the items (with the exception of the Work Avoidance items; these should not be included in a summary score). However, we strongly recommend deriving separate scores for each of the proposed dimensions of reading motivations. The scale scores provide much more information than a total score does. Specifically, they provide information about the pattern of children's responses and how children rate different aspects of their motivation for reading. These profiles could be quite useful for teachers and reading specialists interested in understanding what things children like about reading and what things they don't like about it.

(continued)

SPECIFIC STEPS FOR SCORING THE INSTRUMENT BY HAND

1. Check each questionnaire to be sure that each student completed each item. If some items are left blank, they should not be included in the scoring of the instrument. Each item that is completed should be scored from 1 to 4.
2. If a student circled more than one answer for an item and the answers are adjacent (e.g., circled both 1 and 2 or 3 and 4), take the number closer to the middle. However, if both 1 and 4 were circled, do not count that item.
3. If a student added numbers to the scale (e.g., the student wrote in numbers less than 1 or greater than 4), convert them to the scale. Numbers less than 1 can be scored as 1; numbers greater than 4 can be scored as 4.
4. To create scale scores, use the table (pp. 226–227) to identify the items in each scale. Add the students' responses to the items in each scale (e.g., in the case of the Reading Efficacy scale, add the scores from the four items shown under that heading on p. 226) and divide by the number of items completed (e.g., in the case of the Efficacy scale, divide by 4 if all the items were completed by the student). Dividing by the number of items on each scale means that all the scale scores also will have a range of 1 to 4, which makes them easier to compare.
5. For the Compliance scale, the first two items should be reversed before computing the score here. That is, a score of 1 should be converted to 4, a score of 2 converted to 3, a score of 3 converted to 2, and a score of 4 converted to 1.

SPECIFIC STEPS FOR SCORING THE INSTRUMENT BY COMPUTER

The scales also can be created using different statistical packages, such as SPSS.

1. Follow steps 1 through 3 above.
2. To create scale scores, use the table below to identify the items in each scale. Use your computer program to add the appropriate items for each scale, being sure to reverse the first two items on the Compliance scale.
3. The scale scores can be saved on the computer for later use and analysis.

Interpretation

The scores can be used in several ways. First, individual profiles of the students can be examined. Each profile gives an indication of the kinds of things by which a child is motivated. For instance, does he or she read primarily for curiosity, or to get good grades? Does he or she like to be challenged by reading assignments? These profiles could be used to tailor the curriculum to better match individual student needs, or perhaps to provide special activities for different students. For instance, children who strongly endorse the Reading Challenge items could be given some especially involved assignments. Children strongly endorsing the Reading Recognition items could be given the opportunity to receive some recognition for their work. Children strongly endorsing the Social Reasons for Reading items could be allowed to read more with their peers.

(continued)

Second, the scores also could be grouped and group differences examined to answer questions such as: Are the boys more positively motivated than the girls? Do different things appear to motivate boys and girls most in their reading?

Third, the measure could be given twice or three times over a school year, and patterns of change in different children's motivations could be assessed.

SUBSCALES ON THE MOTIVATIONS FOR READING QUESTIONNAIRE

Reading Efficacy

I know that I will do well in reading next year.

I am a good reader.

I learn more from reading than most students in the class.

In comparison to my other school subjects, I am best at reading.

Reading Challenge

I like hard, challenging books.

If the project is interesting, I can read difficult material.

I like it when the questions in books make me think.

I usually learn difficult things by reading.

If a book is interesting, I don't care how hard it is to read.

Reading Curiosity

If the teacher discusses something interesting, I might read more about it.

If I am reading about an interesting topic, I sometimes lose track of time.

I read to learn new information about topics that interest me.

I read about my hobbies to learn more about them.

I like to read about new things.

I enjoy reading books about people in different countries.

Aesthetic Enjoyment of Reading

I read stories about fantasy and make-believe.

I like mysteries.

I make pictures in my mind when I read.

I feel like I make friends with people in good books.

I read a lot of adventure stories.

I enjoy a long, involved story or fiction book.

Importance of Reading

It is very important to me to be a good reader.

In comparison to other activities I do, it is very important to me to be a good reader.

Compliance

I do as little schoolwork as possible in reading.*

I read because I have to.*

I always do my reading work exactly as the teacher wants it.

Finishing every reading assignment is very important to me

I always try to finish my reading on time

*Reverse the direction of these two items when scoring them.

(continued)

Reading Recognition

I like having the teacher say I read well.

My friends sometimes tell me I am a good reader.

I like to get compliments for my reading.

I am happy when someone recognizes my reading.

My parents often tell me what a good job I am doing in reading.

Reading for Grades

Grades are a good way to see how well you are doing in reading.

I look forward to finding out my reading grade.

I read to improve my grades.

My parents ask me about my reading grade.

Social Reasons for Reading

I visit the library often with my family.

I often read to my brother or my sister.

My friends and I like to trade things to read.

I sometimes read to my parents.

I talk to my friends about what I am reading.

I like to help my friends with their schoolwork in reading.

I like to tell my family about what I am reading.

Reading Competition

I try to get more answers right than my friends.

I like being the best at reading.

I like to finish my reading before other students.

I like being the only one who knows an answer in something we read.

It is important for me to see my name on a list of good readers.

I am willing to work hard to read better than my friends.

Reading Work Avoidance

I don't like vocabulary questions.

Complicated stories are no fun to read.

I don't like reading something when the words are too difficult.

I don't like it when there are too many people in the story.

(continued)

MOTIVATIONS FOR READING QUESTIONNAIRE

Directions

We are interested in your reading.

The statements tell how some students feel about reading.

Read each statement and decide whether it talks about a person who is like you or different from you.

There are no right or wrong answers. We only want to know how you feel about reading.

Here are three examples.

If the statement is **very different from you**, circle a 1.

If the statement is **a little different from you**, circle a 2.

If the statement is **a little like you**, circle a 3.

If the statement is **a lot like you**, circle a 4.

CIRCLE ONE ANSWER FOR EACH QUESTION, USING THESE ANSWERS:	Very different from me	A little different from me	A little like me	A lot like me
1. I like ice cream.	1	2	3	4
2. I like to swim.	1	2	3	4
3. I like spinach.	1	2	3	4
1. I visit the library often with my family.	1	2	3	4
2. I like hard, challenging books.	1	2	3	4
3. I know that I will do well in reading next year.	1	2	3	4
4. I do as little schoolwork as possible in reading.	1	2	3	4
5. If the teacher discusses something interesting, I might read more about it.	1	2	3	4
6. I read because I have to.	1	2	3	4
7. I like it when the questions in books make me think.	1	2	3	4
8. I read about my hobbies to learn more about them.	1	2	3	4
9. I am a good reader.	1	2	3	4
10. I read stories about fantasy and make-believe.	1	2	3	4
11. I often read to my brother or sister.	1	2	3	4
12. I like being the only one who knows an answer in something we read.	1	2	3	4
13. I read to learn new information about topics that interest me.	1	2	3	4
14. My friends sometimes tell me I'm a good reader.	1	2	3	4
15. I learn more from reading than most students in my class.	1	2	3	4

(continued)

228

CIRCLE ONE ANSWER FOR EACH QUESTION, USING THESE ANSWERS:	Very different from me	A little different from me	A little like me	A lot like me
16. I like to read about new things.	1	2	3	4
17. I like hearing the teacher say I read well.	1	2	3	4
18. I like being the best at reading.	1	2	3	4
19. I look forward to finding out my reading grade.	1	2	3	4
20. I sometimes read to my parents.	1	2	3	4
21. My friends and I like to trade things to read.	1	2	3	4
22. It is important for me to see my name on a list of good readers.	1	2	3	4
23. I don't like reading something when the words are too difficult.	1	2	3	4
24. I make pictures in my mind when I read.	1	2	3	4
25. I always do my reading work exactly as the teacher wants it.	1	2	3	4
26. I usually learn difficult things by reading.	1	2	3	4
27. I don't like vocabulary questions.	1	2	3	4
28. Complicated stories are no fun to read.	1	2	3	4
29. I am happy when someone recognizes my reading.	1	2	3	4
30. I feel like I make friends with people in good books.	1	2	3	4
31. My parents often tell me what a good job I'm doing in reading.	1	2	3	4
32. Finishing every reading assignment is very important to me.	1	2	3	4
33. I like mysteries.	1	2	3	4
34. I talk to my friends about what I am reading.	1	2	3	4
35. If I am reading about an interesting topic, I sometimes lose track of time.	1	2	3	4
36. I like to get compliments for my reading.	1	2	3	4
37. Grades are a good way to see how I'm doing in reading.	1	2	3	4
38. I like to help my friends with their schoolwork in reading.	1	2	3	4
39. I read to improve my grades.	1	2	3	4
40. My parents ask me about my reading grade.	1	2	3	4
41. I enjoy a long, involved story or fiction book.	1	2	3	4
42. I like to tell my family about what I am reading.	1	2	3	4
43. I try to get more answers right than my friends.	1	2	3	4
44. If the project is interesting, I can read difficult material.	1	2	3	4
45. I enjoy reading books about people living in different countries.	1	2	3	4

(continued)

CIRCLE ONE ANSWER FOR EACH QUESTION, USING THESE ANSWERS:	Very different from me	A little different from me	A little like me	A lot like me
46. I read a lot of adventure stories.	1	2	3	4
47. I always try to finish my reading on time.	1	2	3	4
48. If a book is interesting, I don't care how hard it is to read.	1	2	3	4
49. I like to finish my reading before other students.	1	2	3	4
50. In comparison to my other school subjects, I am best at reading.	1	2	3	4
51. I am willing to work hard to read better than my friends.	1	2	3	4
52. I don't like it when there are too many people in the story.	1	2	3	4
53. It is very important to me to be a good reader.	1	2	3	4
54. In comparison to other activities I do, it is very important for me to be good at reading.	1	2	3	4

The Reader Self-Perception Scale

Directions for Administration, Scoring, and Interpretation

The Reader Self-Perception Scale (RSPS) is intended to provide an assessment of how children feel about themselves as readers. The scale consists of 33 items that assess self-perceptions along four dimensions of self-efficacy (Progress, Observational Comparison, Social Feedback, and Physiological States). Children are asked to indicate how strongly they agree or disagree with each statement on a 5-point scale (5 = Strongly Agree, 1 = Strongly Disagree). The information gained from this scale can be used to devise ways to enhance children's self-esteem in reading and, ideally, to increase their motivation to read. The following directions explain specifically what you are to do.

Administration

For the results to be of any use, the children must: (a) understand exactly what they are to do, (b) have sufficient time to complete all items, and (c) respond honestly and thoughtfully. Briefly explain to the children that they are being asked to complete a questionnaire about reading. Emphasize that this is not a test and that there are no right answers. Tell them that they should be as honest as possible because their responses will be confidential. Ask the children to fill in their names, grade levels, and classrooms as appropriate. Read the directions aloud and work through the example with the students as a group. Discuss the response options and make sure that all children understand the rating scale before moving on. It is important that children know that they may raise their hands to ask questions about any words or ideas they do not understand.

The children should then read each item and circle their response for the item. They should work at their own pace. Remind the children that they should be sure to respond to all items. When all items are completed, the children should stop, put their pencils down, and wait for further instructions. Care should be taken that children who work more slowly are not disturbed by children who have already finished.

Scoring

To score the RSPS, enter the following point values for each response on the RSPS scoring sheet (Strongly Agree = 5, Agree = 4, Undecided = 3, Disagree = 2, Strongly Disagree = 1) for each item number under the appropriate scale. Sum each column to obtain a raw score for each of the four specific scales.

Interpretation

Each scale is interpreted in relation to its total possible score. For example, because the RSPS uses a 5-point scale and the Progress scale consists of 9 items, the highest total score for Progress is 45 (9 × 5 = 45). Therefore, a score that would fall approximately in the middle of the range (22–23) would indicate a child's somewhat indifferent perception of her or himself as a reader with respect to Progress. Note that each scale has a different possible total raw score (Progress = 45, Observational Comparison = 30, Social Feedback = 45, and Physiological States = 40) and should be interpreted accordingly.

As a further aid to interpretation, Table 2 presents the descriptive statistics by grade level for each scale. The raw score of a group or individual can be compared to that of the pilot study group at each grade level.

(continued)

The Reader Self-Perception Scale scoring sheet

Student name _____

Teacher _____

Grade _____   Date _____

Scoring key: 5 = Strongly Agree (SA)
4 = Agree (A)
3 = Undecided (U)
2 = Disagree (D)
1 = Strongly Disagree (SD)

Scales

General Perception	Progress	Observational Comparison	Social Feedback	Physiological States
1. ____	10. ____	4. ____	2. ____	5. ____
	13. ____	6. ____	3. ____	8. ____
	15. ____	11. ____	7. ____	16. ____
	18. ____	14. ____	9. ____	21. ____
	19. ____	20. ____	12. ____	25. ____
	23. ____	22. ____	17. ____	26. ____
	24. ____		30. ____	29. ____
	27. ____		31. ____	32. ____
	28. ____		33. ____	

Raw score	____ of 45	____ of 30	____ of 45	____of 40
Score interpretation				
High	44+	26+	38+	37+
Average	39	21	33	31
Low	34	16	27	25

(continued)

The Reader Self-Perception Scale

Listed below are statements about reading. Please read each statement carefully. Then circle the letters that show how much you agree or disagree with the statement. Use the following:

> SA = Strongly Agree
> A = Agree
> U = Undecided
> D = Disagree
> SD = Strongly Disagree

Example: I think pizza with pepperoni is the best.   SA   A   U   D   SD

If you are *really positive* that pepperoni pizza is best, circle SA (Strongly Agree).
If you *think* that it is good but maybe not great, circle A (Agree).
If you *can't decide* whether or not it is best, circle U (Undecided).
If you *think* that pepperoni pizza is not all that good, circle D (Disagree).
If you are *really positive* that pepperoni pizza is not very good, circle SD (Strongly Disagree).

	1. I think I am a good reader.	SA	A	U	D	SD
[SF]	2. I can tell that my teacher likes to listen to me read.	SA	A	U	D	SD
[SF]	3. My teacher thinks that my reading is fine.	SA	A	U	D	SD
[OC]	4. I read faster than other kids.	SA	A	U	D	SD
[PS]	5. I like to read aloud.	SA	A	U	D	SD
[OC]	6. When I read, I can figure out words better than other kids.	SA	A	U	D	SD
[SF]	7. My classmates like to listen to me read.	SA	A	U	D	SD
[PS]	8. I feel good inside when I read.	SA	A	U	D	SD
[SF]	9. My classmates think that I read pretty well.	SA	A	U	D	SD
[PR]	10. When I read, I don't have to try as hard as I used to.	SA	A	U	D	SD
[OC]	11. I seem to know more words than other kids when I read.	SA	A	U	D	SD
[SF]	12. People in my family think I am a good reader.	SA	A	U	D	SD
[PR]	13. I am getting better at reading.	SA	A	U	D	SD
[OC]	14. I understand what I read as well as other kids do.	SA	A	U	D	SD
[PR]	15. When I read, I need less help than I used to.	SA	A	U	D	SD
[PS]	16. Reading makes me feel happy inside.	SA	A	U	D	SD
[SF]	17. My teacher thinks I am a good reader.	SA	A	U	D	SD
[PR]	18. Reading is easier for me than it used to be.	SA	A	U	D	SD
[PR]	19. I read faster than I could before.	SA	A	U	D	SD
[OC]	20. I read better than other kids in my class.	SA	A	U	D	SD

(continued)

233

The Reader Self-Perception Scale

[PS]	21. I feel calm when I read.	SA	A	U	D	SD
[OC]	22. I read more than other kids.	SA	A	U	D	SD
[PR]	23. I understand what I read better than I could before.	SA	A	U	D	SD
[PR]	24. I can figure out words better than I could before.	SA	A	U	D	SD
[PS]	25. I feel comfortable when I read.	SA	A	U	D	SD
[PS]	26. I think reading is relaxing.	SA	A	U	D	SD
[PR]	27. I read better now than I could before.	SA	A	U	D	SD
[PR]	28. When I read, I recognize more words than I used to.	SA	A	U	D	SD
[PS]	29. Reading makes me feel good.	SA	A	U	D	SD
[SF]	30. Other kids think I'm a good reader.	SA	A	U	D	SD
[SF]	31. People in my family think I read pretty well.	SA	A	U	D	SD
[PS]	32. I enjoy reading.	SA	A	U	D	SD
[SF]	33. People in my family like to listen to me read.	SA	A	U	D	SD

Reading Activity Inventory

ADMINISTRATION AND SCORING

The Reading Activity Inventory (RAI) is a quick way to find out how frequently and how widely students read and about some of their other activities as well. It consists of 26 questions and can be administered to a class in 20 minutes or less.

Administration

As you distribute the RAI forms, tell students that you want to find out what they read in school and what they do when they are on their own. Explain that the RAI is not a test and that there are no "right" answers. Encourage them to be honest.

The RAI can be administered in two ways: (1) teachers may read the questionnaire aloud to the students, or (2) they may permit students to read and answer the questions silently. We recommend that teachers read a few of the questions aloud and allow students who may not be sure of the definitions of words such as *fiction*, *mystery*, and *biography* to ask questions if they need to. Teachers can model answering the questions by thinking aloud about what they read in their spare time. This procedure might add a few minutes to the administration time but would probably improve the accuracy of the students' answers.

For those questions that request an author, title, or topic, explain that students only have to give one answer, but encourage them to give all three if they can remember.

Scoring

Activities. The Activities questions are coded according to frequency ("How often do you . . . ?") on a scale of 1 to 4 and scored as follows: 1 = Almost never; 2 = About once a month; 3 = About once a week; 4 = Almost every day. The minimum score a student can receive is 5; the maximum score is 20.

School Reading. The School Reading questions are coded according to whether students' reading is consistent with what is being taught in the classroom. This section was developed to see how aware students are of what they are studying in school and how well they understand the format of the questionnaire.

If an answer is consistent, it receives 1 point. For example, assuming that science is being taught in the classroom at the time this survey is administered, the student should circle "yes" to the question "Did you read a science book or a science textbook for school last week?" This answer would receive 1 point. If the student wrote in the title, author, or topic of the science book, that answer would receive 1 point. A "no" answer would receive 0. If the student failed to write in a title, author, or topic, the answer would receive a 0.

Consistency is also examined by questions about frequency, such as "How often do you read a science book or science textbook for school?" Assuming again that science is being taught in the classroom, the student would receive a 1 for circling "About once a week" or "Almost every day." A student with the same instruction who circles "Almost never" or "About once a month" would receive 0.

The minimum score a student can receive is 0; the maximum score is 9.

(continued)

Reading for Personal Interest. Questions about books read for personal interest in the past week are scored: 0 = No; 1 = Yes, without a title given; 2 = Yes, with a title.

Questions about frequency are scored: 0 = circled 1 or 2 and wrote title; 0 = circled 3 or 4 and did not write title; 1 = circled 1 or 2 and did not write title; 2 = circled 3 or 4 and wrote title.

The minimum score a student can receive is 0; the maximum score is 30.

Interpretation

The results of the Reading Activity Inventory can be used to plan instruction for individual students and for whole classes. For example, a student who does not read outside of school but does go to the movies a lot might be motivated to read books that retell the plots of his or her favorite movies. Or the RAI results show that students have little experience following written directions, a teacher might plan a project in which students do something like build a model town or record a videotape, for which they would follow printed instructions. They could then create a companion project in which they themselves write directions to be used by other students.

(continued)

READING ACTIVITY INVENTORY

Directions: We are interested in knowing about your activities and in finding out how often you do them. Circle the answers to some of the questions, and write the answers to the others.

Practice Questions

1. Do you have a first name? (Circle only one.)

   No

   Yes

If yes, write your first name.

First name: _____

	Almost never	About once a month	About once a week	Almost every day
2. How often do you tell another person your first name? (Circle only one.)	1	2	3	4

Questions about Your Activities

	Almost never	About once a month	About once a week	Almost every day
1. How often do you listen to music?	1	2	3	4
2. How often do you watch television?	1	2	3	4
3. How often do you play outside?	1	2	3	4
4. How often do you go to the movies?	1	2	3	4
5. How often do you do chores at home?	1	2	3	4

Questions about School Reading

Directions: In this section, think about the reading you do for school and for homework. Include textbooks and other books in your answers.

6. Did you read a science book or science textbook for school last week? (Circle only one.)

   No

   Yes

If yes, write in the title, author, or specific topic that you read about.
Science book title/author/topic:

_____

	Almost never	About once a month	About once a week	Almost every day
7. How often do you read a science book or science textbook for school?	1	2	3	4

(continued)

8. Did you read a book of literature or fiction last week for school? (Circle only one.)

    No

    Yes

If yes, write in the title, author, or specific topic that you read about.
Fiction book title/author/topic:

_____

	Almost never	About once a month	About once a week	Almost every day
9. How often do you read a literature or fiction book for school?	1	2	3	4

10. Did you read a book about history or a history textbook last week for school?
    (Circle only one.)

    No

    Yes

If yes, write in the title, author, or specific topic that you read about.
History book title/author/topic:

_____

	Almost never	About once a month	About once a week	Almost every day
11. How often do you read a book about history or a history textbook for school?	1	2	3	4

Questions about Reading for Your Own Enjoyment

Directions: In this section, think about books that you read for your own interest that are not assigned for school or homework.

12. Did you read a fiction book, like a mystery or an adventure book, last week for your own interest? (Circle only one.)

    No

    Yes

If yes, write in the title, author, or specific topic that you read about.
Book title/author/topic:

_____

	Almost never	About once a month	About once a week	Almost every day
13. How often do you read a fiction book, like a mystery or an adventure book, for your own interest? (Circle only one.)	1	2	3	4

(continued)

14. Did you read a sports book last week for your own interest? (Circle only one.)

    No

    Yes

If yes, write in the title, author, or specific topic that you read about.
Book title/author/topic:

_____

	Almost never	About once a month	About once a week	Almost every day
15. How often do you read a sports book for your own interest? (Circle only one.)	1	2	3	4

16. Did you read a nature book last week for your own interest? (Circle only one.)

    No

    Yes

If yes, write in the title, author, or specific topic that you read about.
Book title/author/topic:

_____

	Almost never	About once a month	About once a week	Almost every day
17. How often do you read a nature book for your own interest? (Circle only one.)	1	2	3	4

18. Did you read a romance book last week for your own interest? (Circle only one.)

    No

    Yes

If yes, write in the title, author, or specific topic that you read about.
Book title/author/topic:

_____

	Almost never	About once a month	About once a week	Almost every day
19. How often do you read a romance book for your own interest? (Circle only one.)	1	2	3	4

20. Did you read a biography last week for your own interest? (Circle only one.)

    No

    Yes

If yes, write in the title, author, or specific topic that you read about.
Book title/author/topic:

_____

(continued)

	Almost never	About once a month	About once a week	Almost every day
21. How often do you read a biography for your own interest? (Circle only one.)	1	2	3	4

22. Did you read a comic book or magazine last week for your own interest? (Circle only one.)

No

Yes

If yes, write in the title, author, or specific topic that you read about.
Book title/author/topic:

_____

	Almost never	About once a month	About once a week	Almost every day
23. How often do you read a comic book or magazine for your own interest? (Circle only one.)	1	2	3	4

24. Did you read any other kind of book last week for your own interest that was not mentioned? (Circle only one.)

No

Yes

If yes, write in the title, author, or specific topic that you read about.
Book title/author/topic:

_____

	Almost never	About once a month	About once a week	Almost every day
25. How often do you read this kind of book? (Circle only one.)	1	2	3	4
26. How often do you read written directions or instructions that tell you how to do something you enjoy, like for putting together a model airplane, or baking a cake, or some similar activity? (Circle only one.)	1	2	3	4

Title Recognition Test

Name _____

Some of these titles are the names of actual books and some are not. Read the names and put a check mark next to the names of those you know are books. Do not guess, but only check those that you know are actual books. Remember, some of the titles are not those of popular books and can easily be detected.

____ *A Light in the Attic*

____ *By the Shores of Silver Lake*

____ *Call of the Wild*

____ *Curious Jim*

____ *Dear Mr. Henshaw*

____ *Don't Go Away*

____ *Dr. Dolittle*

____ *Ethan Allen*

____ *Freedom Train*

____ *From the Mixed-up Files of Mrs. Basil E. Frankweiler*

____ *Harriet the Spy*

____ *Heidi*

____ *Henry and the Clubhouse*

____ *He's Your Little Brother*

____ *Homer Price*

____ *Hot Top*

____ *How to Eat Fried Worms*

____ *Iggie's House*

____ *Island of the Blue Dolphins*

____ *It's My Room*

____ *James and the Giant Peach*

____ *Joanne*

____ *Misty of Chincoteague*

____ *Ramona the Pest*

____ *Sadie Goes to Hollywood*

____ *Skateboard*

____ *Superfudge*

____ *Tales of a Fourth Grade Nothing*

____ *The Chosen*

____ *The Cybil War*

____ *The Great Brain*

____ *The Hideaway*

____ *The Indian in the Cupboard*

____ *The Lion, the Witch and the Wardrobe*

____ *The Lost Shoe*

____ *The Missing Letter*

____ *The Polar Express*

____ *The Rollaway*

____ *The Schoolhouse*

(continued)

Scoring the Title Recognition Test

✓ A Light in the Attic	___ It's My Room
✓ By the Shores of Silver Lake	✓ James and the Giant Peach
✓ Call of the Wild	___ Joanne
___ Curious Jim	✓ Misty of Chincoteague
✓ Dear Mr. Henshaw	✓ Ramona the Pest
___ Don't Go Away	___ Sadie Goes to Hollywood
✓ Dr. Dolittle	___ Skateboard
___ Ethan Allen	✓ Superfudge
✓ Freedom Train	✓ Tales of a Fourth Grade Nothing
✓ From the Mixed-up Files of Mrs. Basil E. Frankweiler	✓ The Chosen
	✓ The Cybil War
✓ Harriet the Spy	✓ The Great Brain
✓ Heidi	___ The Hideaway
✓ Henry and the Clubhouse	✓ The Indian in the Cupboard
___ He's Your Little Brother	✓ The Lion, the Witch and the Wardrobe
✓ Homer Price	
___ Hot Top	___ The Lost Shoe
✓ How to Eat Fried Worms	___ The Missing Letter
✓ Iggie's House	✓ The Polar Express
✓ Island of the Blue Dolphins	___ The Rollaway
	___ The Schoolhouse

Checked items are actual titles.

_____ No. actual titles/25 _____ No. Foils / 14

Evaluation:

If a child recognizes 6 or fewer, they would be considered to have low literacy exposure, 7–12 titles would be average literacy exposure, and 13 or more would be high literacy exposure.

Adolescent Reading Attitudes Survey

Cicle the number in the box that tells how you feel about each of these activities.

	Very good					Very bad
Reading news online	6	5	4	3	2	1
Reading novels assigned by my teachers	6	5	4	3	2	1
Texting friends	6	5	4	3	2	1
Starting a new book	6	5	4	3	2	1
Reading for information on the Internet	6	5	4	3	2	1
Reading textbooks in school	6	5	4	3	2	1
Instant messaging friends	6	5	4	3	2	1
Reading graphic novels/manga	6	5	4	3	2	1
Researching online	6	5	4	3	2	1
Reading out loud in class	6	5	4	3	2	1
E-mailing friends	6	5	4	3	2	1
Reading novels for fun	6	5	4	3	2	1
Using on online dictionary	6	5	4	3	2	1
Reading a newspaper	6	5	4	3	2	1
Reading for fun on the Internet	6	5	4	3	2	1
Reading during my free time	6	5	4	3	2	1
Using an online encyclopedia	6	5	4	3	2	1
Answering questions about what I read	6	5	4	3	2	1
Reading magazines online	6	5	4	3	2	1
Reading different types of books	6	5	4	3	2	1
Working on an internet project with classmates	6	5	4	3	2	1
Using a dictionary in book form	6	5	4	3	2	1
Reading books online	6	5	4	3	2	1
Reading magazines	6	5	4	3	2	1
Learning from electronic displays, like PowerPoint	6	5	4	3	2	1
Using an encyclopedia in book form	6	5	4	3	2	1
Chatting online about what I'm reading	6	5	4	3	2	1
Going to a bookstore	6	5	4	3	2	1
Playing educational computer games	6	5	4	3	2	1
Someday having a job that requires reading	6	5	4	3	2	1
Finding song lyrics online	6	5	4	3	2	1
Going to a library	6	5	4	3	2	1
Someday having a job that requires reading online	6	5	4	3	2	1
Participating in classroom discussions about what we are reading	6	5	4	3	2	1
Participating in online chat rooms	6	5	4	3	2	1
Getting a book for a present	6	5	4	3	2	1
Discussing class materials online (e.g., writing and reading class blogs, wikis)	6	5	4	3	2	1
Reading from various sources of print to complete class work (articles, historical documents, etc.)	6	5	4	3	2	1
Talking about something I'm reading with friends	6	5	4	3	2	1
Reading to relax	6	5	4	3	2	1
Reading before I go to bed	6	5	4	3	2	1

(continued)

Adolescent Reading Attitudes Survey Scoring Guide

Score each survey as follows:
1. Place the number of each response (1–6) in the white space for each item.
2. Tally the scores in each column.
3. Interpret the score for each column using the scoring guide.

	Recreational print	Recreational digital	Academic print	Academic digital
Reading news online				
Reading novels assigned by my teachers				
Texting friends				
Starting a new book				
Reading for information on the Internet				
Reading textbooks in school				
Instant messaging friends				
Reading graphic novels/manga				
Researching online				
Reading out loud in class				
E-mailing friends				
Reading novels for fun				
Using on online dictionary				
Reading a newspaper				
Reading for fun on the Internet				
Reading during my free time				
Using an online encyclopedia				
Answering questions about what I read				
Reading magazines online				
Reading different types of books				
Working on an internet project with classmates				
Using a dictionary in book form				
Reading books online				
Reading magazines				
Learning from electronic displays, like PowerPoint				
Using an encyclopedia in book form				
Chatting online about what I'm reading				
Going to a bookstore				
Playing educational computer games				
Someday having a job that requires reading				
Finding song lyrics online				
Going to a library				
Someday having a job that requires reading online				
Participating in classroom discussions about what we are reading				
Participating in online chat rooms				
Getting a book for a present				
Discussing class materials online (e.g., writing and reading class blogs, wikis)				
Reading from various sources of print to complete class work (articles, historical documents, etc.)				
Talking about something I'm reading with friends				
Reading to relax				
Reading before I go to bed				
Totals:				

(continued)

Guide to Interpreting Scores

Subscale	Negative	Somewhat negative	Neutral/ indifferent	Somewhat positive	Positive
Recreational Reading in Print Settings	12–24	25–36	37–47	48–59	60–72
Recreational Reading in Digital Settings	9–18	19–27	28–35	36–44	45–54
Academic Reading in Print Settings	10–20	21–30	31–39	40–49	50–60
Academic Reading in Digital Settings	10–20	21–30	31–39	40–49	50–60

CHAPTER TEN

Preparing a Reading
Clinic Report

R eports serve a number of different functions. They can be nothing more than short notes to summarize an assessment for a staff meeting, or they can be more elaborate, formal documents. The reports discussed in this chapter are the more formal kind, reports written about a comprehensive assessment. Because all aspects of the issue being assessed are addressed, as much as possible, this type of report is also useful for communicating with parents, teachers, principals, and others. When composing such a report, it is always best to assume that you do not know who will be reading it, and so you must spell out exactly what actions you took in the assessment process.

Although most teachers will never write such a report, we address the topic for several reasons. To begin with, classroom teachers are sometimes asked to interpret reports written by reading specialists or special educators. Understanding the logic and structure of report writing can be useful for this purpose. Second, we have written this book with a broad readership in mind, and we recognize that the classroom teacher who reads this book today may become the reading specialist of tomorrow. Finally, we include this topic as an exercise in systematic thinking. Writing a formal report requires that you think about the child and your procedures in a comprehensive manner. To write a thorough report, you must ask yourself questions about the child's overall performance and how the different pieces of the assessment puzzle fit together. You must also think about how to communicate this information to a parent or another teacher, explaining what you did and what you found in a clear manner. This is why university reading clinics require such report writing. Following are some suggestions for writing a formal report.

PREPARATION

1. Spread out all the material from your testing—protocols, notes, and so on—on the kitchen table. Ask yourself mentally the questions listed in Table 10.1 about the child's performance. Think about both the level of his or her performance on the various tasks and the quality of that performance (the processes used to produce that performance). You should have an answer to each of these questions before you begin to write your report. These questions will guide you in understanding the assessment materials in front of you.

TABLE 10.1. Guiding Questions for Interpreting a Reading Profile

Question	Source of information
Is the child able to read texts at his or her grade placement with automatic word recognition and adequate expression?	
• Does the child make use of context to monitor his or her reading?	Informal reading inventory; running records (Chapter 3)
• Is the child fluent?	Timed oral reading, fluency scale (Chapter 6)
• Does the child have adequate sight-word knowledge?	Sight-word list such as Dolch or Fry lists (Chapter 5); Informal reading inventory
• Does the child have adequate knowledge of decoding strategies?	Decoding inventories (Chapter 5)
• Does the child have adequate phonological awareness?	Comprehensive Test of Phonological Processing (Chapter 4)
Is the child able to comprehend the language of the text?	
• Does the child have an adequate vocabulary for his or her age and grade?	Formal measures such as the Peabody Picture Vocabulary Test or the Receptive One-Word Vocabulary Test
• Does the child have the background knowledge necessary to understand the particular passage that he or she is reading?	Prereading questions, PreP (Chapter 7)
• Is the child able to use common text structures to aid in comprehension?	Recall; written recall with story map (Chapter 7)
Does the child have adequate knowledge of the purposes for reading and strategies available to achieve those purposes?	
• Does the child have a set of strategies that can be used to achieve different purposes in reading?	Textbook Interview, Index of Reading Awareness (Chapter 8)
• What does the child view as the goal of reading, in general?	Awareness of Purposes of Reading Inventory, Burke Reading Interview (Chapter 8)
• What concepts of print does the child have?	Concepts of print measure, concept of word measure (Chapter 4), observations

BACKGROUND INFORMATION

2. Begin by describing the reason for referral. Couch the comments made by the teacher or parent in terms such as "The teacher reports . . ." and so on. Be careful about "dangerous statements," such as saying that a child is reported to be "hyperactive" or "behaviorally disordered." Unless you are a qualified clinical psychologist who has conducted an appropriate assessment and rendered the diagnosis, you cannot classify children in these ways. Similarly, you cannot classify someone as "speech-impaired" or "intellectually disabled" unless you have appropriate training and have conducted appropriate assessments. Furthermore, do not report intimate family details (e.g., suspected abuse or difficulties experienced by siblings) that might prejudice a person meeting the child for the first time. *Remember that your report may be the first impression that someone gets about this child.* Do not prejudice the reader by making statements that go beyond what you yourself have observed about the child. The statements in the background section should describe behaviors you have seen or reports that you have read. Use professional language to create a portrait of the child, and be careful to distinguish fact from interpretation.

3. Describe the setting in which the assessment was conducted. Was the child cooperative? Were any factors present that might invalidate some of the results? (Did the child respond poorly to interruptions? Was the child too shy to respond in an informative manner?)

TESTS ADMINISTERED

4. List the tests administered, with the results. If the tests do not lend themselves to numerical results, just list the test. Table 10.2 indicates the assessment tasks that are likely to be administered at each grade level, together with the tools we have presented in this book.

OBSERVATIONS DURING TESTING

5. This section, in which you detail your observations, should be the longest of the report. For each area—Oral Reading, Silent Reading, Word Recognition, Decoding, Language, etc.—report *all* of the measures that have an impact on that area. If you administered two oral reading measures, list them both under "Oral Reading." You may use any set of categories or any order that makes sense in presenting your data. If you give a test (such as a phoneme awareness measure) because you noticed a weakness in another area (such as decoding), you might want to order your list so that the reader can follow the progression of your thinking.

6. For each area, do the following:

TABLE 10.2. Basic Assessment Tools

	K–Grade 1	Grades 2–4	Grades 5–8
Concepts about print	• Concepts about print and book-handling tasks (Forms 4.1, 4.2) • Dictation for Phonological Awareness (Form 4.8)		
Phonological awareness	• Tests of Phonemic Awareness (Form 4.7) • Dictation for Phonological Awareness (Form 4.8)		
Development of word recognition	• Isolation: Sight Words (Form 5.1 or 5.2) • Informal Phonics Inventory (Form 5.3) • In Context: Running Records and IRIs	• Isolation: Sight Words (Form 5.1 or 5.2) • Informal Phonics Inventory (Form 5.3) or Z-Test (Form 5.4) • In Context: Running Records and IRIs	*Optional* • Isolation: Test of Word Recognition Efficiency • In Context: Running Records and IRIs
Spelling development	• Elementary Spelling Inventory and Feature Guide (Form 5.6) • In Context: Analyze a writing sample using Qualitative Spelling Checklist (Form 5.7)	• Elementary Spelling Inventory and Feature Guide (Form 5.6) • In Context: Analyze a writing sample using Qualitative Spelling Checklist (Form 5.7)	• Elementary Spelling Inventory and Feature Guide (Form 5.6) *or* Morris–McCall Spelling List (Form 5.8) • In Context: Analyze a writing sample using Qualitative Spelling Checklist (Form 5.7)
Reading fluency	• Prosody rating • Beginning midgrade 1, rate (wcpm)	• Rate (wcpm) • Prosody rating (Table 6.1 or Form 6.1)	• Rate (wcpm)

Comprehension	• Running Record or IRI
	  Error analysis
	  Retelling
	  Prompted recall
		• IRI
		  Retelling
		  Prompted recall
			• IRI
			  Retelling
			  Prompted recall

Strategic reading			• Interview (selections from Chapter 8)
Motivation/ attitudes	• Elementary Reading Attitude Survey (Form 9.3)	• Elementary Reading Attitude Survey (Form 9.3)	• Adolescent Reading Attitudes Survey (Form 9.8)

Note. This table describes the basic assessment tasks that are typically administered at each grade level. The need to administer additional tasks or different tasks may be indicated by a child's performance on a few preliminary assessments.

a. Describe the tests given. Write descriptions in one or two sentences, if possible, that are clear and understandable to parents.
b. Present the quantitative results. At what level is the child? How well did the child score numerically?
c. Present the qualitative analysis of these results—perhaps, for example, a miscue analysis of oral reading, an analysis of a word-recognition list describing patterns that you have seen, an analysis of spelling, and so on. What process was the child using during this activity? Make interpretations. For each interpretive statement, give examples, such as miscues, spellings, word readings, and so forth.

SUMMARY AND RECOMMENDATIONS

7. In the first paragraph, recap the information in the previous sections of the report. *In a report, do not be afraid to be redundant.* Make sure this first paragraph contains a thorough summary of all the areas.

8. Compare the child's performance across the different areas. Look for strengths and weaknesses in his or her reading knowledge and ability. Interpret those strengths and weaknesses, if appropriate.

9. Finally, list and describe the major goals for tutoring. We recommend that you set between three and five goals. Describe each goal briefly and tell why it is important. Then describe sample activities that you plan to use to achieve each goal. You also may append longer descriptions of the activities to the report. These can be your own descriptions or photocopies of activity descriptions. Good sources for such descriptions include the following:

Bear, D. R., Invernizzi, M., Templeton, S., & Johnston, F. (2008). *Words their way: Word study for phonics, vocabulary, and spelling instruction* (4th ed.). Upper Saddle River, NJ: Pearson/Prentice Hall.

Fisher, D., Brozo, W. G., Frey, N., & Ivey, G. (2006). *50 content area strategies for adolescent literacy.* Upper Saddle River, NJ: Merrill/Prentice Hall.

Harvey, S., & Goudvis, A. (2007). *Strategies that work: Teaching comprehension for understanding and engagement.* York, ME: Stenhouse.

Opitz, M. F., Rasinski, T. V., & Bird, L. B. (1998). *Good-bye Round Robin: Twenty-five effective oral reading strategies.* Portsmouth, NH: Heinemann.

Shanker, J. L., & Ekwall, E. E. (2002). *Locating and correcting reading difficulties* (8th ed.). Upper Saddle River, NJ: Merrill/Prentice Hall.

Tierney, R. J., & Readence, J. (2005). *Reading strategies and practices: A compendium* (6th ed.). Boston: Allyn & Bacon.

OTHER POINTS

Be clear and concise, and avoid jargon. If you use a technical term, explain it. The audience is an intelligent layman (parent, teacher, etc.), not the instructor. Make sure you explain yourself clearly and unambiguously. Read through the report after it is drafted and try to misinterpret it—if someone can misinterpret what you say, they will. Be honest and professional in your descriptions. Struggling readers often have difficulty staying on task, avoid taking risks, engage in avoidance behaviors, and have difficulty sustaining their focus. It's important not to characterize those readers as "lazy" or simply "needing to try harder."

Redundancy is fine in a report, because many people do not read the report from beginning to end, but instead look for parts that answer their particular questions or concerns. Positioning information in several places (e.g., a list or chart, the body of the report, a summary) increases the chance that a reader will come across that information. The sample reports in the Appendix contain boilerplate descriptions of the tests used. If you use the same assessments, do not worry about using these descriptions. Because these are the same (presumably), copying the descriptions is not plagiarism, but simply a way to avoid wasting your time and creativity.

APPENDIX

Case Studies

BACKGROUND INFORMATION

Angela was brought to the clinic by her mother after having completed her first-grade year. Angela's mom is concerned about her daughter's reading problems and lack of confidence in reading. She reports that Angela looks at pictures more than words and that she tends to daydream while reading. Her main reason for referring Angela to the clinic is to help her to feel more comfortable with reading and sounding out words.

Her teacher reports that Angela has a good attitude and is usually well behaved. Prior to Christmas she was performing on grade level with only a slight degree of difficulty. During the second semester, however, her comprehension and decoding skills declined slightly below grade level. Her teacher reports that Angela appears to have difficulty applying phonetic skills and lacks self-confidence in the area of reading.

At the testing Angela was very friendly and outspoken. When interviewed concerning her feelings about reading, she expressed some frustration with her problems sounding out words. She does not feel that she is a good reader because sometimes "words don't come" to her and she "can't remember them." She enjoyed elaborating on the examiner's questions and telling stories about herself and her friends.

TESTS ADMINISTERED

Qualitative Reading Inventory
    Word Recognition   preprimer, instructional level
    Oral Reading   preprimer, instructional level

Fry Instant Word List   74/100 correct

Letter Identification   100% correct

Informal Phonics Survey

Consonants	19/20	mastery
Consonant digraphs	5/5	mastery
Short vowels	6/10	needs review
Consonant blends	5/20	needs systematic instruction
Silent *e*	0/4	needs systematic instruction
Vowel digraphs	2/10	needs systematic instruction

Vowel diphthongs	2/6	needs systematic instruction
R-controlled vowels and -al	1/6	needs systematic instruction

Stahl–Murray Test of Phonemic Awareness

Blending	8/15	needs systematic instruction
Phoneme isolation	10/10	mastery
Deletion	0/20	needs systematic instruction

Qualitative Spelling Checklist
    Letter name pattern

Concepts about print test	18/24	5th stanine

OBSERVATIONS DURING TESTING

Word Recognition

The word recognition section of the Qualitative Reading Inventory (QRI) contains eight word lists consisting of 20 words each. The word lists begin with a primer readability level and end with a junior high readability level.

Angela was able to read 16/20 words on the preprimer list automatically or within 1 second. She misread four words. She read 9/20 words from the primer list correctly, putting her at her frustration level—that is, the level at which she would become frustrated if reading independently.

Most of Angela's errors consisted of guesses based on the first letter of a word. For example, she said "please" for *place*, "that" for *thing*, and "so" for *saw*. For *need*, she simply said the letter *n*. Some substitutions showed more awareness of the end of the word: "Oliver" for *other*, "chicken" for *children*, and "when" for *went*.

Oral Reading

The oral reading section of the QRI consists of 42 passages ranging in readability levels from preprimer, primer, and first-grade passages through junior high level. Grade scores are derived from the number of miscues (any deviations from the text) as well as the student's ability to answer comprehension questions. Some comprehension questions have answers that can be found directly in the text, and some have answers that require the student to infer information from the text.

Angela read the preprimer and primer passages. On the preprimer passage with pictures, she made two miscues and answered four out of the five comprehension questions correctly. This story was at her instructional level, meaning she could read and completely comprehend this story with help from a teacher. On the test at the primer level, Angela made 65 miscues. Of these, 43 changed the meaning of the text. She correctly answered three of the six comprehension questions. This story was at her frustration level, meaning that the material was too difficult for her even with assistance.

Because there was a big difference between the number of miscues in the preprimer and primer passages, the examiner gave Angela a preprimer story without pictures. It was thought that perhaps she had relied heavily on picture clues to decode words and answer comprehension questions for the first story. When given the preprimer passage without pictures, Angela made 21 miscues, 19 of which changed the meaning of the text. She answered one out of five comprehension questions correctly. This variance between scores on the two preprimer passages suggests that Angela relies heavily on picture clues to construct meaning when reading.

Before reading a passage, Angela was asked various concept questions about the story topic. She often answered these questions with a rambling, off-subject story related to herself.

> EXAMINER: What is "doing something new"?
>
> CHILD: If you're being picked on and you're doing your work and the teacher tells you to shut the door and people pick on you . . . (*continued*).

When asked to predict what a story would be about, she usually related it to herself and only occasionally to the concept questions or title. When asked to retell the story, she remembered between three and seven story details. She was unable to retell any details from the passage without pictures.

An analysis of Angela's miscues showed that she often made substitutions based on the first letter of the target word—a very similar pattern to the types of miscues she made on the word list. She also made mistakes that were syntactically correct, meaning that when she didn't know a group of words, she constructed a phrase that made structural sense (+ indicates word was read correctly):

> TEXT: He did that every day.
>
> CHILD: + + not see it.
>
> TEXT: His father said, "But pigs can't read!"
>
> CHILD: + + had big teeth + rock.

At this point in her development Angela understands that text carries meaning and that each word is a separate idea, but she often gets frustrated with decoding and then constructs her own meaning using picture clues. This strategy is especially evident in her frustration with the comprehension questions and retelling of the pictureless preprimer story. She knows that letters represent sounds, but she is uncomfortable with decoding individual words. She correctly reads sight words or words whose meanings are indicated by the pictures.

Informal Phonics Survey

At this point, we wanted to determine whether any of Angela's miscues could be due to her not knowing the sounds of written letters. She was therefore given an informal phonics survey, which is a criterion-referenced measure intended to assess the child's knowledge of letter sounds in isolation and in words. Angela knew the sounds of all consonants except the "hard" sounds of *c* and *g*. She had greater trouble with consonant blends. She was confident about the consonant digraphs and could read most short-vowel words. Vowel combinations, such as vowel digraphs, diphthongs, and silent *e* words were difficult for her as well. She misunderstands the role of silent *e*, evidenced by her comment that a silent *e* makes no difference in a word because *e* never makes a sound at the end of a word.

Prereading Knowledge and Abilities

In order to be true readers, children need to have a secure knowledge of three basic concepts. They need to have a secure concept about print, including that words carry meaning, what print is used for, and directionality. They also need to have a comfortable knowledge of letters. Finally, they need to have an awareness of phonemes or sounds in spoken words. This awareness is needed so that a child can match written letters to individual sounds.

Angela was examined in each of these areas. She seemed to have a good idea about print concepts. She was aware of the correct place to start reading and could follow along as the examiner read, matching word to word. She could identify the differences between letters and words and knew the function of periods and commas. She did not notice changes in word order or incorrectly spelled words, but that is not overly surprising considering her age.

Angela was very confident identifying her letter names. She correctly named 54 out of 54 capital and lowercase letters, including irregular forms of *a* and *g*.

The third assessment, the test of phonemic awareness, was given orally to determine whether Angela was aware of sounds in spoken words. Phoneme awareness is the ability to reflect on spoken words and identify the phonemes within those words. This skill is an important prerequisite for learning phonics. The child is assessed on blending sounds into words, identifying letters/sounds in words in isolation, and substituting letter sounds in words.

The first task is a blending activity in which the examiner slowly sounds out a word, and the student must combine the sounds to determine the target word. Angela correctly blended 8/15 words, or 53%. This rating indicates that she needs direct instruction on blending separate sounds into words. In the second task, however, when Angela was given a word and asked to identify the first or last letter of that word, she correctly identified 100% of the onsets and 90% of the rimes. The third task of the test required Angela to delete a sound from a particular word supplied by the examiner. For instance, when given the word *meat*, she was asked to repeat it without the *m*. Angela was unable to understand this task and did not complete this last section of the test.

These results confirm many of the conclusions made earlier from Angela's oral reading. It appears that she is confident pronouncing the initial sounds of words and can also distinguish final sounds. Her difficulty lies in blending sounds together and in separating sounds. In order to determine whether this difficulty carried over to her writing, Angela was given two tests of her invented spelling.

Spelling

Angela was given a list of words to spell. This list was developed in order to evaluate the child's level of invented spelling. It has been found that children go through a developmental sequence in their invented spelling: from prephonemic, in which their writing does not reflect sounds in words; to an early phonemic stage, in which they use an initial consonant to represent a word; to a letter-name stage, in which they use letter names to represent their sounds and often omit vowels; to a transitional stage, in which their spellings reflect all phonemic features.

Angela's spellings were as follows:

Word	Angela's spelling
bed	bed
ship	shepe
drive	grive

bump   bupe
when   wen

Angela also was given a dictation test in which she was asked to write a sentence. The correctness of her spelling was not as important here as her ability to represent all the sounds of the words. Of the 37 sounds included in this sentence, Angela represented all 37, with only two reversals: she wrote "ti" for *it* and "no" for *on*.

Angela's spelling tells us several things. Most of her words were at the letter-name stage, meaning that she included a vowel in each syllable of the word and had progressed beyond using only initial consonants in her spelling. The fact that she could represent all the sounds she heard during the sentence dictation indicates that she can hear and synthesize these sounds.

SUMMARY AND RECOMMENDATIONS

Angela is an end-of-first-grade student having difficulty with reading. She was given the Qualitative Reading Inventory and found to be instructional at the preprimer level. Many of her miscues were guesses based on the first letter of the target word. Although Angela can identify letters and is comfortable with the sounds of consonants, she lacks knowledge about the sounds of vowels and has great difficulty blending sounds together when reading. It is interesting to note that Angela seems able to represent all sounds in her invented spelling when writing, indicating that she has no difficulty hearing the letter sounds. Her difficulty seems to lie in decoding sounds in existing words.

Angela appears to be knowledgeable about basic print concepts, such as directionality, letter identification, and the use of punctuation. She understands that the purpose of print is to convey meaning. However, her struggle with analyzing unknown words hinders her ability to create meaning from text. Her occasional lack of prior concepts and poor ability to predict story outcomes also greatly interferes with her comprehension.

We recommend the following goals and activities for Angela:

1. *Develop decoding ability.* Given that Angela understands many of the basic concepts about print and yet is reading below grade level with a high number of miscues, it appears that she needs direct instruction in decoding unknown words through the explicit teaching of vowel sounds and techniques for blending sounds together. Because she is able to put sounds together to create words in her writing, it seems advantageous to use her invented spellings to help her decode words. Activities with the "making words" approach would work well: having Angela build words with individual letter cards, decode words created by the tutor, sort words with similar characteristics, and explore some reliable rules of phonics (such as the silent *e* rule).

Angela also would benefit from comparing unknown words to words of similar structure that already are part of her sight vocabulary (such as comparing *black* and *sack*). To facilitate this learning, we will use a compare and contrast activity to encourage her to see the similarities between designated key words and new words in her reading.

Another way to help Angela develop word decoding strategies is to have her dictate stories in her own words to the tutor. These stories can then be read, cut apart, sequenced, and reread. Individual words that she dictates can be explored for patterns and phonemic regularity. These activities will help develop Angela's fluency, confidence, and sight-word recognition.

2. *Increase comprehension of text.* Angela's comprehension will increase as her decoding improves. However, she would benefit from direct instruction on applying prediction strategies through reading predictable stories and using picture clues to predict vocabulary. Regularly retelling stories immediately after reading will reinforce comprehension and improve her awareness of story structure.

3. *Develop a sight vocabulary.* Angela already has a good beginning base of sight words, as evidenced by her knowledge of 74/100 words on the Fry list. Given that the fluency of sight-word recognition can greatly influence a student's comprehension, improving Angela's sight-word base will positively affect the other areas in which she needs added instruction. Activities for improving sight-word recognition include use of flashcards in a game called "Three Strikes and You're Out," and "racetrack spelling," in which she will need to correctly say each word, without hesitation, to reach the end of the "track."

4. *Develop oral reading.* Angela's oral reading will improve by asking her to read actual text. She can be taught to apply decoding strategies in context as well as practice her sight words and begin to develop fluency. Along with consistently reading new stories, we will work on improving Angela's oral reading through echo reading, repeated reading, and paired choral reading.

```
┌─────────────────────────────────────────────────────────────────────┐
│  Name: Lee                        Date of report:                     │
│  Grade: 3                         Dates of testing:                   │
│  School: P.S. 555                 Date of birth:                      │
│  Parents:                         Age at testing: 8.4                 │
│  Address:                         Examiner: Megan Monaghan*           │
│  Telephone:                                                           │
└─────────────────────────────────────────────────────────────────────┘
```

BACKGROUND INFORMATION

Lee is an 8-year-old boy in third grade. Lee's teacher, Lindsey, recommended that I work with Lee because he is struggling in literacy and is currently lagging behind his peers. She hopes that one-on-one targeted instruction based on individual assessments will help him improve in reading and writing.

Lee lives with his grandmother. Over the last few years he has switched schools several times, but always seems to return to his current school. Because Lee has transferred schools so many times, a comprehensive record has not been available to Lindsey. Based on running records and conferences with Lee, she determined that Level K was his instructional reading level (Pinnell & Fountas, 1996). Pinnell and Fountas (1996) identify level K as approximately mid-second-grade level. Lindsey indicated that Lee has a hard time retaining directions given to him orally. Directions typically need to be repeated, and he requires frequent reminders to stay on task. She said he sometimes has a hard time staying focused on a single task, and that this is more apparent during English Language Arts than during other times of the day.

Lindsey showed me Lee's reading response journal. His entries are typically one paragraph long, focusing on what he did not understand in the text, compared to the other students in class, who write about a page per entry and reflect upon what was read. Lee is not currently receiving any extra services.

The assessments took place during the third-grade literacy block, which is in the morning. Lee and I sat together in the hallway outside his classroom. He seemed very shy at first, but warmed up to me after we worked together a couple times. When there is a lot of activity going on in the hallway, Lee gets distracted, but responds well to gentle redirection.

TESTS ADMINISTERED

Elementary Reading Attitude Survey

	Raw score	Midyear percentile rank
Recreational Reading	31	57
Academic Reading	32	74
Reading Attitude Total	63	67

---

*Thanks to Megan Monaghan, a graduate student in the New York University Tutoring Practicum, for her contribution. Megan's case study has been used as a foundation, but Lee is a pseudonym and all student information has been extensively revised to create a fictional character.

Qualitative Reading Inventory
  Graded Word Lists

	One	Two	Three
Automatic	80%	80%	40%
Total correct	90%	90%	40%
Level*	IND	IND	FR

Reading Passages

Title	*Who Lives Near Lakes?*	*Mouse in a House*
Readability level	Primer	Grade 1
Total accuracy	100%	98%
Total acceptability	100%	100%
Rate	106 WCPM	117 WCPM
Retelling	44%	36%
Comprehension		
Explicit	4 correct	3 correct
Implicit	2 correct	2 correct
Total	6/6 (100%)	5/6 (83%)
Passage level	IND	INS

Title	*The Brain and the Five Senses*	*Father's New Game*
Readability level	Grade 1	Grade 2
Total accuracy	98%	91%
Total acceptability	100%	93%
Rate	109 WCPM	89 WCPM
Retelling	21%	31%
Comprehension		
Explicit	4 correct	3 correct
Implicit	2 correct	2 correct
Total	6/6 (100%)	5/8 (63%)
Passage level	IND	FR

Title	*Whales and Fish*
Readability level	Grade 2
Total accuracy	89%
Total acceptability	93%
Rate	80 WCPM
Retelling	47%
Comprehension	
Explicit	3 correct
Implicit	2 correct
Total	5/8 (63%)
Passage level	FR

---

*IND, independent (Lee can read successfully without assistance); INS, instructional (Lee can read with assistance from a teacher); FR, frustration (Lee is unable to read the material with adequate word identification or comprehension).

Fry Sight-Word Inventory

First 100 Words

Recognized immediately	96
Recognized with hesitation	2
Incorrect response	2
No response	0

Second 100 Words

Recognized immediately	90
Recognized with hesitation	3
Incorrect response	6
No response	1

Third 100 Words

Recognized immediately	84
Recognized with hesitation	5
Incorrect response	11
No response	0

Elementary Spelling Inventory

Consonants (beginning)	2/2	100%
Consonants (final)	5/5	100%
Short vowels	3/4	75%
Digraphs and blends	6/8	75%
Long vowel patterns	5/6	83%
Other vowel patterns	0/4	0%
Syllable junctures and easy prefixes and suffixes	1/4	25%
Feature points	22/53	42%
Words attempted	15/25	60%
No. of correct words attempted	6/15	40%

Spelling stage: Late within-word pattern

Writing Sample

Qualitative Spelling Checklist	Within-word pattern stage

Dynamic Indicators of Basic Early Literacy Skills: Oral Reading Fluency and Retell Fluency (third grade)

Benchmark 2.1: 78 WCPM
                49 words in retell

Benchmark 2.2: 39 WCPM
                8 words in retell

Benchmark 2.3: 72 WCPM
                25 words in retell

OBSERVATIONS DURING TESTING

Development of Word Recognition

Qualitative Reading Inventory

The Qualitative Reading Inventory (QRI) is an informal assessment that helps teachers determine a child's independent reading level, instructional reading level, and frustration level. The teacher can also assess the child's background knowledge in an area, keep track of reading miscues, learn about the child's fluency, and evaluate the child.

First, the child reads a graded word list. The child's ability to read each graded word list helps the teacher determine the appropriate grade level passage of connected text. Some of the passages in the QRI are narrative and some are expository. In addition to using the word list, the teacher asks the child a few questions to determine whether the child has some prior knowledge about the content of the text. The child reads a story aloud. After the child reads, the teacher asks the student to retell what he remembers from the story. Next, she asks the child a series of comprehension questions about the given passage. Older students have an option of looking back in the story to find the answers to questions they answered incorrectly.

I started the word list at Lee's grade level (grade 3) and then went down to an easier level. Lee read the third-grade reading list at 40% accuracy. This is definitely a frustration level for him. He had a tendency to use initial letters to guess at the words and did not attempt to read five of them. For example, Lee read the word *lion* as "long," the word *rough* as "round," and the word *worried* as "wouldn't." At the second- and first-grade levels, Lee read 80% of the words automatically and 90% with some hesitation. This would be Lee's instructional/independent level for these words.

Fry Sight-Word Inventory

The Fry Sight-Word Inventory assesses a child's ability to recognize 300 words that occur often in text. By looking at Lee's incorrect responses, it can be seen that he relies heavily on initial letters of each word. This was consistent with his word-attack pattern in the QRI graded word list. Examples are included below:

Word	Lee's reading
along	alone
example	explain
life	lift
always	away
while	white
turn	true
Indian	indent

Spelling Development

Elementary Spelling Inventory

The spelling inventory is an assessment that helps the teacher determine the child's stage of spelling development. Each word on the test is more difficult than the previous word and contains features that the teacher can analyze to determine what the child understands about spelling and what is difficult for the child.

Lee has no trouble with beginning and final consonant sounds. He also did well with short-vowel sounds that occur within words. Lee had the most trouble with "other vowel patterns," which include *oi*, *er*, *ew*, and *ar*. Lee also has trouble with word endings. According to the feature guide and error guide that accompany the spelling inventory, Lee is currently in the late within word pattern stage of spelling.

Qualitative Spelling Checklist

The qualitative spelling checklist is an informal assessment that a teacher can use to help determine a child's stage of spelling. It can be used in conjunction with the spelling inventory or it can be used with other writing the student has done. For this assessment, I looked at an expository essay that Lee wrote about his friend Javon. Lee has mastered all of the components in the preliterate, early letter name, and letter name stages of spelling. All short-vowel words were spelled correctly in his essay. In the category of within word pattern, Lee often uses but confuses long vowels and he often spells many single-syllable long vowels correctly, but not consistently. Lee spells all blends and digraphs inconsistently. These features confirm that Lee is currently in the within word pattern stage of spelling. Examples of Lee's spelling errors are shown below.

Word	Lee's spelling
meet	mete
guys	gais
people	popel
reason	reuisn
fight	fitgt
great	grat

Reading Fluency

Dynamic Indicators of Basic Early Literacy Skills: Oral Reading Fluency and Retell Fluency

The Dynamic Indicators of Basic Early Literacy Skills (DIBELS) Oral Reading Fluency and Retell Fluency are assessments of accuracy and reading rate of connected text, as well as a check of comprehension. The child reads a graded passage for 1 minute, then has a minute to retell the events in the passage. The teacher keeps track of any errors the child makes when reading, provides pronunciation of words that are not read within 3 seconds, and keeps track of how many words are included in the child's retelling of the passage.

In the middle of the year at grade 3, students who are reading below 67 words correct per minute (WCPM) are considered at risk; students who are reading between 67 and 92 WCPM are considered at some risk; and students who are reading above 92 WCPM are considered at low risk. Using his median score of 72 correct, as advised on the DIBELS website, Lee is categorized as a student at some risk. If a student is not reading fluently, comprehension will be affected. This can be seen through Lee's retelling. When he read 78 WCPM, his retell consisted of 49 words. However, when Lee read at 39 WCPM, his retell was only eight words long: he did not comprehend this text as well as the previous one.

Qualitative Reading Inventory

During the administration of the QRI, the child reads a passage aloud while the teacher listens and marks down any of the child's miscues. The passage is timed to determine the child's rate of fluency. Lee's fluency increased to 109 WCPM on the first-grade passage of the QRI and to 89 WCPM and 80 WCPM on the second-grade passages. The DIBELS passages were third-grade passages, so it makes sense that he would be able to read easier passages of the QRI more fluently. On both the DIBELS assessment and the QRI, Lee's reading was monotone and lacked expression. His inattention to punctuation and meaning often resulted in awkward word grouping or phrasing.

Comprehension

The QRI graded passages are vehicles that teachers can use to assess many different aspects of reading. The teacher ascertains the student's prior knowledge by asking a few questions and rating the given answers. The child then reads a passage aloud while the teacher listens and records the child's miscues. After the passage is read, the child provides a retelling of the passage and answers comprehension questions.

According to the QRI results, Lee is reading independently at the preprimer and primer grade levels. While Lee's reading accuracy ranged from an independent to an instructional level on the second-grade passages and his reading rate was closer to the expected range for a third-grade student, his comprehension was at the frustration level. Lee had the most difficulty with the inferential questions. In addition, his retellings consisted of a few explicit story details and lacked themes or important story elements. Overall, it seemed as though Lee was making efforts to call words without making sense of the text along the way. First-grade material is likely to be at Lee's independent level. Lee's instructional reading level is second grade. Although he is able to recognize the words in second-grade texts, he will need strong instructional support in comprehending texts at this level.

Motivation/Attitudes

The Elementary Reading Attitude Survey is a quick survey that indicates the student's attitudes toward reading. I read each statement aloud and had Lee choose a Garfield picture that displays the emotion he feels about the statement. Overall, Lee has a positive attitude about both academic and recreational reading when compared with other children in third grade (67th percentile). In general, he has extremely positive feelings about academic reading (74th percentile). Lee does not like reading aloud during class and he also prefers not to read over summer break. Lee enjoys reading during free time at school and at home.

SUMMARY

Lee is a third-grade boy in New York City who enjoys reading, but is currently reading below grade level. Through informal assessment, I have learned a lot about Lee and his abilities as a reader and writer. Lee's instructional reading level is second grade. He is likely to be able to read and understand first-grade texts independently. He has a wonderful attitude about reading. This enjoyment of reading will be a valuable strength as we work together to strengthen some of Lee's reading challenges.

Lee has trouble reading many words that occur frequently in texts that he is exposed to. When approaching unknown words, he overrelies on initial letters. Lee needs practice identifying high-frequency words automatically. He also needs coaching in utilizing his knowledge about both short and long vowels when he comes to an unfamiliar word.

Lee is currently in the late within word spelling stage. He has mastered the short vowels. He needs to refine his knowledge of long-vowel patterns and word endings, especially blends and digraphs. After refining this knowledge, Lee will need to be introduced to other more complex vowel patterns.

Fluency is an area that Lee needs to strengthen. The DIBELS Oral Reading Fluency suggests that Lee is at some risk because of his rate of reading. In addition to this, Lee has trouble reading with prosody; his reading sounds choppy and expressionless. If Lee works on this, his comprehension will greatly improve.

Reading comprehension is an area that requires attention and explicit instruction. Lee's perception of comprehension seems to focus on the repetition of key words and isolated details from the text. He needs practice in identifying themes and the big ideas in texts. Currently, Lee has difficulty extending explicit information in text to generate inferences and personal connections.

RECOMMENDATIONS

There are many areas of literacy that Lee needs to strengthen. I have established a few goals for us to work on in the coming months. If Lee is able to become stronger in these areas, he will begin to catch up to his classmates and, in time, he will be reading at grade level.

Primary Goals

Increase rate, accuracy, and prosodic features of oral reading.
Improve reading comprehension: theme identification, story elements, inferences.

Secondary Goals

Increase automatic recognition of high-frequency words.
Increase accuracy in reading and spelling words with long vowel patterns, diphthongs, and
    consonant blends.

Fluency and Prosody

Fluency and prosody are extremely important when reading. A fluent reader is able to read text so automatically that word recognition is not distracting the reader from making sense of the text. Prosody is also an important component of fluency. The term *prosody* means reading with expression. If a child is reading with prosody, he will sound conversational. Instead of the reading sounding choppy or robotic, the child's phrasing and inflection will reflect the meaning.

Echo Reading

Echo reading has fluency as its main objective. During the lesson the teacher reads first and the student repeats what was read while pointing at the words on the page. This can be done with sentences, paragraphs, or even full pages. The reader will echo not only the actual words, but also the prosody used by the teacher. Echo reading will provide Lee with an explicit model of fluent reading and provide the support he needs when encountering difficult vocabulary.

Partner Reading

During partner reading readers work together as a team to read a given text. Typically, the partners will take turns reading. While one partner reads a portion of the story aloud, the other partner monitors and provides any necessary support. In working with Lee, the use of partner reading will enable us to read lengthier, more sophisticated texts in a reasonable time frame. The use of sophisticated texts will provide the substance needed for comprehension instruction and maintain Lee's good attitude about reading.

Repeated Reading

Repeated reading is when a child reads a piece of text multiple times. By providing repetition, Lee's increasing familiarity with the text will result in increasing fluency. Evidence seems to indicate that with each repetition, the child recognizes the words more quickly and can spend more energy reading with expression and gaining meaning from the text. I plan to use some book series to increase the likelihood that repeated readings help Lee not only with the given text, but also other texts in the series that contain similar language and patterns.

Reading Comprehension

The main goal of reading is to understand what is being read. Lee has difficulty comprehending text, and he retells a story by listing details or exact text phrases. Answering questions about a text is difficult for Lee. He needs instruction that will help him focus on the most important parts of text, and he needs to work on generating and answering comprehension questions.

Story Maps/Five-Finger Retelling

Lee's retellings tend to include every detail he remembers, rather than focusing on the most important aspects of the story. Story maps are graphic representations that allow students to see how information from the story is organized. It focuses on the most important features, including the characters, setting, problem, resolution, and lesson. Instruction and modeling the use of a story map will help Lee identify the key elements in most stories. Once Lee is comfortable with the story-map elements, he can use the five-finger retelling to summarize what he read by including only important elements: characters, setting, problem, resolution, and plot points that are essential to describing these aspects of the text. Lee will better understand what he is reading once he learns to focus on these parts, rather than trying to remember every detail in a story.

Teacher-Generated Questions

Lee needs practice answering both explicit questions (questions that can be answered directly through the text) and inference questions (questions that do not have a concrete answer in the text). Questions should help him focus on important parts of a story. It would be helpful for him to understand the different question types and how to go about answering them.

Development of Word Recognition

According to the QRI graded word lists and Fry's sight-word inventory, Lee is not automatically recognizing as many words as he should for a child in third grade. Both his recognition of high-frequency words and his ability to use word-attack strategies to unlock an unknown word are preventing Lee from being able to read fluently.

"Three Strikes and You're Out"

This activity will help Lee master high-frequency words and other words that cause trouble during oral reading. The words are placed on index cards and practiced during each work session. Upon reading the word correctly three times, the word is "out" and placed in a separate word bank. These words are revisited periodically to confirm mastery.

Word Sorts

Word sorting is a way to engage students in constructing and owning their knowledge about how words work. Children are given lists of words to divide into categories based on features in the words. This type of activity will allow Lee to see many different words and compare how they are similar and different. Lee can apply these patterns to unfamiliar words when he is reading connected text or creating a written composition during writer's workshop. We will begin with a focus on long-vowel words that contain blends and digraphs. As Lee progresses, we will move into the exploration of complex vowel patterns.

SUMMARY OF THE TUTORING

Lee and I worked together twice a week from January 16 until May 1. We had 22 sessions together. I spent the first session observing Lee in his classroom and two sessions administering pretutoring assessments. During most of our time together we focused on fluency and comprehension. During our last two sessions I administered postassessments.

It was a pleasure for me to work with Lee. He was always eager to meet with me in the hallway and take part in our activities. He was never absent or late for school. We normally worked in the hallway and the traffic could be distracting. Over time, he seemed to become more focused and less distracted by other students in the hallway.

Based on the results of initial assessments, my primary goals were to increase Lee's fluency and comprehension. As you can see from the descriptions of the activities below, prosody and text comprehension were always involved in fluency work. Simply reading faster was never an instructional objective.

Echo Reading

Echo reading was a common activity. First we would look at the text selection together and talk about the title and what the selection might be about. If we were reading part of a chapter book, Lee would summarize what had been previously read and make a purposeful prediction about what might be in the next section of text. Typically, I would begin reading a few lines of text or a paragraph. This procedure worked well with a few Nate the Great books by Marjorie Sharmat. We often followed this procedure with poetry. For more difficult poems, I would echo read the poem line-by-line and then repeat by stanza. The repetition helped Lee with unfamiliar words, inflection, and stress as he tried to copy my model. Echo reading also helped Lee increase his rate of reading and confidence level. During our time together Lee became a fan of poetry by Jack Prelutsky and Shel Silverstein.

Assisted Reading: Partner Reading and Paired Reading

In order to engage Lee with easy chapter books, we participated in partner reading and paired reading (Topping, 1987). I wanted Lee to read chapter books so that he would be exposed to greater volumes of words, to provide a scaffolded experience for take-home reading, and to engage in reading fun stories with fairly predictable story structures. Because I only worked with Lee twice a week, the use of easy chapter book series (Nate the Great, Horrible Harry) provided a way to sustain reading when I wasn't present. During the tutoring sessions, assisted reading provided a way to get through a significant amount of text in a short period, while modeling prosodic reading. When Lee and I worked together, we might partner-read the text by taking turns reading alternate pages, or we might do paired reading. During paired reading, we started out reading simultaneously (duet), and Lee later had the option of signaling that he wished to read solo. If he had trouble, I told him the word and we continued in duet until he tapped to indicate his desire to return to solo reading. Assisted reading helped Lee gain confidence in reading aloud and helped him sustain fluent and prosodic reading with engaging chapter books. Reading stopped intermittently for discussion about the characters and events in the book.

Fluency Development Lesson

After working with Lee for a few weeks, I began using a combination of the approaches above in a more intense routine. This approach is an adaptation of the Fluency Development Lesson (Rasinski, Padak, Linek, & Sturtevant, 1994). First, we would read a chapter together using paired reading. Sometimes we would read three or four poems. We discussed the meaning of the chapter or each poem. Then Lee selected his favorite story part or individual poem and read it into a tape recorder. Next, I read it aloud and emphasized inflection, stress, and phrasing. At this point we discussed the relationship of relevant print functions (punctuation, paragraph, or stanza structure), fluency, and meaning. Then we echo-read Lee's selection. After echo reading, Lee and I divided up the lines and took turns reading them. We often did several different arrangements, resulting in multiple repeated readings. Finally, Lee read the poem aloud independently and I recorded him again. At the end of the activity, I played back both recordings and we talked about the differences between the two recordings. Hearing the improvement increased prosodic awareness and was motivational for Lee.

Listening Comprehension

For a portion of each lesson, I read aloud to Lee. This was an opportunity to remind Lee that the purpose of reading is to make sense of the text. During this reading, I asked questions and discussed the vocabulary and characters in the text. This was also the portion of the lesson that included instruction in story elements. Over time, Lee used the five-finger retelling to retell what the important elements: characters, setting, problem, attempts to solve the problem, and resolution.

Word Study

Word-study activities were fast paced and fun for Lee. During each session we did a quick activity to review and increase Lee's automatic recognition of high-frequency words. Lee enjoyed the Three Strikes activity. Fry words and some miscues from his daily reading were incorporated in this game. Each session also included a word sort or game that addressed consonant blends, long-vowel patterns, and diphthongs.

Writing

Although writing was not the main focus of our time together, Lee's teacher asked me to work with him on several occasions in the classroom setting. Lee seemed to have a difficult time getting started on his writing assignments, but with scaffolding and encouragement he was able to do well.

One of Lee's biggest difficulties was staying focused and organized. The writing workshop model in his class was designed to give children time to write every day after mini-lessons. Revising took place after multiple days of writing. Lee had paragraphs on different pages in a seemingly random order. To help Lee, I used small sticky notes to number his pages in the correct sequence. This system seemed to help him focus and aided his ability to revise.

Staying on task during the writing period was difficult for Lee. After the teacher's mini-lesson, I worked with Lee individually to discuss different ways to approach that day's writing task. If I stayed with Lee, he sat and wrote, sometimes asking questions about what he should do next, but usually writing independently. However, if I left his side to assist other students, he often got distracted and stopped writing. In order to motivate Lee, I began using a timer between my drop-ins with him. Explicitly stating expectations for his writing combined with the time limit worked well. Each time I returned to Lee's seat, he had achieved his writing goal!

PRINCIPAL RESULTS

Qualitative Reading Inventory
  Graded Words Lists
    January

	One	Two	Three
Automatic	80%	80%	40%
Total correct	90%	90%	40%
Level	IND	IND	FR

April

	One	Two	Three
Automatic	90%	90%	55%
Total correct	100%	95%	55%
Level	IND	INS	FR

Reading Passages

January

Passage level	Acc	WCPM	Comp	Level
PP	100	126	100%	IND
Primer N	100	97	100%	IND
Primer E	100	106	100%	IND
1 N	100	117	83%	INS
1 E	100	109	100%	IND
2 N	93	89	63%	FR
2 E	93	80	63%	FR

April

Passage level	Acc	WCPM	Comp	Level
Primer N	100	115	100	IND
Primer E	100	102	83	INS
1 N	100	121	100	IND
1 E	100	140	100	IND
2 N	100	120	100	IND
2 E	96	89	75	INS

Fry Sight-Word Inventory

First 100 Words	January	April
Recognized immediately	96	99
Recognized with hesitation	2	1
Incorrect response	2	0
No response	0	0
Total recognized	98	100
Second 100 Words	January	April
Recognized immediately	90	92
Recognized with hesitation	3	6
Incorrect response	6	1
No response	1	1
Total recognized	93	98
Third 100 Words	January	April
Recognized immediately	84	93
Recognized with hesitation	5	5
Incorrect response	11	2
No response	0	0
Total recognized	89	98

Elementary Spelling Inventory

	January		April	
Consonants (beginning)	2/2	100%	2/2	100%
Consonants (final)	5/5	100%	5/5	100%
Short vowels	3/4	75%	3/4	75%
Digraphs and blends	6/8	75%	8/8	100%
Long vowel patterns	5/6	83%	5/6	83%
Other vowel patterns	0/4	0%	3/6	50%
Syllable junctures and easy prefixes and suffixes	1/9	11%	3/9	33%
Feature points	22/53	42%	29/53	55%
Words attempted	5/25	60%	17/25	68%
No. of correct words attempted	6/15	40%	10/17	59%

DIBELS: Oral Reading Fluency and Retell Fluency
    January midyear benchmarks
        Benchmark 2.1: 78 WCPM
                49 words in retell
        Benchmark 2.2: 39 WCPM
                8 words in retell
        Benchmark 2.3: 72 WCPM
                25 words in retell

    April third-grade progress monitoring
        Progress monitoring 1: 126 WCPM
                77 words in retell
        Progress monitoring 2: 106 WCPM
                67 words in retell
        Progress monitoring 3: 82 WCPM
                43 words in retell
        Progress monitoring 4: 79 WCPM
                55 words in retell
        Progress monitoring 5: 100 WCPM
                42 words in retell
        Progress monitoring 6: 128 WCPM
                87 words in retell

Summary of Results

Lee has improved in many areas of reading over the last few months. His assessment scores on measures of comprehension, fluency, and retelling have all increased. According to the QRI results, Lee is reading independently at the primer and first-grade levels. He also read at the independent level in second-grade narrative. Both DIBELS scores and Lee's independent level of functioning on second-grade narrative materials lead me to conclude that Lee is now reading at a third-grade instructional level. He is probably able to read third-grade expository materials when high levels of conceptual support are provided. This indicates reading improvement from his January levels of frustration when reading narrative and expository second-grade materials.

Lee's overall progress in reading may be attributed to improvements in specific reading behaviors. He increased his automatic recognition of high-frequency words. Increased knowledge of particular vowel sounds and spelling patterns was indicated on the Elementary Spelling Inventory (Bear et al., 2008). Lee's choppy reading gave way to fluent reading with natural phrasing. He pays more attention to punctuation and is able to gain and retain more meaning from text.

During the pretest, comprehension questions often had to be rephrased before he was able to frame a response. He no longer needs this scaffolding. Although not every question was answered correctly, he no longer needed to clarify the meaning of the questions. The explicit instruction in reading purposefully has also helped his overall comprehension. Lee still has shown great success over the last few months. According to his teacher, Lee's success has transferred to his literacy performance in the classroom, and she has observed increased engagement and motivation.

FURTHER RECOMMENDATIONS

In the future, Lee should continue many of the same activities he participated in throughout his tutoring sessions. Continuing with a program that includes rereading texts, reading new texts, and developmentally based word study will address many of the reading difficulties that Lee continues to experience.

In addition to the recommendations already given, it is important to note three other suggestions that could not be covered in the short tutoring sessions that I had with Lee but would aid in his development as a reader. These include the application of fluency-oriented approaches with content-area materials, comprehension strategy instruction, and the use of concrete means to demonstrate expectations and progress. These are explained below.

Fluency-Oriented Approaches in Content Areas

One activity that greatly benefits Lee and is a lot of fun for him is my modification of the Fluency Development Lesson (Rasinski et al., 1994). This activity helps Lee in several areas, including fluency, prosody, word recognition, vocabulary, and comprehension. This technique worked very well with Lee during our time together, and it may continue to support Lee's efforts with increasingly difficult text. Continuing this activity will provide a fluency maintenance program and provide the close reading that Lee still needs to support comprehension and vocabulary development. In addition, this technique might incorporate famous speeches and other documents related to content area instruction. The Radio Reading (see Rasinski, 2003) technique would also be a good approach for Lee. During Radio Reading, each student in a small group is assigned to rehearse one section of a larger informational text. Each student assumes responsibility for reading that section of text to the small group and asking one or two comprehension questions based on that segment of text.

Comprehension Strategy Instruction

Lee would benefit from explicit instruction of comprehension strategies such as activating prior knowledge, summarization, questioning, self-monitoring, generating inferences, and text structures. I initiated instruction of narrative text structure and how to answer teacher questions. These two strategies gave Lee greater self-regulation in being able to generate a retelling of a narrative and answering comprehension questions. However, this was a meager beginning. For Lee to make sense of the complex texts that he will encounter in the intermediate grades, he will need far more instruction on the cognitive strategies used by proficient readers to derive meaning and evaluate texts. Tools such as graphic organizers, utilization of short hypertext selections, and conversational application of the strategies might be motivational and effective with Lee. The use of graphic organizers and conversation are also likely to support Lee in translating his comprehension of text to his own written products that reflect his understanding.

Defining a Task

Lee responded well when the expectations and his progress were clearly defined. He was able to use a structure defined by common story elements to improve the quantity and quality of his retellings. Using charts to analyze his errors and prosodic reading improved his fluency in dramatic ways. Even in the classroom, assigning a small, specific composition task within a time frame was met with success. Lee's learning seems to be enhanced when he can have a visual target, graphic representation, or clearly stated goal set before him. These elements might be kept in mind when planning a wide range of instruction for Lee.

References

Adams, M. J. (1990). *Beginning to read: Thinking and learning about print.* Cambridge, MA: MIT Press.

Adams, M. J. (1998). The three-cuing system. In J. Osborn & F. Lehr (Eds.), *Literacy for all: Issues in teaching and learning* (pp. 73–99). New York: Guilford Press.

Afflerbach, P., & Cho, B. (in press). Identifying and describing constructively responsive comprehension strategies in new and traditional forms of reading. In S. E. Israel & G. G. Duffy (Eds.), *Handbook of research on reading comprehension.* New York: Routledge.

Afflerbach, P., Pearson, P. D., & Paris, S. G. (2008). Clarifying differences between reading skills and reading strategies. *The Reading Teacher, 61,* 364–373.

Allington, R. L. (1983). Fluency: The neglected reading goal. *The Reading Teacher, 37,* 556–561.

Allington, R. L. (1984). Content coverage and contextual reading in reading groups. *Journal of Reading Behavior, 16,* 85–96.

Anderson, R. C., & Pearson, P. D. (1984). A schema-theoretic view of basic processes in reading. In P. D. Pearson (Ed.), *Handbook of reading research* (pp. 255–292). White Plains, NY: Longman.

Beach, S. A. (1992). *Toward a model of the development of reader resources in the emergence and acquisition of literacy skill.* Unpublished PhD dissertation, University of California at Riverside.

Bear, D. R., Invernizzi, M., Templeton, S., & Johnston, F. (2008). *Words their way: Word study for phonics, vocabulary, and spelling instruction* (4th ed.). Upper Saddle River, NJ: Pearson/Prentice Hall.

Beaver, J. (2001). *Developmental reading assessment.* New York: Pearson Learning.

Betts, E. A. (1946). *Foundations of reading instruction.* New York: American Books.

Biemiller, A. (1970). The development of the use of graphic and contextual information as children learn to read. *Reading Research Quarterly, 6,* 75–96.

Bloom, B. S. (1969). *Taxonomy of educational objectives: The classification of educational goals.* New York: Longman.

Bradley, B. A., & Jones, J. (2007). Sharing alphabet books in early childhood classrooms. *The Reading Teacher, 60*, 452–463.

Burke, C. L. (1987). Reading interview. In Y. M. Goodman, D. W. Watson, & C. L. Burke (Eds.), *Reading miscue inventory: Alternative procedures*. Katonah, NY: Owen.

Byrne, B. (1998). *The foundation of literacy: The child's acquisition of the alphabetic principle (Essays in developmental psychology)*. Brighton, UK: Psychology Press.

Carbo, M., Dunn, R., & Dunn, K. (1986). *Teaching students to read through their individual learning styles*. Englewood Cliffs, NJ: Prentice Hall.

Chall, J. S. (1996). *Stages of reading development* (2nd ed.). Fort Worth, TX: Harcourt-Brace.

Chomsky, C. (1979). Approaching reading through invented spelling. In L. B. Resnick & P. A. Weaver (Eds.), *Theory and practice of early reading* (Vol. 2, pp. 43–65). Hillsdale, NJ: Erlbaum.

Clay, M. M. (1993a). *An observation survey of early literacy achievement*. Portsmouth, NH: Heinemann.

Clay, M. M. (1993b). *Reading Recovery: A guidebook for teachers in training*. Portsmouth, NH: Heinemann.

Clay, M. M. (2000). *Running records for classroom teachers*. Portsmouth, NH: Heinemann.

Cunningham, A. E., & Stanovich, K. E. (1991). Tracking the unique effects of print exposure in children: Associations with vocabulary, general knowledge, and spelling. *Journal of Educational Psychology, 83*, 264–274.

Cunningham, J. W. (1982). Generating interactions between schemata and text. In J. A. Niles & L. A. Harris (Eds.), *New inquiries in reading research and instruction: Thirty-first yearbook of the National Reading Conference* (pp. 42–47). Rochester, NY: National Reading Conference.

Cunningham, J. W., Erickson, K. A., Spadorcia, S. A., Koppenhaver, D. A., Cunningham, P. M., Yoder, D. E., et al. (1999). Assessing decoding from an onset–rime perspective. *Journal of Literacy Research, 31*, 391–414.

Cunningham, P. M. (1999). *Phonics they use: Words for reading and writing* (3rd ed.). Boston: Addison-Wesley.

Cunningham, P. M. (2001). *Phonics they use*. New York: HarperCollins.

Cunningham, P. M., & Cunningham, J. W. (1992). Making words: Enhancing the invented spelling–decoding connection. *The Reading Teacher, 46*, 106–115.

Dale, E. (1946). The art of reading. *Ohio State University News Letter, 9*, 1.

Davis, A. P., & McDaniel, T. R. (1998). An essential vocabulary: An update. *The Reading Teacher, 52*, 308–309.

Dolch, E. W. (1936). A basic sight vocabulary. *Elementary School Journal, 36*, 456–460.

Donahue, P. L., Voelkl, K. E., Campbell, J. R., & Mazzeo, J. (1999). *NAEP 1998 Reading Report Card for the Nation* (prepublication ed.). Washington, DC: U.S. Department of Education, Office of Educational Research and Improvement.

Duffy, G. G. (2003). *Explaining reading: A resource for teaching concepts, skills, and strategies*. New York: Guilford Press.

Duke, N. (2002, August). *Comprehension*. Paper presented at the Institute for Statewide Literacy Initiatives, Harvard University, Cambridge, MA.

Duke, N. K., Schmar-Dobler, E., & Zhang, S. (2006). Comprehension and technology. In M. C. McKenna, L. D. Labbo, R. Kieffer, & D. Reinking (Eds.), *International handbook of literacy and technology* (Vol. 2, pp. 317–326). Mahwah, NJ: Erlbaum.

Ehri, L. C. (1998). Grapheme–phoneme knowledge is essential for learning to read words in English. In J. L. Metsala & L. C. Ehri (Eds.), *Word recognition in beginning literacy* (pp. 3–40). Mahwah, NJ: Erlbaum.

Ehri, L. C., & Robbins, C. (1992). Beginners need some decoding skill to read words by analogy. *Reading Research Quarterly, 27,* 12–26.

Ehri, L. C., & Sweet, J. (1991). Fingerpoint-reading of memorized text: What enables beginners to process the print. *Reading Research Quarterly, 26,* 442–462.

Elkonin, D. B. (1973). U.S.S.R. In J. Downing (Ed.), *Comparative reading* (pp. 551–579). New York: Macmillan.

English, F. W., & Frase, L. B. (1999). *Deciding what to teach and test: Developing, aligning, and auditing the curriculum.* Thousand Oaks, CA: Corwin Press.

Farr, R. (1992). Putting it all together: Solving the reading assessment puzzle. *The Reading Teacher, 46,* 26–37.

Fountas, I. C., & Pinnell, G. S. (2005). *The Fountas & Pinnell leveled book list, K–8: 2006-2008 edition.* Portsmouth, NH: Heinemann.

Francis, N. (1999). Applications of cloze procedure to reading assessment in special circumstances of literacy development. *Reading Horizons, 40,* 23–44.

Fry, E. B. (1977). Fry's readability graph: Clarification, validity, and extension to level 17. *Journal of Reading, 21,* 242–252.

Fry, E. B. (1980). The new Instant Word List. *The Reading Teacher, 34,* 284–289.

Gambrell, L. B., Palmer, B. M., Codling, R. M., & Mazzoni, S. A. (1995). *Assessing motivation to read* (Instructional Resource No. 14). Athens, GA: National Reading Research Center, University of Georgia and University of Maryland.

Ganske, K. (2000). *Word journeys: Assessment-guided phonics, spelling, and vocabulary instruction.* New York: Guilford Press.

Garner, R., & Kraus, C. (1981). Good and poor comprehender differences in knowing and regulating reading behaviors. *Educational Research Quarterly, 6,* 5–12.

Gaskins, I. W., Downer, M. A., Anderson, R. C., Cunningham, P. M., Gaskins, R. W., Schommer, M., & the teachers of Benchmark School. (1988). A metacognitive approach to phonics: Using what you know to decode what you don't know. *Remedial and Special Education, 9,* 36–41.

Gaskins, I. W., Ehri, L. C., Cress, C., O'Hara, C., & Donnelly, K. (1996). Procedures for word learning: Making discoveries about words. *The Reading Teacher, 50,* 312–328.

Gillet, J. W., & Temple, C. (1990). *Understanding reading problems* (3rd ed.). Glenview, IL: Scott-Foresman.

Goodman, K. S. (1993). *Phonics phacts.* Portsmouth, NH: Heinemann.

Goodman, Y. M., Watson, D. J., & Burke, C. L. (1987). *Reading miscue inventory: Alternative procedures.* Katonah, NY: Owen.

Gough, P. B., Juel, C., & Griffith, P. L. (1992). Reading, spelling, and the orthographic cipher. In P. B. Gough, L. C. Ehri, & R. Treiman (Eds.), *Reading acquisition* (pp. 35–48). Hillsdale, NJ: Erlbaum.

Guthrie, J. T., & McCann, A. D. (1996). Idea circles: Peer collaborations for conceptual learning. In L. B. Gambrell & J. F. Almasi (Eds.), *Lively discussions! Fostering engaged reading* (pp. 87–105). Newark, DE: International Reading Association.

Guthrie, J. T., McGough, K., & Wigfield, A. (1994). *Measuring reading activity: An inventory* (Instructional Resource No. 4). Athens, GA: National Reading Research Center, University of Georgia and University of Maryland.

Guthrie, J. T., Seifert, M., Burnham, N., & Caplan, R. (1974). The maze technique to assess, monitor reading comprehension. *The Reading Teacher, 28,* 161–168.

Harste, J. C., Burke, C. L., & Woodward, V. A. (1982). Children's language and world: Initial encounters with print. In J. A. Langer & M. T. Smith-Burke (Eds.), *Reader meets author/ Bridging the gap* (pp. 105–131). Newark, DE: International Reading Association.

Hasbrouck, J. E., & Tindal, G. (2006). Oral reading fluency norms: A valuable assessment tool for reading teachers. *The Reading Teacher, 59,* 636–644.

Hayes, D. A. (1989). Helping students grasp the knack of writing summaries. *Journal of Reading, 33,* 96–101.

Henderson, E. H. (1981). *Learning to read and spell: The child's knowledge of words.* DeKalb, IL: Northern Illinois University Press.

Henk, W. A., & Melnick, S. A. (1995). The Reader Self-Perception Scale (RSPS): A new tool for measuring how children feel about themselves as readers. *The Reading Teacher, 48,* 470–482.

Hoffman, J. (1987). Rethinking the role of oral reading. *Elementary School Journal, 87,* 367–373.

Hutchins, P. (1968). *Rosie's walk.* New York: Simon & Schuster.

Jacobs, J. E., & Paris, S. G. (1987). Children's metacognition about reading: Issues in definition, measurement, and instruction. *Educational Psychologist, 22,* 255–278.

Johns, J. L. (2005). *Basic Reading Inventory* (9th ed.). Dubuque, IA: Kendall-Hunt.

Johnston, P. H. (2000). *Running records: A self-tutoring guide.* Portland, ME: Stenhouse. [Book and audiocassette]

Koskinen, P. S., Wilson, R. M., & Jensema, C. J. (1985). Closed-captioned television: A new tool for reading instruction. *Reading World, 24*(4), 1–7.

Krahn, F. (1979). *Robot-bot-bot.* Boston: Dutton.

Kuhn, M. R., & Stahl, S. A. (2003). Fluency: A review of developmental and remedial practices. *Journal of Educational Psychology, 95,* 3–21.

LaBerge, D., & Samuels, S. J. (1974). Toward a theory of automatic information processing in reading. *Cognitive Psychology, 6,* 293–323.

Leal, D. J. (1993). The power of literary peer group discussions: How children collaboratively negotiate meaning. *The Reading Teacher, 47,* 114–120.

Leslie, L., & Caldwell, J. S. (2005). *Qualitative reading inventory–4.* New York: Allyn & Bacon.

Leu, D. J., Coiro, J., Castek, J., Hartman, D. K., Henry, L. A., & Reinking, D. (2008). Research on instruction and assessment in the new literacies of online reading comprehension. In L. M. Morrow, C. C. Block, & S. R. Parris (Eds.), *Comprehension instruction: Research-based best practices* (2nd ed., pp. 321–346). New York: Guilford Press.

Manzo, A. V. (1969). The ReQuest procedure. *Journal of Reading, 2,* 123–126.

Manzo, A. V., & Casale, U. P. (1985). Listen–read–discuss: A content reading heuristic. *Journal of Reading, 28,* 732–734.

Martin, B., Jr. (1983). *Brown bear, brown bear, what do you see?* New York: Holt.

McKenna, M. C. (1981). A modified maze approach to teaching poetry. *Journal of Reading, 24,* 391–394.

McKenna, M. C. (1983). Informal reading inventories: A review of the issues. *The Reading Teacher, 36,* 670–679.

McKenna, M. C. (1986). Reading interests of remedial secondary school students. *Journal of Reading, 29,* 346–351.

McKenna, M. C. (2001). Development of reading attitudes. In L. Verhoeven & C. Snow (Eds.), *Literacy and motivation: Reading engagement in individuals and groups* (pp. 135–158). Mahwah, NJ: Erlbaum.

McKenna, M. C. (2002). *Help for struggling readers: Strategies for grades 3–8*. New York: Guilford Press.

McKenna, M. C., & Kear, D. J. (1990). Measuring attitude toward reading: A new tool for teachers. *The Reading Teacher, 43*, 626–639.

McKenna, M. C., Kear, D. J., & Ellsworth, R. A. (1995). Children's attitudes toward reading; A national survey. *Reading Research Quarterly, 30*, 934–956.

McKenna, M. C., Simkin, C. R., Conradi, K., & Lawrence, C. (2008, December). *Development of an adolescent reading attitude survey*. Paper presented at the annual meeting of the National Reading Conference, Orlando, FL.

McKenna, M. C., & Picard, M. (2006/2007). Does miscue analysis have a role in effective practice? *The Reading Teacher, 60*, 378–380.

McKenna, M. C., & Robinson, R. D. (2009). *Teaching through text: A content literacy approach to content area reading*. Boston: Allyn & Bacon.

McKenna, M. C., & Walpole, S. (2005). How well does assessment inform our reading instruction? *The Reading Teacher, 59*, 84–86.

Messick, S. (1993). Validity. In R. L. Linn (Ed.), *Educational measurement* (3rd ed., pp. 13–103). New York: Macmillan.

Morris, D. (1993). The relationship between children's concept of word in text and phoneme awareness in learning to read: A longitudinal study. *Research in the Teaching of English, 27*, 133–154.

Nagy, W. E. (1988). *Teaching vocabulary to improve reading comprehension*. Newark, DE: International Reading Association.

National Reading Panel. (2000). *Report of the subgroups: National reading panel*. Washington, DC: National Institute of Child Health and Development.

Owocki, G., & Goodman, Y. M. (2002). *Kidwatching: Documenting children's literacy development*. Portsmouth, NH: Heinemann.

Palincsar, A. S., & Brown, A. L. (1984). Reciprocal teaching of comprehension fostering and comprehension monitoring activities. *Cognition and Instruction, 1*(2), 117–175.

Paris, A. H., & Paris, S. G. (2001). *Children's comprehension of narrative picture books* (Technical Report No. 3–012). Ann Arbor, MI: Center for the Improvement of Early Reading Achievement,

Paris, S. G. (2005). Reinterpreting the development of reading skills. *Reading Research Quarterly, 40*, 184–202.

Paris, S. G., Lipson, M. Y., & Wixson, K. K. (1983). Becoming a strategic reader. *Contemporary Educational Psychology, 8*, 293–316.

Paris, S. G., Pearson, P. D., Cervetti, G., Carpenter, R., Paris, A. H., DeGroot, J., et al. (2004). Assessing the effectiveness of summer reading programs. In G. Borman & M. Boulay (Eds.), *Summer learning: Research, policies, and programs* (pp. 121–162). Mahwah, NJ: Erlbaum.

Parker, R. I., & Hasbrouck, J. E. (1992). The maze as a classroom-based reading measure: Construction methods, reliability, and validity. *Journal of Special Education, 26*, 195–218.

Pearson, P. D., & Gallagher, M. C. (1983). The instruction of reading comprehension. *Contemporary Educational Psychology, 8*, 317–344.

Perfetti, C. A., Beck, I. L., Bell, L., & Hughes, C. (1987). Phonemic knowledge and learning to read are reciprocal: A longitudinal study of first-grade children. *Merrill-Palmer Quarterly, 33*, 283–319.

Peterson, B. (1991). Selecting books for beginning readers. In D. E. DeFord, C. A. Lyons, & G. S. Pinnell (Eds.), *Bridges to literacy: Learning from Reading Recovery* (pp. 119–147). Portsmouth, NH: Heinemann.

Peterson, J., Greenlaw, M. J., & Tierney, R. J. (1978). Assessing instructional placement with an IRI: The effectiveness of comprehension questions. *Journal of Educational Research, 71,* 247–250.

Phelan, P. (Ed.). (1996). *High interest–easy reading: An annotated booklist for middle school and senior high school* (7th ed.). Urbana, IL: National Council of Teachers of English.

Pinnell, G. S., & Fountas, I. C. (1996). *Guided reading: Good first teaching for all children.* Portsmouth, NH: Heinemann.

Pressley, M., & Woloshyn, V. (1995). *Cognitive strategy instruction that really improves children's academic performance.* Cambridge, MA: Brookline Press.

Pugh, K. R., Mend, W. E., Jenner, A. R., Katz, L., Frost, S. J., Lee, J. R., et al. (2001). Neurobiological studies of reading and reading disability. *Journal of Communication Disorders, 34,* 479–492.

Rasinski, T. V. (2003). *The fluent reader: Oral reading strategies for building word recognition, fluency, and comprehension.* New York: Scholastic.

Rasinski, T. V., Padak, N., Linek, W., & Sturtevant, E. (1994). The effects of fluency development instruction on urban second grade readers. *Journal of Educational Research, 87,* 158–164.

Raygor, A. (1977). The Raygor readability estimate: A quick and easy way to determine difficulty. In P. D. Pearson (Ed.), *Reading: Theory, research, and practice: Twenty-sixth yearbook of the National Reading Conference* (pp. 259–263). Clemson, SC: National Reading Conference.

Rayner, K., & Pollatsek, A. (1989). *The psychology of reading.* Mahwah, NJ: Erlbaum.

Read, C. (1971). Pre-school children's knowledge of English phonology. *Harvard Educational Review, 41,* 1–34.

Rhodes, L. (1981). I can read: Predictable books as resources or reading and writing instruction. *The Reading Teacher, 34,* 511–518.

Riccio, C. A., & Hynd, G. A. (1996). Neuroanatornical and urophysiological aspects of dyslexia. *Topics in Language Disorders, 16*(2), 1–3.

Riedel, B. W. (2007). The relation between DIBELS, reading comprehension, and vocabulary in urban first-grade students. *Reading Research Quarterly, 42,* 546–567.

Rigby Education. (2001). *Rigby PM benchmark kit.* Barrington, IL: Author.

Rosenshine, B., Meister, C., & Chapman, S. (1996). Teaching students to generate questions: A review of the intervention studies. *Review of Educational Research, 66,* 181–221.

Rosner, J. (1975). *Helping children overcome learning difficulties.* New York: Walker.

Scarborough, H. S., & Brady, S. (2001). *Toward a common terminology for talking about speech and reading: A glossary of the Phon words and some related terms.* Unpublished manuscript.

Schumaker, J. B., Deshler, D. D., Alley, G. R., Warner, M. W., & Denton, T. H. (1982). Multipass: A learning strategy for improving reading comprehension. *Learning Disability Quarterly, 5,* 295–304.

Shankweiler, D., & Liberman, I. Y. (1972). Misreading: A search for causes. In I. F. Kavanaugh & I. G. Mattingly (Eds.), *Language by eye and by ear* (pp. 293–317). Cambridge, MA: MIT Press.

Shaywitz, S. E. (1996). Dyslexia. *Scientific American, 275*(5), 98–104.

Shin, J., Deno, S. L., & Espin, C. (2000). Technical adequacy of the maze task for curriculum-based measurement of reading growth. *Journal of Special Education, 34,* 164–172.

Shinn, M. R. (Ed.). (1989). *Curriculum-based measurement: Assessing special children.* New York: Guilford Press.

Shinn, M. R. (1992). Curriculum-based measurement of oral reading fluency: A confirmatory analysis of its relation to reading. *School Psychology Review, 21*, 459–479.

Silvaroli, N. J. (1977, April). *Norm-referenced tests do not diagnose.* Paper presented at the A. Sterl Artley Symposium, University of Missouri–Columbia.

Smith, F. (1988). *Understanding reading* (4th ed.). Mahwah, NJ: Erlbaum.

Spear-Swerling, L., & Sternberg, R. J. (1996). Off track: When poor readers become "learning disabled." Boulder, CO: Westview Press.

Stahl, S. A. (1999a). Different strokes for different folks? A critique of learning styles. *American Educator, 23*(3), 27–31.

Stahl, S. A. (1999b). *Vocabulary development.* Cambridge, MA: Brookline Press.

Stahl, S. A., Duffy-Hester, A. M., & Stahl, K. A. D. (1998). Everything you wanted to know about phonics (but were afraid to ask). *Reading Research Quarterly, 33*, 338–355.

Stahl, S. A., & Heubach, K. M. (2005). Fluency-oriented reading instruction. *Journal of Literacy Research, 37*, 25–60.

Stahl, S. A., & McKenna, M. C. (2001). *The concurrent development of phonological awareness, word recognition, and spelling* (Technical Report No. 01–07). Ann Arbor, MI: Center for the Improvement of Early Reading Achievement. Available online at *www.ciera.org/library-larchi ve/2001-07/200 lO7.htm*

Stahl, S. A., & Murray, B. A. (1994). Defining phonological awareness and its relationship to early reading. *Journal of Educational Psychology, 86*, 221–234.

Stahl, S. A., & Murray, B. A. (1998). Issues involved in defining phonological awareness and its relation to early reading. In J. Metsala & L. C. Ehri (Eds.), *Word recognition in beginning literacy* (pp. 65–88). Mahwah, NJ: Erlbaum.

Stanovich, K. E. (1980). Toward an interactive–compensatory model of individual differences in the development of reading fluency. *Reading Research Quarterly, 16*, 32–71.

Stanovich, K. E. (1986). Matthew effects in reading: Some consequences of individual differences in the acquisition of literacy. *Reading Research Quarterly, 21*, 360–407.

Stanovich, K. E. (1991). Word recognition: Changing perspectives. In R. Barr, M. L. Kamil, P. B. Mosenthal, & P. D. Pearson (Eds.), *Handbook of reading research* (Vol. 2, pp. 418–452). New York: Longman.

Sulzby, E. (1985). Children's emergent reading of favorite storybooks: A developmental study. *Reading Research Quarterly, 20*, 458–481.

Taylor, B. M. (1986). Teaching middle grade students to summarize content textbook material. In J. F. Baumann (Ed.), *Teaching main idea comprehension* (pp. 195–209). Newark, DE: International Reading Association.

Topping, K. (1987). Paired reading: A powerful technique for parent use. *The Reading Teacher, 40*, 608–614.

Torgesen, J., & Wagner, R. (1999) *Comprehensive Test of Phonological Processing.* Austin, TX: PRO-ED.

Torgesen, J., Wagner, R., & Rashotte, C. (1999). *The Test of Word Reading Efficiency (TOWRE).* Upper Saddle River, NJ: Pearson.

Torgesen, J. K., & Bryant, B. R. (2004). *TOPA-2+: Test of Phonological Awareness* (2nd ed.). Austin, TX: PRO-ED.

Treiman, R. (1993). *Beginning to spell: A study of first-grade children.* New York: Oxford University Press.

Tuinman, J. J. (1971). Asking reading-dependent questions. *Journal of Reading, 14*, 289–292.

Uhry, J. K. (1999). Invented spelling in kindergarten: The relationship with finger-point reading. *Reading and Writing: An Interdisciplinary Journal, 11,* 441–464.

U.S. Department of Education, National Center for Education Statistics. (1995). *Listening to children read aloud.* Washington, DC: Author.

Vygotsky, L. (1978). *Mind in society.* Cambridge, MA: Harvard University Press.

Wallach, M. A., & Wallach, L. (1979). Helping disadvantaged children learn to read by teaching them phoneme identification skills. In L. B. Resnick & P. A. Weaver (Eds.), *Theory and practice of early reading* (Vol. 3, pp. 197–216). Hillsdale, NJ: Erlbaum.

Walpole, S., & McKenna, M. C. (2006). The role of informal reading inventories in assessing word recognition. *The Reading Teacher, 59,* 592–594.

Watkins, J. H., McKenna, M. C., Manzo, A. V., & Manzo, U. C. (1994, April). *The effects of the listen–read–discuss procedure on the content learning of high school students.* Paper presented at the meeting of the American Educational Research Association, New Orleans, LA.

Wylie, R. E., & Durrell, D. D. (1970). Teaching vowels through phonograms. *Elementary English, 47,* 787–791.

Yussen, S. R., & Ozcan, N. M. (1996). The development of knowledge about narratives. *Issues in Education, 2,* 1–68.

Zutell, J., & Rasinkski, T. (1989). Reading and spelling connections in third- and fifth-grade students. *Reading Psychology, 10,* 137–155.

Zutell, J., & Rasinkski, T. (1991). Training teachers to attend to their students' oral reading fluency. *Theory into Practice, 30,* 211–217.

Index

Page numbers followed by *f* indicate figure, *t* indicate table